CU00920698

THE "RUSSIAN IDEA" IN INTERNATIONAL RELATIONS

The "Russian Idea" in International Relations identifies different approaches within Russian Civilizational tradition – Russia's nationally distinctive way of thinking – by situating them within IR literature and connecting them to practices of the country's international relations.

Civilizational ideas in IR theory express states' cultural identification and stress religious traditions, social customs, and economic and political values. This book defines Russian civilizational ideas by two criteria: the values they stress and their global ambitions. The author identifies leading voices among those positioning Russia as an exceptional and globally significant system of values and traces their arguments across several centuries of the country's development. In addition, the author explains how and why Russian civilizational ideas rise, fall, and are replaced by alternative ideas. The book identifies three schools of Russian civilizational thinking about international relations – Slavophiles, Communists, and Eurasianists. Each school focuses on Russia's distinctive spiritual, social, and geographic roots, respectively. Each one is internally divided between those claiming Russia's exceptionalism, potentially resulting in regional autarchy or imperial expansion, and those advocating the Russian Idea as global in its appeal. Those favoring the latter perspective have stressed Russia's unique capacity for understanding different cultures and guarding the world against extremes of nationalism and hegemony in international relations.

This book will be of interest to students and scholars of Russian foreign policy, Russia–Western relations, IR theory, diplomatic studies, political science, and European history, including the history of ideas.

Andrei P. Tsygankov is Professor of International Relations and Political Science at San Francisco State University. Recent publications include *Russian Realism: Defending "Derzhava" in International Relations* (2022) and *Russia and America: The Asymmetric Rivalry* (2019).

WORLDING BEYOND THE WEST

Series Editors: Arlene B. Tickner, Universidad del Rosario, Colombia, David Blaney, Macalester College, USA and Inanna Hamati-Ataya, Cambridge University, UK

Historically, the International Relations (IR) discipline has established its boundaries, issues, and theories based upon Western experience and traditions of thought. This series explores the role of geocultural factors, institutions, and academic practices in creating the concepts, epistemologies, and methodologies through which IR knowledge is produced. This entails identifying alternatives for thinking about the "international" that are more in tune with local concerns and traditions outside the West. But it also implies provincializing Western IR and empirically studying the practice of producing IR knowledge at multiple sites within the so-called "West."

The Kyoto School and International Relations
Non-Western Attempts for a New World Order
Kosuke Shimizu

Russian Realism
Defending "Derzhava" in International Relations
Andrei P. Tsygankov

Globalizing International Theory
The Problem with Western IR Theory and How to Overcome It
Edited by A. Layug and John M. Hobson

The "Russian Idea" in International Relations
Civilization and National Distinctiveness
Andrei P. Tsygankov

For more information about this series, please visit: www.routledge.com/ Worlding-Beyond-the-West/book-series/WBW

CONTENTS

TABLES

PREFACE

This book continues with the topic of Russian international relations IR theory. While the first volume (Tsygankov 2022) analyzed "Russian Realism," the present book considers "Civilizational" approaches. Following nineteenth-century writer Fyodor Dostoyevsky, Russian philosophers and IR thinkers commonly employ the notion of the "Russian Idea" (RI) to describe the country's nationally distinctive way of thinking. This volume aims to identify different schools and ideas within the RI, or "Russian Civilizational," tradition by situating them within the IR literature and connecting them to practices of the country's relations with the outside world.

The Civilizational tradition is the second broad school of thought that emerged several centuries ago, alongside Statism or Realism, that focuses on Russia's national interests and protection of state sovereignty. The Civilizational tradition also differs from that of "Russian Westernizers," who emphasize Russia's similarities and the importance of catching up with the West. I plan to explore ideas of Westernizers in a future separate volume.

Parts of several chapters draw on my previously published articles: "Mastering Space in Eurasia" (*Communist and Post-Communist Studies* 36, 1, 2003, pp. 101–127); "Finding a Civilizational Idea" (*Geopolitics* 12, 3, 2007, pp. 375–399); "The Heartland No More" (*Journal of Eurasian Studies* 3, 1, 2011); "Crafting the State-Civilization," (*Problems of Post-Communism* 63, 3, 2016, pp. 146–158); "In the Shadow of Nikolai Danilevskii: Universalism, Particularism, and Russian Geopolitical Theory," (*Europe-Asia Studies* 69, 4, 2017, pp. 571–593, copyright © 2017 University of Glasgow, reprinted by permission of Taylor & Francis, www.tandfonline.com, on behalf of University of Glasgow); and "Constructing National Values" (*Foreign Policy Analysis* 17, 4, 2021; CC-BY 4.0). I thank the publishers for permission to use these materials in the book.

At Routledge, I express my deep gratitude to the editors of the Worlding Beyond the West series – Arlene Tickner, Inanna Hamati-Ataya, and David Blaney – for their support and interest in Russian IR. I also wish to thank Emily Ross, Hannah Rich, and all at the press for their advice, assistance, performing editorial services, and preparing the manuscript for publication.

While researching and writing the book, I had numerous conversations with my father and frequent co-author, Pavel Tsygankov, my wife, Julia Godzikovskaya, and many friends and colleagues in Russia and the West. I thank them all for their willingness to listen and offer suggestions for improving the book.

I dedicate this book to all those in the broadly defined IR community who recognize the value of nationally distinctive thinking about the world and do not reduce such thinking to national exceptionalism.

In transliterating names from Russian, I have used "y" to denote "ы", to denote "ь" and "ъ", "yu" to denote "ю", "ya" to denote "я", "i" to denote "й" and "ий", "iyi" to denote double "и", "e" to denote "э", "kh" to denote "х", "zh" to denote "ж", "ts" to denote "ц", "ch" to denote "ч", "sh" to denote "ш", and "sch" to denote "щ". I have also used "Ye" to distinguish the sound of "e" (such as "Yevropa") in the beginning of a word from that in the middle of a word (such as "vneshnei"). Everywhere, I did not distinguish between "e" and "ё". Spelling is retained in quotations.

Reference

Tsygankov, Andrei P. 2022. *Russian Realism*. London: Routledge.

1
INTRODUCTION

The idea of a nation is not what it thinks of itself in time, but what God thinks of it in eternity.

Vladimir Solovyev (1989, 220)

This book studies the role of ideas in sustaining social communities across time and space. In particular, I am interested to learn how ideas formulated by non-Western nations reflect and preserve their national unity and the sense of cultural distinctiveness. Russian IR theory has come to accept the importance of *samobytnost*, or national distinctiveness (Tsygankov and Tsygankov 2021). Following the end of the Cold War, scholars have increasingly studied cultural and civilizational interactions to understand sources of foreign policy and patterns of inter-state relations (Huntington 1996; Inayatullah and Blaney 2004; Hall and Jackson 2007; Katzenstein 2010; Spruyt 2020; Chebankova and Dudkevitch 2021). To contribute to our understanding of these processes, I focus on Russian civilizational ideas and conditions under which they serve as guides in national development. Such ideas are often formed by intellectuals, whose concepts and theories are then borrowed by politicians.[1] Concepts and theories subsequently play the role of springboards (Goldstein and Keohane 1993) for becoming "isms," each carrying names of powerful intellectuals – Marxism, Leninism, Keynesianism, Ghandism, Confucianism, and the like.

The Russian Question in the World

Like other nations, Russia strives to protect its values and interests worldwide. The two – values and interests – are interrelated, yet distinct. National interests develop in the context of the contemporary international system and are based on a nation's historically formed self-perception. The idea of a nation is more

DOI: 10.4324/9781003377573-1

historically continuous and results from collectively overcoming challenges – wars, revolutions, economic, demographic, and other crises. By addressing these challenges, a nation builds a character and develops a particular combination of values or long-term preferences. These long-term preferences greatly assist a nation in deciding and sustaining what it is and what it wants to accomplish in the contemporary world.

Following the Soviet disintegration in 1991, Russia was immediately guided by the idea of joining the Western community of nations. Russian leadership assumed that the country's historically developed system of values, which included the concept of a strong, socially responsible state and great power, would be compatible with Western institutions of liberal democracy, free-market economy, and international security preferences. The reality proved different. Russia's insistence on playing a unique role in European and Eurasian affairs came into conflict with the West's idea of expanding its political, economic, and military institutions, resulting in multiple crises in Russo-West relations.

Having reached no understanding with the West, Russia reframed its national idea. It challenged Western liberal ideology and capitalized on historically established values of conservative family values, national sovereignty, a strong state, and great power (Tsygankov and Tsygankov 2021). Because of the contemporary conflict between Russia and the Western nations, the latter have increasingly framed these values as "autocratic" and incompatible with Western values (Tsygankov 2019; Diesen 2022; Sakwa 2023). In the meantime, Russia's insistence on its distinct interests and active rapprochement with China and other non-Western nations have led some observers to define Russia's values in terms of their Eastern or Eurasian opposition to those of the Euro-Atlantic West (Lewis 2018; Lukin and Yakunin 2018).

In the second half of the 2010s, Russia capitalized on "conservative" values, further challenging Western liberalism. The crisis within the European Union, Brexit, and the election of Donald Trump as US president, strengthened the Kremlin's perception that the age of liberalism is over and the world is entering a new era of nationalism and nationally defined values. Russia cultivated special relations with Euro-skeptics and critics of the liberal West in France, Germany, and other countries. Russia also improved ties with the conservative and friendly governments in Hungary, Italy, and Serbia but maintained semi-frozen relations with pro-American Poland and the Baltics.

In 2021, following the election of Joe Biden as US president, Russia's anti-Western turn led to a new crisis in relations with the West. The Kremlin was determined to protect its sovereignty and interests by refusing to discuss with Western officials issues of human rights, such as jailing the opposition leader Aleksei Navalny, expulsion of Western diplomats, sanctions against top-level European officials, and shielding the Russia-friendly Belarus from the EU criticisms of Belarus's fraudulent presidential elections of August 2020. Soon after a short period of seemingly improving relations with the United States and a productive bilateral meeting in Geneva in June 2021, Putin formulated new demands for Russia's security from the United States and NATO, including ending the alliance's policy of admitting new members, such as Ukraine and Georgia. He did not find the Western response sufficient. He remained convinced that NATO-Ukraine cooperation and Kyiv's possible preparations for using force in Donbas constituted an existential threat to national security. Russia's decision to attack Ukraine on February 24, 2022, reflected the deep sense of insecurity and perceived encroachment on Russia's interests and values by hostile Ukraine and the Western powers (Gotz and Staun 2022; Kuzio 2022; Tsygankov 2023).

This discourse and actions of Russia merit further investigation. The struggle for values and ideas intensifies as the world transitions toward a new international system. The involvement of larger societies and emotions, such as those concerning the Russia-Ukraine war, is likely to complicate the processes of resolving interstate disagreements, especially if such emotions are based on nationalist indignation and scapegoating of others. These developments beg the question of what it is that different nations are bringing to the contemporary world, aside from the distinct preferences of political elites. Precisely what is the national idea of Russia in this world? Disagreements between Russian elites and those of the West are not conclusive in answering the questions of values and a national idea by which Russia stands, except for rejecting liberalism and strengthening relations with non-Western nations.

Perhaps this question will be clarified by Russia's contemporary reassessment of its thirty years of experience with post-Soviet development, during which Russia defined itself in terms of relations with Western values. The war in Ukraine in 2022 has brought this period to its closure. Contemporary Russia is less interested in having its values recognized by the West than in protecting its national security interests from perceived encroachment by Western powers. After years of conflict and disagreement following the Cold War, Russia does not expect to agree on important economic and political issues with the West. However, Moscow feels threatened by the Western economic and military policies, and the Kremlin hopes to develop a greater sense of security from what it sees as the West's relentless global expansion.

Russia's international activities are increasingly organized outside the Western countries to reassess the nation's values and rebuild its internal foundations for future development (Krickovic and Pellicciari 2021; Diesen and Lukin 2021). As the world is becoming increasingly multipolar, Russia's search for security from the West is translating into renewed efforts to strengthen political and economic relations with countries in Eurasia, Asia, the Middle East, and other regions. Russia's new "National Security Strategy" adopted in July 2021 indicated that, while aiming to deter the West, Moscow plans to considerably expand economic, political, and military ties with non-Western nations such as China, India, Turkey, and Iran. In relations with these nations, Russia does not feel that its security is threatened, and it is ready to develop multiple projects to build a post-Western world order on multipolar and multilateral foundations. The fact that none of these nations have supported the West and Ukraine in their confrontation with Russia strengthens the Kremlin's determination to limit relations with Western nations.

Overall, Russia has made essential headway in overcoming its mental and material dependence on the West. In the future, this development may translate into a renewed effort to challenge Western policies and areas of global activities in partnership with non-Western nations such as China, India, Turkey, Iran, South Africa, and others. Alternatively, if Russia's capacity is limited, its future strategy may be defined by the need to reassess the capabilities of global power and focus on internal state-building. Russian scholars have argued for such a strategy since the 1990s by criticizing what they saw as the Kremlin's obsessive focus on containing the West globally.[2]

In Russian history, the country has known periods of internal concentration or foreign policy retreats from active involvement with European/Western relations. The notion of concentration results from Alexander II's course following the Crimean War in the mid-nineteenth century. Having lost the war, Russia chose to withdraw from active participation in European affairs] while embarking on "Great Reforms" at home, including lifting restrictions on economic freedom, censorship, and political centralization. The intention was to rebuild domestic foundations to return to great-power politics and revive Russia's pre-war interests and status.

Russia knew periods of relative isolation from the West even before the post-Crimean period. In the fifteenth century, Ivan III refused to cooperate with Catholic Rome by proclaiming the independence of Russia's interests and values and engaging in Eurasian expansion. Russians later reformulated the idea as that of the "Third Rome" that followed Byzantium rather than the Catholic faith and political tradition. However, Muscovy collapsed following a crisis of Ivan IV's rule resulting in the period of political disorder known as *Smuta*, or "Time of Troubles." Russia, again, retreated from active foreign policy until 1654, when it incorporated Ukraine, assisting the Romanov's rulers in confirming the identity of an East Christian empire in the post-Muscovy period. In the eighteenth century, Catherine the Great needed to withdraw from the Seven Years' War to minimize the risk of a major war and address pressing economic issues. Each of these periods was required to deal with various nation-building issues, including territorial unity, economy, finance, and demography.

Arguing the "Russian Idea" (RI)

Historical retreats to recover internal ideas and values became possible because there was something to salvage. Orthodox Christianity served as the foundation of the concept of Russia for centuries. Russian philosophers stressed those foundations as permanent regardless of their interpretation. In the words of the country's leading thinker, Vladimir Solovyev (1989, 220), "The idea of a nation is not what it thinks of itself in time, but what God thinks of it in eternity."[3] However, while grounded in Orthodox Christianity, Russia's system of values changed on various occasions to solve contemporary tasks. Today, as the international system is becoming increasingly post-Western, conditions emerge for Russia's new intellectual justification of its role in the world.

Russian philosophers Vladimir Solovyev and Nikolai Berdyayev employed the expression "Russian idea" (RI) to capture the nationally distinctive way of thinking. They followed the Russian writer Fyodor Dostoyevsky, who was the first to coin the term in 1860 (Gulyga 2003, 13). Even before Dostoyevsky, Russian thinkers constantly debated what counted as the country's values and national mission. The purpose of the present volume is to identify different approaches within the RI, or "Russian Civilizational" tradition by situating them within the IR literature and connecting them to practices of the country's relations with the outside world.

Scholars of Russian values and ideology or the RI have produced considerable research. In the West, many of them have concentrated on Russia's historically distinct ideas formed by Orthodox Christianity and exceptional conditions separating the country from the outside world, especially the Western European region. These ideas have translated into the missionary belief in protecting those people who culturally gravitate to Russia while living outside its borders (Duncan 2000; Curanovic 2020). The cultural appeal of Russia has been geographically limited, having its roots in Eastern Christian influence in Eurasia and Eastern/Central Europe.

In political affairs, the described cultural and ideological affinity has often resulted in a particular form of nationalism that some scholars call imperial (Kolstø and Blakkisrud 2016; Laruelle 2019; Kuzio 2022 Melvin 2022). The Russian state has preserved essential characteristics of a traditional land-based multinational empire and, therefore, hardly qualifies as fitting with a Western-style nation-state. Scholars of Russian nationalism have studied various dimensions of the country's missionary worldview and expansionist foreign policy (Tuminez 2000; LeDonne 2004; Van Herpen 2015; Grigas 2016). These dimensions have come under new scrutiny following Russia's invasion of Ukraine in 2022 (Burbank 2022; Snyder 2022).

Scholars of Russian political theory have traced Russian ideas and policies to diverse concepts of national values – conservative (Dunlop 1983; Pipes 2008; Robinson 2019; Diesen 2020), liberal (Weidle 2000; Chebankova 2014; Malinova 2009), socialist (Kolakowski 1976; Agurski 1987; Malia 1999; David-Fox 2015), and others. Scholars have produced overviews of Russian political ideas and identities (Berlin 1969; Billington 1970, 2004; Walicki 1990; Gulyga 2003; Riasanovsky 2005; Chebankova 2020; Bykova, Forster, and Steiner 2021). Concerning international relations, Russian ideas fall into several broad traditions or schools – Westernizers, Slavophiles, Communists, and Eurasianists. Although their main origins are in the nineteenth to early twentieth centuries, some of their roots can be traced to significant state-building periods, during which Russian leaders had to make strategic choices of international orientation. For example, the idea of Russia as independent from the West found its expression in the fifteenth-century decision by Ivan III to decline Rome's invitation to a close partnership.

In this book, I focus on those traditions of Russian thought that have been critical of the West and its dominant ideas – Slavophiles, Communists, and Eurasianists.[4] Slavophiles emerged in the first half of the nineteenth century to stress Russia's particular spiritual roots (Riasanovsky 1954; Rabow-Edling 2006; Engelstein 2009). Communists prioritized social justice and equality (Agurski 1987; Malia 1999). Finally, Eurasianists focused on Russia's special geographic and spatial conditions as responsible for forming national values and the RI (Hauner 1990; Bassin, Glebov, and Laruelle 2015). All these currents of thought have sought to highlight the distinctiveness of Russia as a civilization or a system of values with national and global appeal. All of them have argued the importance of combining the values of spirituality, social justice, and political independence advocating the notion of the integral (*tselostnyi*) Russia and the integral personality.[5] Therefore, my presentation of Slavophiles, Communists, and Eurasianists as stressing one of these values over others should be viewed mainly as a methodological choice that serves the purposes of analysis.

The analysis of distinctive Russian thinking fits with the recent turn in IR theory aimed at reassessing the foundations of knowledge about international relations. Scholars have produced significant research about the West's ideas and their reception by non-Western cultures and/or civilizations (Katzenstein 2010; Spruyt 2020; Buzan & Acharya 2021). They have shown that this reception has met a complex reaction and opposition partly because these ideas and the recipient cultures often result from the ethnocentric reading of national values (Hobson 2012; Grovogui 2006). Scholars have further demonstrated the difficulties of developing a cross-national dialogue that is complicated by differences in religions, social customs, historical traditions, and political systems (Inayatullah and Blaney 2004). Civilizational ideas are often framed in exceptional terms, allowing a limited space for learning from other cultures (Cha 2015). At the same time, such ideas may have global characteristics so long as their content appeals to the outside world. The extent to which such ideas are capable of dialogue remains debatable.

Exceptionalism and Global Dialogue

Echoes of the identified IR discussion can be found in the research on the RI. Many scholars have studied the RI as defined by claims to national exceptionalism, potentially resulting in regional autarchy or imperial expansion. Scholarship that stresses themes of exceptionalism is abundant in both Russia and the West. In Russia, the nationally exceptional mode of thinking has progressed since the maxim, "Moscow is the Third Rome."

The mirror-image position is presented in the West. It is similar to the one formed in Russia, except it views the RI from its own pejorative and ethnocentric perspective – as enslaving, dark, and dangerous for humanity rather than contributing to liberation and enlightenment of the outside world (Smith 2019). Russia's contentious, conflictual relations with the West, the Ottoman Empire, and other civilizations have reinforced this kind of thinking. It remains popular in various social and political circles and feeds off the renewed Russo-Western conflict (Sakwa 2023).

The second position presents the RI as global in its appeal and potentially transformative, even while rooted in a special religious tradition and particular geographic settings and historical conditions. Those favoring such a perspective have stressed Russia's unique capacity for understanding different cultures and guarding the world against extremes of nationalism and hegemony in international relations. The nation's cultural renaissance is associated with Alexander Pushkin's poetry, "The Wanderers" art, Piotr Tchaikovsky's music, and Fyodor Dostoyevsky's literature. It was widely recognized as reflecting the perception of Russia as a global bridge, not a fortress. In philosophy, the most prominent voice favoring such perception and advocating Russia's capacity to bridge Catholic Rome and Orthodox Christianity was Vladimir Solovyev. In the late nineteenth – early twentieth centuries, he battled with the national fortress mentality as advanced by Russian Pan-Slavists and radical critics of Christian Europe.

In this book, I trace the intellectual evolution and the social conditions for both interpretations of the RI. I situate my analysis in contemporary IR discussions. The vital debate in IR concerns relations between global and Western knowledge, on the one hand, and locally grounded approaches, on the other. The two sides are connected in various ways. Their relations include dialogue and mutual adaptation but can also be based on alienation and exceptionalism. Some who embrace and celebrate cultural differences still demonstrate a commitment to global knowledge (Buzan and Acharya 2021). Others remain skeptical that such knowledge is possible, arguing its deep cultural roots – Western or non-Western.

In addition to exploring the position of dialogue among Russian thinkers, I study the nature of exceptionalist attitudes by contrasting the two sides' arguments and the social conditions responsible for their principal divergence. To identify progress in the development of global IR knowledge, we ought to understand both positions and the relevant social contexts of their emergence.

These contexts are both internal and external. European/Western developments have deeply influenced Russia, but they have been processed inside the country based on its historical experience and cultural and political conditions. The exceptionalist interpretations of the RI have emerged or been revived under conditions of Russia–West conflict and polarization. In contrast, the dialogue perspectives drew their inspiration from the relative openness of the West and Western intellectuals to outside influences.

Today's Russia, again, demonstrates both positions. The ongoing conflict between Russia, on the one hand, and the United States and European powers, on the other, has revived the discourse of national exceptionalism inside the country, particularly concerning the West. Within these circles, Russia is presented as a conservative autarchic civilization principally opposed to political, economic, and cultural developments within Western societies (Linde 2016; Kuzio 2022).

Russian exceptionalism expresses itself in two ways: defensive and expansionist. The two attitudes manifest themselves in all civilizations, Western and non-Western (Cha 2015). Defensive exceptionalism is akin to the siege fortress mentality that aims to preserve national values in a community with fixed cultural, political, and economic boundaries shielded from the outside, particularly from the Western world. Defensive exceptionalism is a form of nationalism under perceived self-weakness and inability to expand national values abroad. On the other hand, the expansionist form of exceptionalism assumes both the need and ability to promote a civilization's "universal" values and ideas.

However, Russian thinkers have also continued to produce ideas of cross-cultural dialogue and global understanding. Such theories stress the capacity of Russia to initiate political and civilizational dialogues in the world by capitalizing on the nation's geographical position between Europe and Asia, the religious tolerance, and the political and economic status of a "semi-periphery" between the Western center and the non-Western periphery in the global economy (Gefter 1991; Shakhnazarov 2000; Tsygankov 2008; Malyavin 2015). Russia has engaged in various political and cultural dialogues in the Middle East, the Caucasus, and greater Eurasia. It has contributed to the development of multilateral formats in Asia. Under some conditions, Russia can revive the dialogue with the West and contribute to a mutual understanding between Western and non-Western nations preventing the development of a dangerous economic and military conflict.

Dialogue, of course, is not synonymous with replacing the values of one nation with those of another. Like exceptionalism, dialogue is a complex concept that incorporates different dimensions. It refers to various forms of international communication, exchange of ideas, and mutual learning. Scholars identified dialogue and communication based on rational interests, shared values, and the capacity for empathetic understanding of others (Inayatullah and Blaney 2004; *Hamati-Ataya* 2011; Pasha 2011; Petito 2016). Dialogue can be limited and extensive, with the capacity to penetrate different areas and dissolve previously existing social boundaries and barriers. In international relations, a deep cross-cultural dialogue is constrained by historically formed values and national priorities. The remaining chapters of the book will demonstrate that dialogues proposed within Russian civilizational traditions also have limitations. Slavophiles, Communists, and Eurasianists each have their versions of engaging nations outside Russia in dialogue and learning from them. However, their proposed engagement and learning have often meant to be conducted on Russia's terms or without threatening what their authors see as the nation's fundamental values and moral principles.

Given the depth of the country's conflict with the West, the exceptionalist position prevails in Russia. It remains to be seen how the RI will progress in the future. Some of its advocates have described Russia's ability to change the world through the force of a positive example. Others have been skeptical. Most, however, have agreed that Russia can "teach the world some important lesson," as famously diagnosed by Pyotr Chaadayev.

Organization of the Book

In this book, I trace the intellectual evolution and social conditions for both exceptional and global interpretations of the RI. I develop my argument in several steps.

Chapter 2 provides an overview of civilizational ideas and their role in the global world. I explain their roots and significance for constructing national identity and foreign policy. I also explain how civilizational ideas rise and fall by utilizing insights from the ontological (in)security theory and using examples from Russian, Chinese, and Western experiences. I then apply the conceptual framework for understanding Russia's civilizational position in the international system and the renewed search for national identity. I contrast my explanation with those stressing predominantly political and culturally essentialist factors. I further develop a classification of the leading intellectual currents among Slavophiles, Communists, and Eurasianists for their subsequent analysis in Chapters 3–5. The classification aims to position Russian civilizational ideas in terms of their nationally exceptional and global content and their inter-relations in various historical contexts. Finally, I briefly describe Russia's search for new civilizational ideas of exceptionalist and global varieties following the Soviet dissolution.

The subsequent Chapters 3–5 review Russia's main civilizational schools – Slavophile, Communist, and Eurasianist – each stressing the RI's spiritual, social, and spatial dimensions. Therefore, I define each of these schools as sufficiently inclusive of incorporating diverse thinkers who sometimes disagree with each other. Adopting such a broad definition allows me to identify: Slavophiles as all those who stress Russia's spiritual/Christian foundations; Communists as all those focusing on the country's distinctive egalitarian economic and social institutions; and Eurasianists as all those concentrating on geoeconomic and geopolitical relations within the region that differentiates and connects Europe, Asia, and the Middle East. I identify leading exceptionalist and global voices within these civilizational schools and trace their arguments across several centuries of Russia's historical development. My goal here is to identify exciting and potentially fruitful ideas for understanding the contemporary debate on RI.

Chapter 3 analyzes Slavophile ideas that have reflected Russia's spiritual conditions associated with Orthodox Christianity and the commune-based free peasant labor. I review the evolution of Slavophile thought from the first half of the nineteenth century to the post-Soviet developments. Such developments include: the early Slavophiles (Aleksei Khomyakov and Konstantin Aksakov); Pan-Slavists (Nikolai Danilevsky and Ivan Aksakov); Vladimir Solovyev and his followers, such as Nikolai Berdyayev; the critics of the Soviet system (Ivan Ilyin and Alexander Solzhenitsyn); and more recent figures (Alexander Panarin).

I selected these figures to illustrate the diversity of Slavophile arguments developed by leading figures across time. While convinced of their values' superiority over Western ones, Slavophiles diverged concerning preferred relations with European nations. For instance, Khomyakov, Kireyevsky, and Solovyev believed in reviving Christian ideas jointly with Europe. However, Pan-Slavists and anti-Soviet Slavophiles were motivated by their alienation from Europe and sought to preserve Russianness in separation from the West. Finally, I select the figure of Panarin to demonstrate the complexity of the post-Soviet search for national identity. Initially a supporter of pro-Western development, Panarin became disillusioned and shifted to the position of strengthening Russia as an anti-Western Orthodox empire.

The chapter explains the described divergence in Slavophile thinking by Russian thinkers' perceived conditions of Western civilization and Russia. Russia-European political conflicts have contributed to the rise of exceptionalist ideas that aimed to preserve the perceived authenticity of Christian ideals. Russian thinkers developed defensive (fortress) and offensive (expansionist) ideas of an exceptionalist nature as Russia and the West diverged in their political and social directions. The revolutionary upheavals of the 1840s or liberal political protests of the 2010s were perceived as the retribution of the European continent for abandoning traditional values in favor of "corrupting" individualism and secularism.

Chapters 4 and 5 follow the framework of Chapter 3 by analyzing the development of Communist and Eurasianist thought, respectively. Unlike the spiritual emphasis of Slavophiles, Communists and Eurasianists stress the distinctiveness of Russia's social and spatial conditions in forming national values. My purpose here, as in the previous chapter, is to demonstrate the diversity of these civilizational schools' arguments and explain the historical and political context in which these arguments are formed.

For analyzing Communists (Chapter 4), I have selected arguments by the nineteenth-century thinkers, Bolsheviks, and Soviet Marxists of the late Soviet and post-Soviet periods. While Bolsheviks developed exceptionalist ideas of offensive (the World Revolution) and defensive (Socialist in One Country) nature, some of the late Soviet thinkers sought to position the Soviet Union's dilemmas as requiring dialogue with the West. The post-Soviet conditions also produced ideas ranging from exceptionalism to global dialogue.

For analyzing Eurasianism (Chapter 5), I have assessed ideas that emerged in the late nineteenth century and shaped the school's further development throughout the twentieth and early twenty-first centuries. Eurasianism is primarily known for its defensive exceptionalist orientation, although some Eurasianist theories demonstrate expansionist and globally dialogical approaches. For example, in some of Eurasianism's versions, the contemporary idea of the "greater Eurasia" positions Russia as economically, politically, and culturally open to outside influences rather than as an autarchic region isolated from the West.

The concluding chapter summarizes my findings on Russian civilization ideas, reflects on their various criticisms, and discusses the implications of the book's argument for the future relations of Russia with the outside world. I also reflect on the impact of the Russia-Ukraine war on Russian thinking and its potential to contribute to building a more secure and integrated world. Such a world can only result from global dialogues initiated from below or civilizational ideas that remain open to the outside world and capable of cross-cultural conversation.

Notes

1 The reverse is also true.
2 Tsygankov 2022, chap. 5 documents this criticism by Russian scholars.
3 *Italics* as in the original.
4 I will consider Westernizers in a separate volume. As a school with a particular influence among educated Russian elites, they merit a special investigation.
5 For analyses of Russian thinking as searching for integral or holistic personality in harmony with the outside world, see Gulyga 2003; Hahn 2022.

Further Reading

Russia-West: Relations and Perception

Dowling, M. 2021. *Writing Russia The Discursive Construction of AnOther Nation*. Routledge.
Malia, M. 1999. *Russia Under Western Eyes*. Cambridge, MA: Harvard University Press.
McDaniel D. 1996. *The Agony of the Russian Idea*. Princeton, 1996.
Peris, D. 2021. Custiniana: The many histories of a single trip to Russia 180 years ago, and why it matters today. *Kritika: Explorations in Russian and Eurasian History* 22, 2.
Smith, M. 2019. *The Russia Anxiety*. New York: Penguin
Tsygankov, A. 2012. *Russia and the West from Alexander to Putin*. Cambridge UP.
Sakwa, R. 2023. *The Russia Scare*. Routledge.

Russian Political Thought and IR Theory

Berlin, I. 1969. *Russian Thinkers*. New York: Penguin.
Bykova, M. F., M. Forster, and L. Steiner, (eds.) 2021. *The Palgrave Handbook of Russian Thought*. Palgrave.
Chebankova, E. 2020. *Political Ideologies in Contemporary Russia*. McGill-Queen's University Press.
Diesen, G. 2020. *Russian Conservatism*. Boulder, CO: Rowman & Littlefield.
Gulyga, A. 2003. *Russkaya ideya i eye tvortsy*. Moscow: Eksmo.
Kaczmarska, K. 2020. *Making Global Knowledge in Local Contexts*. Routledge.
Kelly, I. 1998. *Toward Another Shore: Russian Thinkers Between Necessity and Chance*. Yale UP
Kochtcheeva, L. 2020. *Russian Politics and Response to Globalization*. Palgrave.
Leatherbarrow, W. and D. Offord, eds. 2010. *A History of Russian Thought*. Cambridge UP.
Lebedeva, M. 2019. *Russian Studies of International Relations*. New York: Ibidem.
Lynch A. 1987. *The Soviet Study of International Relations*. Cambridge UP.
Morozov, V. 2015. *Russia's Postcolonial Identity*. Palgrave.

Oskanian, K. 2021. *Russian Exceptionalism between East and West*. Palgrave.

Neumann, I. B. 2015. *Russia and the idea of Europe*, 2nd ed. London: Routledge.

Pipes, R. 2008. *Russian Conservatism and Its Critics*. New Haven: Yale UP.

Riasanovsky, N. V. 2005. *Russian Identities*. Oxford UP.

Robinson, P. 2019. *Russian Conservatism*. Cornell UP.

Tsygankov, A. 2022. *Russian Realism*. London: Routledge.

Weigle, M. A. 2000. *Russia's Liberal Project*. Pennsylvania State University.

Walicki, A. 1990. *A History of Russian Thought from Enlightenment to Marxism*. Stanford.

Russian Nationalism and Messianism

Brudny, I. 2000. *Reinventing Russia: Russian Nationalism and the Soviet State*. Harvard UP.

Curanovic, A. 2020. *The Sense of Mission in Russian Foreign Policy*. Routledge.

Duncan P. J. S. 2000. *Russian Messianism*. Routledge.

Dunlop, J. 1983. *Russian Nationalism*. Princeton UP.

Kolstø, P. and H. Blakkisrud, eds. 2016. *The New Russian Nationalism*. Edinburgh: Edinburgh University Press.

Kuzio, T. 2022. *Russian Nationalism and the Russian-Ukrainian War*. Routledge.

Lohr, E. 2003. *Nationalizing the Russian Empire*. Harvard UP.

Laruelle, M. 2019. *Russian Nationalism*. London: Routledge.

Suslov, M. 2020. *Geopolitical Imagination: Ideology and Utopia in Post-Soviet Russia*. New York: Ibidem, Columbia UP.

Tuminez, A. S. 2000. *Russian Nationalism since 1856*. Boulder, CO: Rowman & Littlefield.

Dialogue and Exceptionalism in International Relations

Acharya, A. 2011. Dialogue and discovery. *Millennium* 39, 3.

Callahan, W. A. 2008. Chinese visions of world order: Post-hegemonic or a new hegemony?, *International Studies Review* 10, 4.

Cha, T. 2015. The formation of American exceptional identities, *European Journal of International Relations* 21, 4.

Chakrabarty, D. 2000. *Provincializing Europe: Postcolonial Thought and Historical Difference*. Princeton University Press.

Grovogui, S. 2006. *Beyond Eurocentrism and Anarchy*. Palgrave.

Habermas, J. 1990. *The Philosophical Discourse of Modernity*. Cambridge: Polity Press.

Hamati-Ataya, I. 2011. The "Problem of Values" and international relations scholarship. *International Studies Review 13*.

Hutchings, K. 2011. Dialogue between whom? *Millennium* 39, 3

Inayatullah, N., and Blaney, D. L. 2004. *International Relations and the Problem of Difference*. Routledge.

Pasha, M. K. 2011, Western nihilism and dialogue. *Millennium* 39, 3.

Petito, F. 2016. Dialogue of civilizations in a multipolar world. *International Studies Review* 18, 1.

Said, E. W. 2003 (1979). *Orientalism*. London: Penguin Books.

Tickner, J. A. 2011. Dealing with a difference. *Millennium* 39, 3.

Tripathi, 2021. International relations and the 'Global South.' *Third World Quarterly* 42, 9.

Yong-Soo, E. 2019. Global IR through dialogue. *The Pacific Review.*

References

Agurski, Michael. 1987. *The Third Rome: National-Bolshevism in the USSR*. Boulder, CO: Westview.

Bassin, Mark, Sergei Glebov, and Marlene Laruelle, eds. 2015. *Between Europe and Asia*. DeKalb: Northern Illinois University Press.

Berlin, Isaiah. 1969. *Russian Thinkers*. New York: Penguin.

Billington, James. 1970. *The Icon and the Axe: An Interpretive History of Russian Culture*. Vintage.

———. 2004. *Russia in Search of Itself*. Washington, DC: The Woodrow Wilson Center. 2004.

Burbank, Jane. 2022. The Grand Theory Driving Putin to War. *New York Times*, March 22.

Buzan, Barry and Amitav Acharya. 2021. *Re-Imagining International Relations*. Cambridge UP.

Bykova, M. F., M. Forster, and L. Steiner, eds. 2021. *The Palgrave Handbook of Russian Thought*. Palgrave.

Cha, T. 2015. The formation of American exceptional identities, *European Journal of International Relations* 21, 4.

Chebankova, Elena. 2014. Contemporary Russian Liberalism. *Post-Soviet Affairs* 30, 5.

Chebankova, Elena. 2020. *Political Ideologies in Contemporary Russia*. McGill-Queen's University Press.

Chebankova, Elena and Piotr Dudkevitch, eds. 2021. *Civilizations and World Order*. Routledge.

Curanovic, Alica. 2020. *The Sense of Mission in Russian Foreign Policy*. Routledge.

David-Fox, Michael. 2015. *Crossing Borders: Modernity, Ideology, and Culture in Russia and the Soviet Union*. University of Pittsburgh Press.

Diesen, Glenn. 2020. *Russian Conservatism*. Boulder, CO: Rowman & Littlefield.

———. 2022. *Russophobia*. Palgrave.

Diesen, Glenn, and Aleksandr Lukin, eds. 2021. *Russia and Eurasia in the New World*. Palgrave.

Duncan, Peter J. S. 2000. *Russian Messianism*. Routledge.

Dunlop, John. 1983. *Russian Nationalism*. Princeton UP.

Engelstein, Laura. 2009. *Slavophile Empire: Imperial Russia's Illiberal Path*. Ithaca, NY: Cornell University Press.

Gefter, Mikhial. 1991. *Is tekh i etikh let*. Moskva: Progress.

Goldstein, Judith and Robert O. Keohane, eds. 1993. *Ideas and Foreign Policy*. Ithaca, NY: Cornell University Press.

Götz, Elias and Jørgen Staun. 2022. Why Russia attacked Ukraine: Strategic culture and radicalized narratives, *Contemporary Security Policy*.

Grigas, A. 2016. *Beyond Crimea: The New Russian Empire*. New Haven: Yale University Press.

Grovogui, S. 2006. *Beyond Eurocentrism and Anarchy*. Palgrave.

Gulyga, Arseny. 2003. *Russkaya ideya i eye tvortsy*. Moscow: Eksmo.

Hahn, Gordon M. 2022. *Russian Tselostnost': Wholeness in Russian Culture, Thought, History, and Politics*. Europe Book.

Hall, Martin and Patrick T. Jackson, eds. 2007. *Civilizational Identity*. Palgrave.

Hamati-Ataya, Inanna. 2011. The "Problem of Values" and international relations scholarship. *International Studies Review* 13.

Hauner, Milan. 1990. *What Is Asia to Us?* London: Routledge.

Hobson, J. M. 2012. *The Eurocentric Conception of World Politics: Western International Theory, 1760–2010*. Cambridge: Cambridge University Press.

Huntington, Samuel P. 1996. *The Clash of Civilizations and the Remaking of World Order*. New York: Simon & Schuster.

Inayatullah, Naeem and Blaney, David L. 2004. *International Relations and the Problem of Difference*. Routledge.

Katzenstein, Peter J., ed. 2010. *Civilizations in World Politics*. New York: Routledge.

Kolakowski, Leszek. 1976. *Main Currents of Marxism*. Oxford UP.

Kolstø, Paul and Helge Blakkisrud, eds. 2016. *The New Russian Nationalism*. Edinburgh: Edinburgh University Press.

Krickovic, Andrej and Ian Pellicciari. 2021. From Greater Europe to Greater Eurasia. *J. of Eurasian Studies*.

Kuzio, Taras. 2022. *Russian Nationalism and the Russian-Ukrainian War*. Routledge.

Laruelle, Marlene. 2019. *Russian Nationalism*. London: Routledge.

LeDunne, John P. 2004. *The Grand Strategy of the Russian Empire, 1650–1831*. New York: Oxford University Press.

Lewis, David G. 2018. Geopolitical Imaginaries in Russian Foreign Policy. *Europe-Asia Studies* 70, 10.

Linde, Fabian. 2016. The Civilizational Turn in Russian Political Discourse. *Russian Review* 74, 4.

Lukin, Aleksandr and Vladimir Yakunin. 2018. Eurasian integration and the development of Asiatic Russia. *Journal of Eurasia Studies* 9.

Malia, Martin. 1999. *Russia Under Western Eyes*. Cambridge, MA: Harvard University Press.

Malinova, Ol'ga. 2009. Россия и «Запад» в XX веке: трансформация дискурса о коллективной идентичности. Moscow: РОССПЭН.

Malyavin, Vladimir. 2015. *Evraziya i vsemirnost': novyi vzglyad na prorodu Evraziyi*. Moscow.

Melvin, Neil. 2022. Nationalist and Imperial Thinking Define Putin's Vision for Russia. *RUSI*, March 2.

Pasha, Mustafa. K. 2011, Western nihilism and dialogue. *Millennium* 39, 3.

Petito, F. 2016. Dialogue of civilizations in a multipolar world. *International Studies Review* 18.

Pipes, Richard. 2008. *Russian Conservatism and Its Critics*. New Haven: Yale UP.

Rabow-Edling, Sarah. 2006. *Slavophile Thought and the Politics of Cultural Nationalism*. Albany, NY: SUNY Press.

Riasanovsky, Nicholas. 1954. *Russia and the West in the Teaching of the Slavophiles*. Harvard UP.

———. 2005. *Russian Identities*. Oxford UP.

Robinson, Paul. 2019. *Russian Conservatism*. Cornell UP,.

Sakwa, Richard. 2023. *The Russia Scare*. Routledge.

Shakhnazarov, Georgi. 2000. *Otkroveniya i zabluzhdeniya teoriyi tsivilizatsi*. Moscow: Sovremennyi gumanitarnyi universitet.

Smith, Mark. 2019. *The Russia Anxiety*. New York: Penguin.

Snyder, Timothy. 2022. The War in Ukraine Is a Colonial War. *The New Yorker*, April 28.

Solovyev, Vladimir. 1989. Русская идея. Том 2 // Сочинения в 2 томах. Moscow: Nauka.

Spruyt, Hendrick. 2020. *The World Imagined: Collective Beliefs and Political Order in the Sinocentric, Islamic and Southeast Asian International Societies*. Cambridge UP.

Tsygankov, Andrei P. 2008. Self and Other in International Relations Theory. *International Studies Review*.

———. 2019. *The Dark Double*. Oxford UP.

————. 2022. *Russian Realism*. Routledge.

————. 2023. The West, Russia, and Ukraine: The Roots of the Conflict. Ms. under review.

Tsygankov, A. and P. Tsygankov 2021. Constructing National Values. *Foreign Policy Analysis*.

Tuminez, Astrid. 2000. *Russian Nationalism since 1856*. Boulder, CO: Rowman & Littlefield.

Van Herpen, Marcel H. 2015. *Putin's Wars: The Rise of Russia's New Imperialism,* 2nd ed. Boulder, CO: Rowman & Littlefield.

Walicki, Andrzej. 1990. *A History of Russian Thought from Enlightenment to Marxism*. Stanford, 1979.

Weigle, Marsha A. 2000. *Russia's Liberal Project*. Pennsylvania State University.

2
RUSSIAN CIVILIZATIONAL IDEAS

> [W]e are called to solve most of the problems of the social order, to complete most of the ideas that have arisen in old societies, to answer the most important questions that occupy humanity.
>
> *Pyotr Chaadayev (1991, 150)*

With Pyotr Chaadayev, many Russian thinkers believe in their country's unique mission and the ability "to answer the most important questions" of humanity. However, the belief in a global mission has not been shared by others who have thought about their country as a self-sufficient civilization developing in isolation from the West. For instance, according to Ivan Ilyin (1992, 328), the meaning of the Russian idea is limited to Russia, which must strive to create an original Russian spiritual culture rather than teach others or learn from them.[1]

This chapter discusses the nature of global and nationally exceptionalist ideas of civilization as articulated in various historical and cultural settings. I discuss the content of such ideas and the conditions of their rise and fall using examples from the West, Russia, and China. I also introduce a typology of civilizational ideas based on their content and degree of openness.

This framework is then applied to the leading schools of Russian civilizational thinking. Global or dialogical thinking among Slavophiles, Communists, and Eurasianists has developed in the context of Russia's internal confidence and perception of the outside world – until recently, the West – as sharing some essential values with Russia. Alternatively, exceptionalist thinking results from the nation's internal weakness and perception of a hostile international environment. Historically, the country's meaningful outside world has been constructed around the West. Today, however, Russian leadership is increasingly positioning the country vis-à-vis non-Western nations in Eurasia and outside. Dialogue and exceptionalism are now progressing in both Eastern and Western global contexts.

DOI: 10.4324/9781003377573-2

Civilizational Ideas in the Global World

This section explores the content and variety of civilizational ideas, including American, European, Soviet, and Chinese. In particular, I analyze the content and conditions for the rise and decline of the theories of "the end of history" (Francis Fukuyama), the "clash of civilizations" (Samuel Huntington), the "world system" (Immanuel Wallerstein), the "international society" (Hedley Bull), the "new thinking" (Mikhail Gorbachev), and Tianxia as developed by Chinese scholars. Some of these ideas are more globally appealing than others. The section reflects on why some have gradually lost their international appeal while others have not. I also discuss the insufficiency of existing explanations articulated by cultural essentialists, realists, and liberals.

Civilizational Idea: The Global and the Exceptional

Every large nation tends to assume that its values are not limited to national boundaries but have certain universal qualities. This vision is sustained in ideas that aim to capture meanings developed across time and space in response to various historical developments. I refer to these ideas as civilizational. Civilizational ideas are national to the extent that they express the nation's internally formed values. These values result from everyday spiritual, religious, and historical experiences, linking large groups of people with systems of meaning and understanding of the global world and their place in it. Civilizational ideas stress the originality of national values vis-à-vis other nations and nationalities. Such ideas express the nation's "broadest cultural identification" (Huntington 1997, 41, 43) and can be formulated by stressing religious traditions, social customs, and economic and political values. For example, in the case of China, civilizational identity is largely determined by ethnicity, while religious and political influences primarily determine Russia's identity.

Civilizational ideas are national and global insofar as they capture the internal values' international dimension. Although these values are formed by national history, no nation is entirely divorced from others, and all nations have something important to say about the outside world. In turn, the latter can help legitimize an idea by extending the external recognition of the values and cultural characteristics expressed by the idea.

Some ideas are more influential than others. No nation is a monolith, and civilizational ideas compete for dominance in the political space. Such ideas seek to appeal to many people separated by various political and cultural boundaries. There are liberals striving for greater openness and renewal of values within each national community, and conservatives who argue reliance on predominantly national experience and defend the national values' inner unity. Each community also has its radicals who advocate a complete break with national experience to embrace other peoples' values. For instance, in the first half of the nineteenth century, Russian philosopher Pyotr Chaadayev admired Western

Catholicism rather than Orthodox Christianity and the values inspired by the dominant Russian religion. Extremely critical of his country's experience, he summarized it in the following words: "We live only in the present time, within its closest limits, without a past and a future, and *amid dead stagnation*" (Chaadayev 1991, 22–24).[2]

Civilizational ideas prove influential in the national context if they successfully serve three related functions – cultural, explanatory, and normative. First, having roots in a national experience, a civilizational idea functions as a cultural bridge by connecting historical meanings into a coherent narrative that provides philosophical foundations for social and political elites and everyday meanings for broader segments of the population. Second, a civilizational idea has explanatory power by providing a worldview that answers questions about the current international system – its structure, principles, and behavioral rules. Third, a civilizational idea contains a normative vision of a desired future by suggesting recommendations and answering the "what to do" questions. A practical policy and grand strategy are normally based on an idea that expresses national values. For instance, Russia cannot achieve great-power status by becoming another America or China in terms of borrowing their ideas and values. These countries have gained their upper place in the international system by building on their own historically developed ideas. A well-developed idea provides coherence to a nation's foreign policy over a considerable time and justifies various policy actions, such as global adaptation, isolation, or nationalist revenge and offensive.

Civilizational ideas can be differentiated in terms of their international ambitions and have appeal. Some establish boundaries and call for geographically and regionally confined policies, while others are globally expansionist and unlimited in their political ambitions. Civilizational ideas also differ regarding their appeal or receptiveness to the outside audience. Some are globally appealing, whereas others are culturally ethnocentric or exceptional.

In the American context, the ideas of the "end of history" by Francis Fukuyama and the "clash of civilizations" by Samuel Huntington are examples of ideas that, respectively, are more expansionist and less expansionist. While differing in content and degree of self-intended exceptionalism, both ideas are culturally ethnocentric and unacceptable to non-Western cultures. Francis Fukuyama's theory was formulated in the Western context of the late 1980s and justified the global spread of Western-style market democracy after the end of the Cold War. On the contrary, Huntington drew the attention of the academic and political community to elements of global disorder that were perceived as increasingly dominant in the mid-1990s. Both theories have been widely discussed in non-Western societies, particularly in Russia, which makes it possible to trace how some Western ideas are perceived in other sociocultural contexts (Tsygankov 2004).

Non-Western cultures have been critical of both ideas as reflecting the West's cultural standards. For example, in Russia, Fukuyama's idea was rejected twice – before and after the collapse of the Soviet Union. Over time, the criticism has intensified. At first, some liberal intellectuals put forward arguments similar to the "end of history." Still, most researchers have rejected it as limiting Russia's freedom and her contribution to the world. After the Soviet disintegration, Russia grew even more critical and perceived Fukuyama's idea as incapable of accommodating Russia's legitimate interests in the post-Cold War world.

Huntington's theory was different, yet Russia was also critical of it. Unlike Fukuyama, Huntington defended Western values as culturally exclusive and geographically limited. While advocating an alarmist vision of the world order, Huntington hoped to convince Russia of the need for an alliance with the West in the face of the threat from "Confucian-Islamic" civilization. However, most Russian scholars who discussed Huntington's idea pointed to its potential to destabilize the Eurasian region and the world, undermining the pluralism of civilizations, creating unnecessary enemies in China and the Muslim world, and exploiting Russia's internal vulnerability.

An example of a more appealing idea is the world system theory developed by Immanuel Wallerstein (2004). While critical of Fukuyama and Huntington, many Russian intellectuals have been receptive to Wallerstein. The latter criticized the two authors and the international system the West established as divided between the prosperous Western "core" and the dependent non-Western "periphery." Wallerstein argued for a transformation of the system into one that is more egalitarian and receptive to all nations' participation in the world. In Russia, most international affairs scholars view Wallerstein as a greater authority than Fukuyama and Huntington. He is perceived as less ethnocentric and more open to understanding by non-Western cultures and civilizations.[3]

Another example of an expansionist yet globally appealing idea has been that of international society. While being developed by British scholars during the 1970s and 1980s, the concept remains influential today worldwide. Its authors, Bull and Watson (1984, 2), traced the emergence and development of the universal society of states and people. They viewed the world as still considerably controlled by Europe and were open about describing the relationships between Europe and the world as "Eurocentric" (Ibid.). Although such emphasis displays elements of ethnocentrism, the approach is culturally more inclusive than those of Fukuyama and Huntington. Bull and Watson acknowledged the global and the European community without unequivocally committing themselves to one or the other. They also appreciated both the tensions and mutual learning between Europe and non-European societies. For example, they recognized, albeit rather implicitly, that during the international society's expansion, Europeans had to adjust their rules and values and did not merely export them to the rest of the world (Ibid., 6). As a result, the idea of international society has been favorably received in Russia. Influential IR scholars have adopted its language and promoted the vision of a pluralistic international society in their work.[4]

By building on the initial openness of the idea, other scholars developed it into the Western global society approach, which argues for the emergence of new structures and institutions of governance at the supranational and transnational levels (Held 1995; Linklater 2013, 2020). The global civil society school recognizes the pluralism of local cultures and identities and proposes that this plurality of identities flourish, not disappear, during the globalization era. However, the theory's call for transcending the currently existing system of nation-states (Held 2000, 283) makes it more West-centric and less appealing from the standpoint of non-Western nations. While different from Fukuyama's institutional universalism, the idea of global society also reflects the West's civilizational standards and encourages cross-cultural divisions worldwide.

An example of a non-Western civilizational idea is the theory of the *Tianxia* (literally "all under Heaven") system based on Chinese Confucianism and recommended for stabilizing human relations within and outside nations. The theory may be viewed as a non-Western equivalent of a globally ambitious yet ethnocentric idea. The theory rejects the notion of a balance of power reflecting Western values and proposes hierarchical principles as a foundation of harmony in the world (Shih 2014, 129–130). Chinese scholars have positioned the Tianxia theory as a country's distinct contribution to IR theory, alongside the themes of humane authority and relationality. Within Chinese approaches, the idea of Tianxia is compared to Western liberal cosmopolitanism (Hwang 2021).

The idea of Tianxia developed out of China's disappointment with West-centered globalization. Initially, Chinese intellectuals followed Chairman Deng Xiaoping's idea of combining nationalism and globalization by preserving what he defined as a "socialist spiritual civilization" under Communist Party rule (Hughes 1997, 104–105). However, following the student protests in Tiananmen Square and the collapse of the Soviet system, Deng grew pessimistic that such a combination was possible, and he concluded – not unlike Huntington – that the Cold War would be followed by new violent conflicts (Ibid., 107). The Tianxia idea is yet another attempt to combine the national and the global, but this time on Chinese hierarchical principles. By comparison, Chinese relationality is viewed as global yet non-ethnocentric and appropriate for a cross-national dialogue (Hwang 2021). Such dialogue is often proposed in non-Western intellectual and political contexts.

Rise and Fall of Civilizational Ideas

Conditions responsible for the rise and fall of civilizational ideas are both domestic and foreign. A civilizational idea can strengthen the inner confidence of the national "Self" and relations with the "Significant Other." A more confident nation is likely to produce global and culturally open ideas, especially if the outside audience is receptive to such ideas. Global ideas propose solutions to national problems by engaging with the outside world – ideally by not sacrificing the nation's values and interests but adapting those to fit new international realities.

However, a global civilizational idea can lose its initial appeal if it fails to match the nation's expected domestic- and foreign-relations direction. National anxieties and insecurities tend to activate defensive and nationally exceptional ideas. Scholars have documented how outside changes challenge distinct national identities creating various dislocations and anxieties in people's consciousness, defined as the condition of ontological insecurity (Kinnvall 2004; Mitzen 2006; Steele 2007; Zarakol 2011; Berenskoetter 2014; Bettiza 2014; Steele and Homolar 2019) and "identity crisis" (Guzzini 2012). In response to the condition, a process of the Self's identity (re)formulation gets activated, during which people adapt to the outside world by searching for meaningful symbols and behavioral norms. One scholar argues that the nation is a bounded community with a biographical narrative, which gives meaning to its collective spatiotemporal situatedness (Berenskoetter 2014).

For example, if the West serves as the nation's significant Other, then the West's recognition or lack thereof shapes the global or nationally exceptional nature of the Self's ideas. Western actions that are widely perceived within the nation as disrespectful of its values are likely to undermine the appeal of global ideas leading to a nationalist mobilization. Although national identity is a continuum of different schools and traditions, actions by the Other can push the national diversity of approaches toward a nationalist consensus vis-à-vis the Western other. Influenced by different events, each school will become concerned with perceived Western pressures, thereby forming conditions for a more coherent, consensus-based foreign policy and the emergence of nationally exceptional civilizational ideas.

Examples to illustrate the rise or fall of global civilizational ideas may include the Soviet "New Thinking," Western liberal globalization, and the already-cited Chinese idea of Tianxia. Each in their way, they emerged to capitalize on the Self's internal confidence and growing external recognition.

The Soviet New Thinking emerged in the second half of the 1980s when the reformer Mikhail Gorbachev came to power and proposed changes known as *Perestroika*. By introducing the new idea, Gorbachev wished to overcome the Cold War hostilities and develop international cooperation in arms control, environment, and economic development. New Thinking diagnosed international problems as global that could be resolved only through global efforts, "We are all passengers aboard one ship, the Earth, and we must not allow it to be wrecked. There will be no second Noah's Ark" (Gorbachev 1987, 12). Scholars analyzed the vision as reflecting the Soviet desire to improve world status through an innovative strategy of engaging the West rather than merely cooperation on Western terms (Larson and Shevchenko 2003).

The New Thinking declined because the conditions that favored its emergence evaporated. The idea emerged in the context of domestic confidence and was based on Gorbachev's faith in the Soviet system's viability and superiority to that of Western "capitalism." While critical of the Soviet system's performance, he believed in its reform and in the global potential of combining democracy and an egalitarian economy. However, the reforms did not develop the way Gorbachev expected. They led to a sharp decline in living standards, the emergence of political instability, and ethnic conflicts within the Soviet Union

(Tsygankov 2019, chap. 2). In addition, external support for the ambitious idea of changing the world was missing. Western leaders viewed the New Thinking with suspicion and did not support the vision of global unity based on contributions by both capitalist and socialist systems (Marcetic 2022).

The idea of liberal globalization appeared in the context of the West's confidence and growing international recognition. Following the end of the Cold War and the Soviet disintegration, Western nations appeared triumphant and convinced that their domestic institutions were universally applicable. Many non-Western leaders shared the feeling and aspired to build similar institutions and join West-centered international organizations. The above-discussed "end of history" drew initial interest and was widely discussed worldwide. However, in the second half of the 2000s, the idea of liberal globalization confronted a growing list of problems, including the 2008 global financial crisis, the domestic and global adverse reactions to the US military interventions, and the growing internal divisions within Western societies.

The above-discussed idea of Tianxia is yet another example of a global idea articulated by Chinese intellectuals. The idea has emerged and is being widely discussed in the context of the country's confidence as the world's potential superpower. Internationally, the idea is yet to gain sufficient recognition. The extent of Tianxia's influence on Beijing's policies deserves to be investigated further. However, even assuming such influence is considerable, reactions across the globe to China's developmental strategy and ideas of "peaceful rise" and "global harmony" are mixed. The country's global projects, such as the new Silk Road, have generated interest in some parts of the world, while others have been suspicious and resentful.

Global ideas that aim to build bridges across diverse cultural communities lose their initial appeal in response to crises of domestic confidence and resulting ontological insecurity in the world. Developments in the United States and Russia can illustrate these developments resulting in a decline in domestic confidence and international support.

The Western liberal idea of globalization began to decline in the late 2000s. During the 2010s, the more nationally exceptional ideas challenged the liberal idea. The unexpected developments in European societies and the election of Donald Trump as the US president in November 2016 caught many by surprise while reflecting the rise of new nationalist ideas. The latter expressed a polarization and lack of confidence within Western societies faced with new economic, political, and migration-related issues. Skepticism toward the West-centered globalization in Europe and other parts of the world has become an essential driver of the re-nationalization and regionalization of politics, pushing toward new international divisions and areas of competition. The Trump phenomenon is now studied as "authoritarian populism" in American and European politics (Norris and Inglehart 2019).

Russia turned to more nationally exceptional ideas, even before Trump, by stressing the prominence of political sovereignty and cultural difference from the West. Russian intellectuals have searched for nationally distinct values in the context of domestic weakness and lack of Western recognition of Russia's international interests. Russian intellectuals have actively promoted the vision of a fortress as a protective response to pressures from an alien Western civilization demanding compliance with its values and interests. Major currents in Russian IR have accepted the importance of national distinctiveness by providing their justification for the new discursive turn (Tsygankov and Tsygankov 2021). During the 1990s, Russia transitioned from a communist system. However, it soon concluded that the West-recommended reforms undermined state sovereignty and weakened the state's capacity to modernize based on domestic needs. As a result, although initially an admirer of the West, Russia has emerged as a critic actively seeking to carve out its own economic and political niche in global markets and political institutions. Vladimir Putin's increasingly anti-Western and nationalist state aims to protect its development path by dictating the conditions of domestic and foreign participation in the Russian business and energy sectors. Western economic sanctions imposed on Russia following its annexation of Crimea and invasion of Ukraine further pushed the Kremlin away from Western markets. In political affairs, Russia has embraced anti-Americanism and sought to protect itself against Western democratization pressures by warning outsiders against interference with Russia's domestic developments and by restricting the activities of Western NGOs and pro-Western opposition inside the country.

Alternative Explanations

The explanation of civilizational "ideas" rises and falls as resulting from foreign (Western) recognition, and domestic confidence can be objected to on at least three substantive grounds: essentialist, realist, and liberal.

Cultural essentialists[5] view civilizational ideas as reflecting civilization's ontological coherence and propensity to protect or promote their cultural values. According to this perspective, all ideas are culturally exceptional and incapable of cross-cultural enrichment or dialogue. If there are natural and distinctive boundaries between civilizations, as Samuel Huntington and others argued, one cannot but remain skeptical regarding possible cross-civilizational cooperation and learning. Hence Huntington's (1997) argument about conflicts that are likely to occur between Western and Orthodox Christianity in Europe; between Orthodox and Muslim people in Europe and Eurasia; between Muslims and Hindus in Asia; between China and America; and between Japan and the United States in the global scale.

Realist explanations stress the role of geopolitical conditions in determining the rise and fall of civilizational ideas. To realists, ideas reflect the power position of a country within the international system. The rising power status is likely to result in the emergence of global ideas, which the outside world will recognize insofar as the world recognizes the nation's material and political capabilities. Unlike cultural essentialists, realists, by focusing on states and governments, underestimate the autonomous role of cultural values and ideas. Analyzing the world in terms of "nation-states," realists neglect potentially critical differences between nations' and states' values and priorities. For example, in his book, John Mearsheimer (2018) criticized liberalism from the positions of realism and nationalism by not exploring the principal differences between realism and nationalism. Even when realists add to their analysis variables such as ideology and political culture, they view their role in world affairs as secondary to that of power and the structure of the international system.

Finally, liberals and liberal constructivists view civilizational ideas as resulting from varying political contexts, processes, and elites' choices. Liberals are uncomfortable with the national as defined by historical and cultural values. Instead, they prioritize individual rights, viewing those as natural and existing before politics and community.[6] While essentialists overestimate civilizations' coherence, liberals underestimate the continuity of cultural contexts in developing nationally distinct values and ideas. In their assessment, local cultural differences notwithstanding, the world is forming a single "culture of modernity" that sets standards for others to follow (Finnemore 1996; Katzenstein 2009). Another aspect of liberal constructivist thinking is a top-down approach to forming, sustaining, and changing cultural structures. For instance, some studies present civilizations as imagined and governed by political and intellectual elites with little room allocated for mass social values and perceptions (Jackson 2007; Hall and Jackson 2010). The emphasis here is on civilizations' agency and capacity to act under specific procedures and processes via influential agents.

My argument incorporates and moves beyond essentialist, realist, and liberal constructivist approaches. In contrast to essentialism, civilizations are not once and forever established coherent entities acting like super-states in a zero-sum world. Rather, civilization, as Arnold Toynbee (1948, 55) wrote, "is a movement and not a condition, a voyage, and not a harbor." Multiple ideas commonly represent civilizations, some of which are global and some are nationally exceptional. How and why these ideas prevail and become nationally dominant is a complex process in which cultural memory, power status, and leaders' choices play distinctive roles. Elites, intellectuals, and political leaders make choices by stressing some values and memories over others. Using available material and ideational resources, different coalitions form to promote their visions in public and private spaces. However, elites and leaders do not have all the flexibility to favor some ideas over others in shaping social discourses. Foreign pressures, power status, the influence of historically established values, and nationally persistent memory are also critically important. The world, therefore, remains in a state of irreducible cultural diversity not to be subsumed under the broader context of modern rationality.

Explaining Russian Civilizational Ideas

This section applies the above-developed concepts of global dialogue and national exceptionalism to Russia. Russian civilizational ideas progressed by responding to the country's dilemma of relations with the country's Western other. Preserving national distinctiveness while strengthening ties with the West has been a constant challenge. Western perception – favorable or unfavorable – has been essential, leading to global and exceptionalist thinking inside Russia.

Russia's Civilizational Dilemma

Russia's civilizational discourse complexity results from its original institutions and ambivalent relations with Western/European others. Russia seeks to preserve its institutions while obtaining recognition from and developing ties with the outside world. The challenge is to reconnect to the "significant Other" while retaining those historical values that have defined Russia as a nation.[7] Europe created a larger meaningful environment in which Russia's rulers defended their core values. Although Europe's recognition of Russia as one of its own was never unproblematic (Neumann 1999; Malia 1999; Smith 2019), Russia's leaders identified with European ideas. Some rulers – most prominently Alexander II – attempted again to redefine the country's identity in line with the new European ideas of Enlightenment, Constitutionalism, and Capitalism. Others sought to defend old Europe and preserve the basic features of the autocratic regime. In the early twentieth century, the Bolsheviks made the critical identity choice by pronouncing Russia the Soviet Union and proclaiming a break with the "bourgeois" Europe. The Soviet disintegration revealed the situation of identity crisis in which a nation with seemingly European roots is attempting to reconnect with its significant Other after decades of lacking recognition from it.

The roots of this civilizational dilemma are old. At least since Czar Peter the Great, Europe figured prominently in Russia's debates on national identity. In the early nineteenth century, the Russian philosopher Pyotr Chaadayev famously expressed his ambivalence regarding his nation's belongingness to Europe, the latter being commonly assumed by his contemporaries. Since then, Russia has been in, of, and for Europe, as it was outside and against it. In attempting to preserve what they saw as their lifestyle, Russian rulers successfully adapted to the growing power of Christianity while preserving the ambivalent attitude toward the European civilization. However, when the egalitarian ideals of the French revolution of 1789 split Europe into progressive and anti-revolutionary camps, Russia had to make a choice. The Bolshevik Revolution of October 1917 reflected the struggle between the two Europes and the resulting crisis of Russia's external identification.

In the absence of the czar's ability to answer the newly emerged identity questions, the Bolsheviks made the critical identity choice by proclaiming

Russia's break with its "bourgeois" past and, in 1922, pronouncing it the Soviet Union. Unlike some previous critics of the two Europes, the Bolsheviks adopted not merely a *non*-European, but an *anti*-European identity.[8] Their socialist identity vision implied the perceived superiority of Russia relative to the liberal and autocratic Europe. Over the decades of revolutionary transformations, the Soviet system obtained the qualities of a distinctive civilization (Kotkin 1990; Sinyavski 2001; Kara-Murza 2002). Its disintegration in 1991 meant a collapse of the previously established system of values, not just of hierarchically established political relations between the core and the periphery (empire).

That system of cultural values reflected a belief in the common destiny of Russia and other nationalities living in the geographical space of the former USSR, and people across that space widely shared that belief. Even in the highly politicized discourse of Perestroika, many polls of the general public demonstrated the resilience of this civilizational thinking and the potential for its continuous support. For instance, during the referendum on 17 March 1991, which took place in the context of Gorbachev's struggle for a renewed Union and was conducted in all of the Soviet republics except the three Baltics, Armenia, Georgia, and Moldavia, 147 million people voted, and 76.4 percent approved the preservation of the Union.[9] Prominent intellectuals and politicians on both conservative and reformist sides, too, showed their commitments to preserving core elements of this civilizational system. Gorbachev himself signaled his support for newly reformulated civilizational ideas and renewed union of Eurasianist nature.[10]

The situation of cultural and political ambivalence stimulated civilizational thinking in post-Soviet Russia. Several Civilizational schools or perspectives have defined Russia's cultural status and determined its appropriate goals and international strategy. Some argued that the "return" to Europe was the only available option and a viable civilizational project. Others have cautioned that cultural integration with Europe cannot come true without sacrificing a considerable part of Russia's values, including a strong state, Orthodox religion, and collectivist economy. This debate has deep intellectual and historical roots, and it delineates what may be seen as Russia's civilizational dilemma: How can one connect with the European Other while preserving its Self?

Exceptionalism and Dialogue

Russian civilizational ideas can be usefully classified using concepts of exceptionalism and dialogue. While the former presents Russia as a community with fixed cultural, political, and economic boundaries shielded from the outside, particularly the Western world, the latter makes sense of the country in terms of its relative openness to outside influences. Therefore, the first essential criterion for classifying Russian thinking is exclusiveness–inclusiveness vis-à-vis the nation's historically prominent significant Other, the West.

The second criterion concerns Russia's internal institutions – spiritual, economic, political, and spatial or geographic. While seeking the West's recognition, Russia has historically preserved its cultural and political values. Some of these values included the idea of a strong state. Others included a commitment to Orthodox Christianity and special relations with non-Russian nationalities and non-Western nations. Russian Slavophiles have stressed the country's unique spirituality. Communists have emphasized the distinctiveness of Russia's economic institutions with their roots in peasant communes. Finally, Eurasianists have drawn attention to Russia's geoeconomic and geopolitical relations within the region that differentiates and connects Europe, Asia, and the Middle East.

The above-introduced external exclusion–inclusion and internal institutional criteria yield nine schools of Russian civilizational thinking (please see Table 2.1).

Westernizers include those who strongly favor Western civilization, albeit for different reasons. Conservative Westernizers connect with the West's conservative values, such as those of Christianity, the monarchical system, or traditional family values. For example, the early nineteenth-century Russian Westernizers were not liberal and, instead, sought to present Russia as a loyal member of the family of European monarchies. A different group of Westernizers identifies with the West's social institutions, such as constitutional freedoms, free markets, and individual political equality. After the Great Reforms era and Russia's shifting its relations from Germany to France and Britain under Alexander II, the Czarist government seemed more willing to embrace the new European values of constitutionalism. Even Westernizers within the Soviet system saw Russia as not standing too far apart from Europe by emphasizing social-democratic ideas. Finally, some Westernizers stress the spatial or geographic dimension of their gravitation to the West by stressing Russia's Europeanness regarding extensive relations with European nations.

On the other side of the exclusion–inclusion spectrum are those who visualize Russia as an anti-Western fortress capable of protecting and/or expanding the nation's values abroad. Their perception of Russian spiritual, social, and

TABLE 2.1 Russian Intellectual Currents

	Europe/West		*Non-West*
	←⋯⋯⋯⋯⋯⋯⋯⋯⋯⋯⋯⋯⋯⋯⋯⋯⋯⋯⋯⋯⋯→		
	ASSIMILATION	*DIALOGUE*	*EXCEPTIONALISM*
Spiritual	Conservative	Early Slavophiles	Late Slavophiles
Social	Westernizers	Global Communists	National & Revolutionary
Spatial	Liberal Westernizers	Advocates of a	Communists
	Europeanists	Greater Eurasia	Eurasianists &
			Neo-Eurasianists

spatial roots is radically different from that of Westernizers. They present Russia's Orthodox Christianity, communal values in politics and economics, and Eurasian foreign relations as principally superior to the West. Slavophiles, especially those of the late nineteenth century, strongly desired to separate Russia from Western Europe and build a unique unity with the Slavic peoples of eastern Europe and the Balkans. Russian Communists wanted Russia to preserve its original social and political institutions while showing the world a path to a more progressive development than the one presented by the West. Finally, Eurasianists argued for severing foreign relations with Europeans and capitalizing on Russia's special, historically sustained ties in Asia and the Muslim world.

Between those positioning Russia as pro-Western and those viewing it in anti-Western terms are those favoring dialogue with the West without sacrificing Russia's historically developed values. Within the identified civilizational currents stressing authentic Russian values – Slavophiles, Communists, and Eurasianist – there were those insisting on the importance of a dialogue with and learning from the West. Some early Slavophiles – Vladimir Solovyev, and his followers – advocated a spiritually centered dialogue with Europeans. A distinct group of Russian Communists argued for a dialogue with Left forces in the West to realize what they saw as Russia's global mission. Finally, some Eurasianists advanced the idea of Russia as a part of a greater Eurasia and a geocultural bridge to connect Europe and Asia. All three schools believed in Russia's capacity to lead the world to a better future.

Rise and Fall of Russian Ideas

Following the above-introduced framework, I explain the rise and fall of Russian civilizational ideas by developments within the West and inside Russia. In this volume, I do not analyze the ideas of Westernizers and instead focus on those intellectual currents that have proceeded from the nation's cultural distinctiveness – spiritual, social, and spatial.[11]

Russian ideas of a fortress and separation from the West have responded to the perceived decline of conditions that once united Russia with its significant Other, such as Christian roots, shared monarchical legacy, and diplomatic relations. If the West was perceived as a weak relative to Russia, the authors of such ideas argued for expanding areas of Russian values at the expense of those of the West. If instead, the West was viewed as not only culturally alien but also strong and assertive, the stress according to Russian authors has been on defending their civilizational fortress from Western encroachment.

Alternatively, those Russian ideas that stressed an interaction and dialogue with the West have responded to the perceived similarity of Russian and Western values and conditions, and Russia's confidence in showing the way to improve relations and understanding with the West.

The Slavophile ideas have emerged in the context of Europe's growing secularism and liberalism. Like the Russian writer Fyodor Dostoyevsky

(2006), Slavophiles viewed Europe as their "second fatherland" and reacted to the weakening of Christian ideals in Europe. In the perception of the early Slavophiles, the revolutionary upheavals of the 1840s were the retribution of the European continent for abandoning traditional religious values in favor of "corrupting" individualism, secularism, and the nation-state. They warned against the temptations of materiality and argued for following the "Russian path" based on Christian and communal values. The late Slavophiles showed an even greater disappointment in Europe and argued for uniting all Slavs under the leadership of Russia.

Russian Communists, beginning with Alexander Hertzen, were disillusioned with European socio-economic changes and the development of private–property-based institutions. They viewed the revolutions of the 1840s as paving the way to the abandonment of the ideals of social equality and shared economic prosperity. In different historical periods, Communists were united by a belief in their country's distinctiveness and superiority as the leader of the world's egalitarian development. Inspired by the perceived rise of socialism in Europe, some Russian communists argued for strengthening relations with the West. Others were pessimistic and wanted Russia to advance socially egalitarian ideas in separation from the West. Joseph Stalin (2002) was especially known for advocating Soviet independence through a "revolution in a single country." The support for Stalin's ideas declined in the context of European unity and prosperity during the 1970s.

Eurasianism reacted to European decline and instability in the late nineteenth century – the first decades of the twentieth century. Weakened by the First World War, the European nations proved unable to defeat Bolshevism, and so offered a compelling alternative. Most Eurasianists were immigrants to Europe from Soviet Russia who rejected the Bolshevik system yet remained suspicious of European liberalism. They built on the late Slavophiles' views of Europe as threatening Russia's cultural identity. Most Eurasianists had limited expansionist ambitions. Instead, they strived to secure Russia's geopolitical and geocultural status as a unique, self-sufficient civilization. Only some, like Pyotr Suvchinsky and Alexander Dugin, advocated Eurasia's "revolutionary" expansion.

Slavophiles, Communists, and Eurasianists

Russian civilizational schools developed in varying historical contexts preserving elements of change and continuity. Many Slavophiles, Communists, and Eurasianists have viewed the world in nationally exceptionalist terms, often justifying the government's anti-Western policies. However, all three schools have also devised ideas of dialogue and engagement with the outside world.

Slavophiles and the Spiritual

Historical conditions for Slavophiles' emergence and development have had to do with the particular character of Russia's Christianity. Initially progressing under the influence of Byzantium (Florovsky 1983; Averintsev 1990), Russian Orthodox Christianity had developed critical special features. Until the 17th century, it successfully resisted the attempts of the authorities to subjugate the Church in the manner of the eastern empire. The period of Russia's occupation by the Golden Horde weakened Byzantine influence, thereby contributing to the emergence of indigenous Orthodox Christian thinking in Russia. At the end of the fifteenth century, following the fall of Byzantium and the end of Mongol domination, attitudes toward spiritual self-sufficiency grew stronger among the Russian princes. The rise of Muscovy and its improved reputation since the battle of Kulikovo created the political conditions for establishing such self-sufficiency. The Russian state now desired ideological autonomy, which was claimed by Ivan the Third in his refusal to accept the patronage of Catholic Rome. The "Moscow as the Third Rome" doctrine reflected spiritual and political demand for independence from European influence. According to one of the scholars of the doctrine, "the unification of individual principalities under the leadership of Moscow provided the powerful impetus to the political thought of the Russian people at the end of the 15th century" (Kirillov 1914, 2).

The subsequent political and ideological paths of Russia and Europe were increasingly different. Russia accepted and internalized the norm of the absolutism of European states. However, it refused to accept the movement toward democratization and secularization. Instead, the Russian state increasingly followed the Byzantine practice of subordinating the church to political interests. In contrast, church circles continued to cherish the idea of the symphonic or harmonious unity between the state and the church. Another factor that separated Russia and Europe concerned their diverging geopolitical interests. In the mid-nineteenth century, the difference in interests resulted in the Crimean War.

Russia's new ideas sought to respond to the demand for spiritual and political independence vis-à-vis the European continent. Without breaking all the existing spiritual relations with Europe, the Slavophile school set out to substantiate the unique nature of Russia's influence on the outside world. The Slavophiles reacted to the trend of European secularization and wished to revive Christian ideals spiritually and in public life. Some of them believed in creating a theocratic system. Others argued that the church could regain its influence, not through involvement in public affairs, but by focusing on the salvation of souls. Without directly participating in political and economic life, the church was expected to contribute to forming a socially just order by concentrating on improving its moral and ethical foundations.

In response to the European revolutions of the 1840s, the early Slavophiles split into those who desired a new dialogue with Europe and those who wanted to protect Russia from "pernicious" continental influences. While critical of Europe, Ivan Kireyevsky and Nikolai Khomyakov did not separate Russia from it. Instead, they were eager to demonstrate what they viewed as the advantages of the Russian spiritual and economic experience. Another group included Konstantin Aksakov, who valued the development of Russia in separation from

Europe. Most Slavophiles were also critical of Peter the Great and his role in establishing of the Russian state as dependent on European developments, including the revolutions. While supporting the autocratic state, they defined it in their way without compromising the principles of the church's spiritual autonomy and the economic community's freedom.

In the final quarter of the century, following the spread of secular and leftist ideas in Europe and the growing confrontation between Germany and France, another deep divide emerged within the Slavophile school. Philosopher Vladimir Solovyov went further than the early Slavophiles in asserting Russian spiritual unity with Europe. He advanced the idea of a new reunification with the European continent on theocratic foundations. The reaction to the European processes by Pan-Slavists, headed by Ivan Aksakov, was radically different. In no way supportive of France, they were especially critical of Germany, arguing the principal differences between the Slavic and Romano-Germanic cultural types. Pan-Slavists advocated the integration of Russia only with the Slavic peoples, refusing to unite with the rest of the European peoples.

The next crucial ideological division within Slavophile thought occurred due to the Bolshevik Revolution of 1917. Solovyov's followers, including Nikolai Berdyaev and Christian socialists, sought to emphasize in their work the cultural connection between Russia and Christian Europe and defended the spiritual freedom of the individual from the encroachments of the authorities. Developing the "Russian idea" as the idea of global unity, they advocated a "true kingdom" of spiritual freedom rather than capitalism and individualism (Berdyayev 1995; Fedotov 1991). In turn, monarchical and imperial Russian supporters adopted an entirely different attitude toward Europe during the interwar period. Russian philosopher Ivan Ilyin (1992) and his supporters argued for isolation from "Russophobic" Europe. They saw threats coming not only from Bolshevism but also from the West.

In the post-war period, Alexander Solzhenitsyn and Russian nationalist thinkers like Igor Shafarevich had much to agree with Ilyin (Brudny 1999). None of them wanted to strengthen the spiritual connection with the European continent in the way that the early Slavophiles or followers of the religious renaissance desired. Very few inside Russia supported a spiritual dialogue with Europe. They included people such as Grigory Pomerants (1990; 2004), who was in the position of dissident within the Soviet system. Most Slavophile thinkers were skeptical of such dialogue, with Europe aware of Russia's great geopolitical, cultural, and political differences, such as its imperial structure and strong state.

After the collapse of the Soviet Union, Slavophile thought found itself in new conditions. On the one hand, in the absence of censorship, opportunities arose for the development of the previously existing nativist, or the "village" direction of the magazines *Moskva, Nash Sovremennik,* and others. On the other hand, the period of strict Soviet censorship deepened the polarization of intellectual discourse, influencing Slavophile thought as well. The above-noted confrontation between supporters and critics of dialogue with Europe progressed further, deepening the crisis of Russian identity.

For example, the ideas of Ilyin and Solzhenitsyn were adopted by supporters of restoring the empire within the Soviet borders (Panarin 2014; Narochnitskaya 2004; Nazarov 2005). Ilyin and Solzhenitsyn condemned the Soviet empire as not serving the interests of the Russians. By contrast, the new Slavophiles emphasized the continuity of Russia's history and values insisting on the vital significance of the Soviet period. They presented the latter as a short but victorious time. The Soviet victories built on victories of the southern Novgorod principalities, the colonization of the North, the monastic lifestyle, the resistance to the Mongol occupation, the gathering of Russian lands under the banner of the Third Rome, and the revival of the country after the Time of Troubles (Kholmogorov 2006a; *Russkaya doktrina* 2007). While praising national sovereignty, the new Slavophiles do not emphasize the legal foundations of power (as Ilyin did) or the division of labor between state and society (like the early Slavophiles). Instead, they highlight the imperial state's economic, political, and cultural self-sufficiency (*Russkaya doktrina* 2007, 16–17).

Concerning the West, the position of new Slavophiles is partly consonant with the views of the late Slavophiles and Solzhenitsyn. They are convinced of a deep crisis in Western civilization and of the opportunities that this crisis presents for Russia (Ibid., 11). They expect that in the face of the progressive decline of Western countries, Russia will be able to restore its imperial self-sufficiency. After the annexation of Crimea by Russia, some of the new Slavophiles advocated a different model for developing the historically Russian territories, including the east of Ukraine. They supported economic and civilizational self-sufficiency and isolationist foreign policy toward unfriendly states (Remizov 2016; Kholmogorov 2006a, 2006b). According to the new Slavophiles, the Russian state is not a European nation but a self-sufficient Eurasian empire that develops strategic ties with non-European countries (*Russkaya doktrina* 2007, 297, 313).

Regarding the ideas of spiritual dialogue with Europe, they were not in great demand in post-Soviet Russia. Instead, there appeared theories of "fatigue" from the "imperial" state and of the anti-imperial nationalism of Russians. Their supporters criticized the traditional imperial state in Russia as resulting from the Muscovite system (Solovei 2005, 2008) or the religious schism (Glinchikova 2008). They postulate a principal conflict between the state and society in Russian history. Accusing the state of betraying its people, they insist on the people's right to free themselves from the dominance of the state and "empire." Some call to establish Russia anew as a decentralized and racially "white" polity by abandoning territories populated by non-Russian nationalities in the northern Caucasus (Barry 2019; Blakkisrud 2022).

These anti-imperial ideas are radically different from their predecessors. The latter would have hardly endorsed the idea of a racially pure and decentralized Russia. Even those Slavophiles who were critical of the state recognized it "as a necessary, inevitable evil" (the wording of Konstantin Aksakov cited in Zhaba

1954, 48). They never proposed to abandon any Russian territories and did not call to return to pre-Petrine, let alone pre-Muscovy Russia.[12]

Communists and the Social

The Russian notion of equality combines the traditions of the peasant commune with Western egalitarian ideas. Peasant communes arose in Russia in ancient times, leaving a significant imprint on the development of Russian thought. The commune adhered to the principle of fair income distribution and elected local authorities. Russian tsars, beginning with Ivan the Terrible, exploited the commune for various purposes – from collecting taxes to recruiting soldiers – thereby contributing to its conservation. In particular, the authorities encouraged the principle of mutual or collective responsibility (*krugovaya poruka*) for the payment of taxes and redemption payments because there was no other way to collect debts in the case of communal land use. As an economically and politically autonomous institution, the commune arose before the autocracy, but it survived the advent of serfdom (Milov 2006). Even when the latter was abolished, the commune did not disappear. Instead, it was transformed into societies for former landlord peasants from 300 to 2,000 people.

The historical processes of the second half of the nineteenth century undermined the commune's foundations, pushing Russia onto the path of industrial-capitalist development. At the end of the century, state intervention in the affairs of the commune increased. The agrarian reform of Pyotr Stolypin reduced the role of the commune in the country's economic life. The conservative nature of the reform and the active development of capitalism contributed to the emergence and activism of the Left political forces. The ideas of Karl Marx spread among the intelligentsia. Even populists or those speaking on behalf of the peasant masses became interested in Marxism. Some populists, like Vera Zasulich, entered into correspondence with Marx. They were interested in his attitude to the commune and the possibilities of its combination with socialism. Others, in particular Nikolai Danielson, acted as translators and distributors of Marx's principal work, *Capital* (Anikin 1990, 380–386). Further historical developments contributed to the weakening of not only populism but also moderate forces within the government and the opposition. Following Russia's participation in devastating World War I, the country went through the Bolshevik Revolution, and the movement along the path of capitalism was interrupted.

The attitudes of dialogue with and alienation from Europe can be traced at different times. In the second half of the nineteenth century, the rise of industrial capitalism affected Russian anarchism, which exemplified both attitudes toward Europe. For instance, like many Pan-Slavists, Mikhail Bakunin was highly critical of Germany and Austria. However, unlike Pan-Slavists, he desired the revolutionary collapse of monarchy in Europe and Russia. Another representative of anarchism, Prince Peter Kropotkin, advocated the gradual transformation of Russian and European societies based on principles of Christian morality. His ideas turned out to be consonant with the ideas of Leo Tolstoy and the Russian religious renaissance associated with Vladimir Solovyev and his supporters.

During the same time, the populist movement advocated the social liberation of the Russian people. Like the anarchists, the populists were critical of the Russian state but were politically more conservative and advocated separation from Europe based on traditional peasant values. The influential thinker Alexander Herzen, who emigrated to Europe, argued for the development of Russia in a break from Europe to preserve the peasant commune. Several populists, such as Pyotr Lavrov and Nikolai Mikhailovsky, promoted the idea in their writings. They contrasted capitalism with the development of a free and integral personality whose integrity results from the commune's development and is not fragmented by modern industrial civilization.

Among Marxists, the division also concerned the attitude toward Europe. Marxists did not agree with populists and anarchists in their rejection of industrial civilization. At the beginning of the twentieth century, classical Marxists, like Georgy Plekhanov, advocated the development of relations with European social democrats and expected the gradual maturation of capitalism in Russia. The more radical wing, associated with Vladimir Lenin and Leon Trotsky, argued for seizing power in Russia and developing the country on an industrial basis while bypassing the stage of capitalism through the organization of concentrated state power.

Later, following the Russian Revolution, the Bolsheviks were also not united in their views. Some considered the country's development part of global and European processes. They expected that further development of Soviet socialism would be possible only if there were external conditions for this and the support of the left forces of Europe. Lenin, Trotsky, and Nikolai Bukharin proceeded from such understanding during the 1920s. They considered the development of the world communist movement necessary for the preservation of socialism in the USSR.[13] On the other hand, Josef Stalin spoke from an isolationist position and argued for building communism in isolation from the outside "hostile capitalist" world. To him, the Western world was the primary source of threat, and the main priority was to create a national military and civilian industry.

The disagreement between isolationists and supporters of dialogue continued in the last decades of Soviet development. Nikita Khrushchev and later Mikhail Gorbachev argued for coexistence and cooperation with Western countries. Advocates of a more isolationist position, such as Richard Kosolapov, the editor of the leading Communist Party journal, *Kommunist*, supported the political course of Leonid Brezhnev (Marchenko 2020). Like Stalin in the earlier historical period, they defended independent development based on the already established foundations of the socialist system.

After the collapse of the Soviet system, the controversy between isolationist and globally oriented-leftist ideas continued. At the same time, their positions were radicalized due to Russia's renewed search for national identity and a place in international relations.

The isolationists continued the movement begun by Stalin towards nationalism and opposition to the West. This thinking was often represented by those ideologically and politically associated with the Communist Party of the Russian Federation. Communists argued that Russia was still in a hostile world and needed to be economically and politically self-sufficient (Zyuganov 1999, 2002). Fear of the West and globalization was central to their thinking. In line with the traditional Bolshevik views of global capitalism, they were convinced of the deep crisis of Western civilization, seeing in this crisis opportunities for Russia. According to this view, as an independent Eurasian power, Russia is principally different from the West (*Russkaya doktrina* 2007, 11).

The global trend within the new left movement searched for a new subject for the global revolutionary process. Unlike the isolationists, the globally minded thinkers were convinced of the importance of external support for the defeat of capitalism. They found a new revolutionary class in various social movements advocating global egalitarian ideas. Unlike isolationists, this group accepted European values (democracy, human rights), but considered them insufficient for socialist development in Russia and the world. Theorists like Boris Kagarlitsky (2003, 2010) argued for transforming the entire system of global capitalism, of which Russia was an integral part. In their view, without such a transformation, Russia would remain integrated into the system of exploitation or non-equivalent socio-economic exchange between the capitalist center and the periphery.

Eurasianists and the Spatial

The emergence of Eurasianism also resulted from the weakening of Russia's relations with Europe. Following World War I, the European states failed to defeat Bolshevism but emerged relatively united in defeating Germany. Eurasianists reacted to the West's growing power and geopolitical ambitions. The Eurasian thought was built on the assumption that geopolitical and cultural conflicts were at the core of Russian and European differences. Eurasianists viewed Russian and European interests as competitive and shaped by the difference in religious and socio-economic institutions.

Central to Eurasianist thinking is the search for a strategy for geopolitical survival in the face of Western pressure and the West's drive for global expansion. In their view, Russia's survival as a unique imperial state required that it understands and exploits its particular geographic and geocultural position. Determined to understand the motives for Western actions in the world, the Eurasianists evaluated all historical events through the lens of conflict with Western expansionism. Such events included the competition between imperial Russia and European countries, the revolution of 1917, the Bolshevik regime, the Cold War, and the post-Cold War order following the end of the US–Soviet confrontation. In response to perceived pressures from the geopolitically alien West, some Eurasianists argued for Russia's geopolitical self-sufficiency. In contrast, others promoted global revolutionary expansion in partnership with the West's internal critics.

The Eurasianist movement went through several stages, reacting to significant changes in the world. The theme of self-sufficiency and "local development" (*mestorazvitiye*) was strong in the classical Eurasianism of Nikolai Trubetskoy and Petr Savitsky after the Bolshevik Revolution.[14] The Eurasianists were critical of Europe and its instability and of Bolshevik Russia, from which they were forced to immigrate. Their suspicion toward Europe had roots in geopolitical tensions of the older period expressed in theories of their nineteenth-century thinkers, such as Nikolai Danilevsky and Konstantin Leontyev. These thinkers opposed "Europeanization" mainly in the context of Russian–European competition for the Balkans. The Eurasianist Nikolai Trubetskoy, who did not sympathize with the Bolsheviks, was nevertheless convinced of the danger presented by Europe to Russia's cultural identity.

Already at this stage, some among the Eurasianists opposed isolation from Europe and advocated an active, revolutionary transformation of the West. Such thinking was adopted by the left wing of Eurasianism, associated with Lev Karsavin, Pyotr Suvchinsky, Dmitry Svyatopolk-Mirsky, and others. Some within this group tried cooperating with the Soviet authorities, advocating the revolution as a cleansing process and renewal of Russian statehood.

During the Soviet period, Eurasianist thought was officially banned. Its most important representative was the marginalized geographer Lev Gumilyov. In the meantime, the geopolitical analysis favored by Eurasianists retained its significance within state institutions associated with military planning, particularly the military's general staff. While Gumilev, who considered himself a student of Savitsky and Trubetskoy, was working on the ideas of Russia's self-sufficiency and separation from the "alien" "super ethnicity" of Europe, the planners of the general staff were looking for ways to oppose the geopolitical plans of the United States globally.

After the collapse of the USSR, the idea of revolutionary expansion found its development in the works of Alexander Dugin. The latter contrasted the countries of the "Atlantic" geopolitical orientation to the Eurasianists represented by land-based powers. In his analysis, the United States and Great Britain were natural leaders of the former, while Russia was the leading power of the Eurasianist orientation. Such a globally minded approach was met with resistance from supporters of rebuilding geopolitical unity within the borders of the USSR and preserving stability within the post-Soviet territorial space. Others, like Vadim Tsymbursky, prioritized Russia's internal development and geopolitical self-sufficiency. In his geopolitical analysis, Russia's geopolitical position as an "island" protected the country from most important external threats and providing it with the opportunity for development (Mezhuyev 2012, 2015; Tsygankov 2022, chap. 6).

The position of global dialogue with Europe and the West turned out to be less influential in Eurasianism. Nevertheless, some Russian thinkers associate

Eurasianism with the ability of Russia to mediate between Europe and Asia. In late Soviet times, the historian Mikhail Gefter and other thinkers expressed ideas for such a dialogue and mediation. After the collapse of the Soviet system, Alexander Panarin and others expressed similar views, although Panarin later moved to other, more radical positions.[15] At a later stage, Sergei Karaganov and other experts in Moscow promoted the perspective of "greater Eurasia" in part to preserve Russia's relations in Asia and Europe.

Civilization and the Russian Idea Today

This final section discusses new developments in Russian civilizational thinking shaped by post-Soviet conditions, such as global economic interdependence and growing political instability. These conditions have introduced new versions of exceptionalism and dialogue within Russian IR. I begin by analyzing the idea of state-civilization in Russian official circles. I then describe exceptionalist discourses in Russian IR as shaped by the historical influence of the school, the Kremlin's propaganda, and the West's actions after the Cold War. I also demonstrate the persistence of the dialogue ideas articulated by supporters of Russia's engagement with the outside world. With the decline of the West's appeal to Russia, some Russian intellectuals advocate intensifying dialogue with non-Western societies while not breaking all the relations with the West.

The Rise of Civilizational Thinking

Politicians and intellectuals in Russia have applied different meanings to the term "civilization." Some think of civilization as a global phenomenon and associate it with joint human achievements by concentrating on results, not the sources of such achievements. To others, civilization implies tolerance in treating those who are culturally different. For example, Russian politicians frequently speak of the importance of civilized dialogue between various ethnic communities inside and outside the country. Finally, the language of local cultural distinctiveness (*samobytnost'*), or cultural self-standing, highlights local values and moral norms as they differ from those shared in other parts of the world.

The rise of civilization as a culturally distinctive entity vis-à-vis Western and non-Western nations after the Soviet dissolution can be traced to the mid-2000s. Since then, politicians from the relatively marginal to the established have begun to regularly link Russia's foreign policy to its cultural/civilizational values. Officials, including Vladimir Putin and others, advance the notion of Russia-civilization in their speeches and public writing. Some of them, such as Russia's foreign minister Sergei Lavrov (2008), wrote about it even earlier, arguing that "competition is becoming truly global and acquiring a civilizational dimension; that is, the subject of competition now includes values and development models."

Before Putin's election for the third term as Russia's president in 2012, the Kremlin's discourse was largely shaped by the ideas of adjustment to the international community and protecting national interests (Tsygankov 2016a). However, since then, he has advanced the idea of state-civilization, recognizing ethnic Russians as "the core [*sterzhen'*] that binds the fabric" of Russia as a culture and a state (Putin 2012a). Being especially concerned with national unity, Putin pointed to the "deficit of spiritual values" and recommended strengthening "the institutions that are the carriers of traditional values," especially family and schools. In multiple statements, he has further criticized what he sees as Europe's departure from traditional religious and family values. In one speech, he declared "the desire for independence and sovereignty in spiritual, ideological and foreign policy spheres" as an "integral part of our national character" (Putin 2013b).

The discourse of distinctiveness from the West grew more robust in the context of the Ukraine crisis and reached its highest strength following Russia's invasion of Ukraine in 2022. Putin sought to justify the incorporation of Crimea in terms of consolidating Russia's civilizational values on imperial nationalist grounds (Putin 2014) and described the values of Ukrainian authorities as Nazi-like and anti-Russian (Putin 2022).

The described civilizational turn ended Russia's attempts to reach an understanding with the West. Before 2012, Putin and his predecessors talked about the imperatives of modernization and associated civilization with present-day human achievements. Such was the discourse of Dmitry Medvedev (2009). He responded to the global financial crisis by criticizing Russia's domestic conditions, such as "a primitive economy based on raw materials and endemic corruption," and proposing the upgrading of the economic and political system, technological changes, strengthening of the judiciary to fight corruption, and "modernization alliances" with the United States and other Western nations.

Outside the official circles, the discourse of Russia as a local civilization emerged in the 1990s and consolidated in the second half of the 2000s (Tsygankov and Tsygankov 2014). During the 1990s, Russian intellectuals actively debated the above-described ideas of Fukuyama and Huntington by viewing them as insufficiently sensitive to Russia's cultural conditions. During the 2000s, Russian intellectual discourse grew anti-Western by building on domestic exceptionalist thought. One survey of Russian IR theorists teaching in Moscow, St. Petersburg, Nizhny Novgorod, Kazan', Irkutsk, Tomsk, and Vladivostok found that Russian academics find particular promise in those thinkers who theorize the nation as a unique system of values. (Ibid.) The findings from the survey are further supported by an analysis of citations from *Russia and Europe* (1869 [1990]), by Danilevsky, whose work has been cited considerably more frequently since the second half of the 2000s.

Three factors are responsible for the rise of local civilizational discourse in Russia: the historical tradition of viewing the country's development as culturally distinct; the state efforts to capitalize on such distinctiveness at the expense of common global values; and the actions by others – in particular the West – that serve to reinforce the civilizational thinking.

The historical tradition of viewing Russia as a particular system of values has progressed since at least the nineteenth century. It has been available for borrowing by Russian thinkers since the end of the Cold War. Under the vacuum of values caused by the Soviet dissolution, Russia attempted to re-formulate its national identity by building on some ideas of pre-Soviet thinkers. Below, I elaborate on various civilizational concepts – both exceptionalist and non-exceptionalist.

The state's role is also significant as a necessary impetus for civilizational thinking. Scholars point to the government's need to obtain additional legitimation in the eyes of domestic audiences and to the tendency of Russian academics to develop theories and concepts reflecting the government's concerns, such as those with the US dominance in international relations (Omelicheva and Zubytska 2016). The Russian government may exploit social science by cultivating the dependence of academia on state funds and reducing academic freedom. At the same time, the state's role is limited. The emergence of Russian civilizational thinking predates the government's attempts to introduce state-civilization language by some five to ten years. Such thinking has gradually influenced the Russian state, contributing the political support to its further proliferation. Therefore, the government has not been responsible for the civilizational ideas but has increased their appeal by promoting them publicly.

Finally, the West's ideas and foreign policy have contributed to Russia's rise in civilizational thinking. Western exceptionalist thinkers, such as Fukuyama and Huntington, have contributed to the rise of exceptionalism in Russia (Tsygankov 2004). Actions by Western nations that could be construed as external pressures and disregard for Russia's interests and values have further alienated Russia from its significant Other. The above-described Slavophile, Eurasianist, and Communist theories also historically resulted from various competitive interactions with the West. Pressures on Russia to comply with West-centered norms and policies gradually increased since the 1990s, taking the form of the expansion of NATO and global democracy promotion and reaching their culmination in sanctions against the Russian economy and military support for Ukraine following the Kremlin's annexation of Crimea, support for eastern separatism in the country, and Russia's invasion of Ukraine in 2022. The United States and European countries pursued policies of expanding both NATO and the EU by inviting Ukraine, but not Russia, to consider joining the organizations.[16] In addition, during the Ukrainian revolutions of 2004 and 2013–2014, the West extended political support to those candidates who favored strengthening ties with Western organizations at the expense of Ukraine's relations with Russia and the Russia-initiated Eurasian Union.[17]

The Dominance of Exceptionalism

The identified factors have strengthened Russia's civilizational identity and encouraged the development of civilizational theories. Among these theories, those of exceptionalist nature dominate the academic and public space. Like

Samuel Huntington (1997), many Russian thinkers and academics view their culture in essentialist and ethnocentric terms (Gumilev 1990; Yerasov 2002; Narochnitskaya 2004; Panarin 2006; Dugin 2013; Ivannikov 2022). To them, cultures are real ontological entities with distinctive values-based boundaries between them and a propensity for cross-cultural conflicts. In addition to many intellectuals and politicians, many Orthodox priests, including Patriarch Kirill, also endorse the idea of Russia's religion-centered civilizational distinctiveness.[18]

Scholars have documented the rising influence of Russian IR scholars of culturally essentialist thinkers such as Lev Gumilev (Bassin 2016), Nikolai Danilevsky (Tsygankov 2017), and others (Laruelle 2008; Linde 2016; Robinson 2019). The intellectual prominence of Danilevsky has been especially notable. He was the first to advocate for a culturally particularistic alternative and Russia's ability to progress separately from European civilization. Ideas he formulated in his main book, *Russia and Europe* ([1869] (1990) have anticipated those expressed by Oswald Spengler, Arnold Toynbee, and Samuel Huntington. Many Russian authors found a key intellectual foundation in the book that provided them with relevant theoretical arguments and conceptual apparatus. Proposed culturally relativist concepts included those of the geopolitical "island" (Tsymbursky 2007), "Orthodox civilization" (Panarin 2002), "Eurasian empire" (Dugin 2002), and others. Exceptionalist discourses then influenced the Kremlin, which provided an environment favorable for the discourses' further proliferation.

Rather than trying to assess the complexity of the modern world's boundaries, Russian thinkers seek to strengthen the country's identity as a fortress by bridging diverse exceptionalist narratives. For example, the Izborsky club has tried synthesizing Orthodox and Eurasianist ideas of Russia's civilizational distinctiveness. The club's founder is Aleksander Prokhanov, the editor of the radical newspaper *Zavtra* with long-standing sympathy for imperial and Eurasianist ideas. A prominent activist and writer, Prokhanov is an advocate of bridging Soviet and Eurasianist ideas with those of tsarist Russia. For example, while endorsing the idea of Russia's cultural self-standing, the two camps did not agree on the role of ethnic Russians in the new civilization. The Russian Orthodox Church has positioned Russia as an essentially white, European nation that has historically had to coexist with and be tolerant of Islam. Eurasianists saw Europe as the most prominent threat. They argued that in the process of interaction with Muslim people, Russia became a special cultural symbiosis of Slavic and Turkic influences (Tsygankov 2016b).

Since the second half of the 2000s. Russian exceptionalist thinkers have argued for strengthening Slavic, Orthodox Christian, and Eurasian values under the leadership of Russia. Some of them have advocated global conservative alliances to defeat liberalism (Drobnitsky 2017) and the unification of all Slavic and Christian lands in Europe (Kholmogorov 2019). They have argued that Russia cannot coexist with the West peacefully and that any such existence is merely an illusion (Ivannikov 2022). According to this reasoning, attempts to integrate into the global capitalist system after the Cold War provided the West with an opportunity to destroy Russia. To pursue national survival, it must leave the system and build a self-sufficient civilization (Ibid.).

Russia's growing confrontation with and subsequent invasion of Ukraine has further strengthened the exceptionalist discourse. Its advocates have presented the relations with Ukraine as a decisive moment in establishing Russia's civilizational differences from contemporary Europe and America. According to them, Russia, a conservative religious power, now had to defeat global liberalism and unite all lands that share its values (Kholmogorov 2019; Dugin 2022). Other exceptionalist thinkers have been more defensive and concerned with protecting such values from foreign interference. Conservative intellectual Boris Mezhuyev (2019) proposed the concept of "civilizational realism" as the guide for thinking about Russia in Eurasia. In his view, a Russia-influenced Eurasia is vital within the culturally shared boundaries, including all those gravitating to Russia in eastern Ukraine and elsewhere. As an area of vital interests and values, Eurasia must be protected by all possible means and by making its external red lines unambiguously clear. Mezhuyev proposed that Russia should not annex these territories, yet do everything in its power to protect them from being incorporated by unfriendly governments such as the one in Kyiv (Ibid.).

The Persistence of Dialogue

Despite the prevalence of exceptionalism, dialogical thinking continues to progress in Russian academic and intellectual discussions about international relations. The notion of dialogue assumes the need to frame the interests and values of a nation as relatively open to engagement with others. Dialogical reasoning critically reflects any locally centered knowledge and analyzes the national and the global as constantly interacting. All local knowledge and experiences have something valuable to offer, and they must learn from each other in addressing the world's problems. Because the nation is never entirely isolated from its environment, managing all social issues ultimately requires international and global coordination. The dialogue perspective is non-essentialist and dialectical. It is, therefore, principally different from exceptionalism, whether the latter takes the form of cultural isolationism or universalism/expansionism.

An expression of a search for dialogical approaches in Russian IR is an attempt to develop a national perspective on international affairs as sensitive to domestic and global realities. The Russian–Western political conflict has forced many academics in Russia to critically reassess West-centered IR perspectives as insufficiently global and open to dialogue. Many Russian scholars navigate the broad middle ground between the described camps of isolationism and West-centered universalism and tend to be supportive of a nationally sensitive integration and a sustained dialogue with the global IR community. To bring the 'Russianness' out, they advocate a more robust interaction of Russian IR theorists with those specializing in Russian political philosophy. They see the weakness of Russian IR not only in insufficient integration with global developments but also in its lack of knowledge of Russia's intellectual roots (Tsygankov and Tsygankov 2014, 2021). Such roots include the above-described schools of thought that focus on the spiritual dimension of national development (Slavophiles), social and economic justice (Communists), and special regional/geographic conditions (Eurasianism).

Unlike exceptionalists, supporters of dialogical approaches argue the importance of understanding these national ideas in the context of global processes and global problems. Such processes and issues include political and economic instability, poverty, diseases, arms races, terrorism, climate change, and so forth. In their assessment, the challenge is establishing a legitimate international order and global cooperation in the interests of all civilizational and other communities' economic, social, and cultural prosperity. In addition to acquiring deep knowledge about national values, traditions, and ideas, meeting such a challenge requires a sophisticated understanding of the global. Russian IR continues to wrestle with the notion by engaging with both domestic and foreign scholarship on global processes (Gorbachev 2003; Gadzhiyev 2007; Akopov 2013; Sadykova 2014; Lebedeva and Kharkevich 2016; Shestopal 2020; Bakurkov and Tyapin 2021; Chebankova and Dutkiewicz 2022).

The global, therefore, does not exist by itself and must be viewed as existing in constant interaction with the national. This intellectual perspective is consistent with a scholarly critique of attempts to build a globally applicable IR theory (Acharya and Buzan 2021). For instance, the German IR theorists F. Anderl and A. Witt (2020) pointed out the need to problematize the global and question its understanding as structurally unchanged and ontologically independent. Their proposed solutions include theorizing the historical and current conditions of the "global" and analyzing the purposes and interests they serve (Ibid., p. 48).

Such thinking allows a dialogical perspective on civilizations that stresses their complexity and interdependence. Russian values and cultural orientations are rooted in varying national and regional experiences but cannot be comprehensively summarized in terms of "Europe," "Eurasia," and so forth. National value systems are also not radically opposed to one another. In a transcontinental and geographically diverse country such as Russia, maintaining close ties with one part of the world can be combined with equally meaningful cooperation with others. Russia can be close to the East and the West while remaining in Russia. Awareness of itself as a civilization with an independent system of political, economic, historical, and cultural values does not mean that Russia has no shared values with other countries and regions (Hale and Laruelle 2020). The world of values does not resemble Huntington's (1997) perspective of the clash of civilizations. Civilizations compete and overlap, actively interact with each other, and engage in complex and hierarchical relations.

Russia has special opportunities for dialogue with others as a country at the geographical intersection of the Western, Eastern, and Asian parts of the world. Such conversations can be built at multiple levels. Russia may find it easier to communicate with some parts of the world in some dimensions than others. For example, it has clashed with Western nations over human rights issues while sharing many historical, cultural, and political characteristics with them. On the other hand, Russia's propensity to have more substantial state control over the economy brings the country closer to non-liberal systems in the world.

Appreciation of such complexity of civilizations is reflected in the work of several contemporary scholars in Russia. One example is the research on civilizations by a group of sociologically minded academics in St. Petersburg (Maslovskiy 2020; Braslavskiy and Kozlovsky 2021; Kozlovsky 2021). Influenced by the Western sociological analysis of multiple modernities, these Russian scholars view the country's development as resulting from the modern worldwide processes, domestic tradition, and "cultural resources" (Braslavskiy and Kozlovsky 2021, 154).[19] They further identify various layers of internal civilizational complexity involving center-periphery relations, the elite-society dimension, and others (Ibid.). Finally, following the research on "inter-civilizational encounters" by Johann Arnason (2001, 2003), they study the external complexity and interdependence of civilizations.

Another example is the research under the Moscow Institute of Philosophy umbrella and the journal *Problemy tsivilizatsionnogo razvitiya* (*Problems of Civilizational Development*). With an interdisciplinary nature, the research incorporates work by philosophers and social scientists. Building mainly on Russian intellectual sources, these scholars aim to reassess the country's cultural foundations and secure its position as a civilization in the context of global development while not becoming dependent on China or the West (Smirnov 2018–2024).

Conditions of Dialogical Thinking

The country's location at the intersection of cultures and civilizations explains the persistence in Russian IR of dialogical thinking about the world. Such a location stimulates the development of global thinking. The tradition of such thinking is too rich and complex to describe here fully. It has roots in centuries-long intellectual exchanges with European and non-European philosophy and social science, which has produced an indigenous way of comprehending the world. Some concepts of Russian thinking about the world include the ideas of all-unity (*vseyedinstvo*) and collective personality (*sobornost'*). These concepts assume a combination and interaction of global, local, and individual and are rooted in the early Slavophile and Christian socialist philosophy.[20] They are firmly established in the Russian mind due to the accomplishments of writers such as Alexander Pushkin, Fyodor Dostoyevsky, Lev Tolstoy, and others. They serve as antidotes to exceptionalist thinking and continue to be critical of such thinking for its extremist tendencies and lack of self-awareness (Nikol'sky 2022; Tsipko 2022).

In the twentieth century, other Russian thinkers developed dialogical thinking under the influences of Hegelian dialectics, hermeneutics, and existentialism. Works about the dialogue of cultures by Mikhail Bakhtin, Yuri

Lotman, Vladimir Bibler, Genrikh Batishchev, and others have produced important insights into inter-civilizational relations influencing Western, Soviet, and post-Soviet researchers. Many – geographers, psychologists, physicists, mathematicians, mineralogists, and others – have developed an acute sense of global responsibility. Thinking of Vladimir Vernadsky, Andrei Sakharov, Piotr Kapitsa, Nikita Moiseyev, and others has influenced Mikhail Gorbachev, who proposed his version of globally dialogical thinking.[21]

Russia's special geographic and geocultural position in the international system undermines the discourse of cultural exceptionalism while encouraging a constant search by the political authorities for strategies to adapt to the inter-civilizational environment. Dialogue is a requirement of such adaptation. While engaged in conflict with the West, Russia actively interacts with non-Western nations in Eurasian and global settings. Russia has already mediated multiple conflicts in the Caucasus and the Middle East. Moscow has also contributed to developing multilateral formats in the former Soviet region, East Asia, and outside by helping to establish international forums and organizations such as the Eurasian Economic Union, Shanghai Cooperation Organization, BRICS (Brazil, Russia, India, China, and South Africa) and others.

The contemporary world combines processes of conflicts, diversity, and global interdependence. Despite various national and cultural barriers, this is the world of late modernity, in which technologies such as the Internet, social media, and artificial intelligence allow much greater circulation of information and ideas than during the Cold War. Partly for this reason, economic, political, and ideological boundaries are less pronounced than several decades ago. As a result, even in its conflictual relations with the West, Russia is engaged in competition over status, economic development, and media positioning rather than existential national survival.

Public opinion polls consistently show that Russians know their special values and history and the importance of building strong relations with neighbors. For example, despite the problematic relations with European nations, the number of Russians who believe their country remains part of Europe has been consistently high throughout the post-Soviet years (Aris 2022). However, the same Russians may believe in their country's growing ties with Asian nations. Overall, Russia abandoned the initial efforts to become a part of the Euro-Atlantic civilization and now aims to develop more balanced relations with different parts of the world while preserving its internal strength and power capabilities.

Notes

1 Next chapter analyzes Ilyin's views in greater details.
2 Chaadayev later recognized Russia's capacity for change and setting an example for others.
3 For instance, a prominent academic journal published a round table devoted to Wallerstein's ideas, in which only one participant expressed criticism (*Kosmopolis*, Winter 2003–2004, 1 (7)).

4 For example, see the work by Aleksei Bogaturov (analyzed in Tsygankov 2022, chap. 4).

5 The most known proponent of this approach is Samuel Huntington (1997). For similar perspectives, see Gress 1998; Buchanan, 2002; Blankeley, 2005. Many Russian scholars also employ essentialist approaches (Tsygankov 2017).

6 As Andrew Moravcsik writes, people have tastes, commitments, and endowments, which they bring *to* politics (Cited in Simpson 2008).

7 Russia's debate on belongingness to Europe is centuries-old (Narochnitskaya 2004; Neumann 2015).

8 In response to the crisis of European identity, some Russian intellectuals began advocating a break with both the old – nationalist and new – liberal Europes as early as in the 1840s–1850s. Alexander Herzen, for instance, grew disappointed with European conservative restorations and – long before the Bolsheviks – turned to socialism arguing for Russia's own, non-European way of "catching up" economically and socially. The Bolsheviks pushed this line of thinking to its extreme.

9 The wording of the question was as follows, "Do you support the preservation of the union as a renewed federation of sovereign republics in which the rights of a person of any nationality are fully guaranteed?" The Yeltsin-led Democratic Russia has actively campaigned against the referendum (Kotz and Weir 1997, 147).

10 On several occasion, Gorbachev used the term Eurasia in his speeches and writings. For example, in October 1988 in his welcoming message to foreign guests attending the Asia-Pacific Region conference in Vladivostok, he stressed that "the Soviet Union was a Eurasian state ... to serve as a hopeful bridge bringing together two great continents" (as cited in Hauner 1990, 249). And in his *Perestroika* book of 1987 edition he upgraded his "common European home" formula by adding the Asian dimension, "The Soviet Union is an Asian, as well as European country" (Ibid, 11). Gorbachev's principal foreign policy advisor Georgi Shakhanazarov wrote later about his regret that the post-Soviet Commonwealth of Independent States was not named "the Commonwealth of Euro-Asian States," which "would have emphasized the unique feature of our country that for centuries has been a bridge between the two great continents and civilizations" (2001, 486). Gorbachev's liberal foreign minister Eduard Shevardnadze too referred to the Soviet Union as a "great Eurasian space" and a "world of worlds" (*mir mirov*). Citing the Russian philosopher Georgi Fedotov, Shevardnadze said Russia had to politically live in a complex world of both European and Asian nations (Cit. in Otunbayeva 1991, 186–187). Gorbachev's difference from conservative opposition was about methods of unifying the Soviet space, rather than about the principal need to have such unity. Among the Westernizers, Andrei Sakharov defended the notion of Eurasia and even has written his own project of "Constitution of the Union of the Soviet republics of Europe and Asia" (Sakharov 1990, 266–276).

11 I plan to explore the ideas of Westernizers in a separate volume.

12 For example, the Christian socialist thinker Georgy Fedotov wrote in his essay "Will Russia Exist?" about his deep fear of "separatisms" that had grown stronger after the revolution and were tearing apart the body of Russia (Fedotov 1990, 173)

13 Before and immediately following the revolution, they even believed in the inevitable world revolution.

14 Chapter 5 provides greater details.

15 Next chapter analyzes Panarin's ideas in greater details.

16 Both Yelstin and Putin raised the possibility of joining NATO, yet it was never serious considered by the alliance.

17 For analyses of Western and Russian policies in Ukraine, see Sakwa 2015; Charap and Colton 2017; Toal 2017; Hahn 2018; Gotz and Stoun 2022.

18 In particular, Kirill endorsed *Russkaya doktrina* (2007).

19 Russian sociological tradition was nationally established even before the Bolshevik Revolution. Some Russian sociologists such as Pitirim Sorokin (1957, 1959) anticipated ideas of multiple modernities and cross-cultural dialogue.

20 For Russian religious thought, see Emerson, Pattison, and Poole 2020; Bykova, Forster, and Steiner 2021.

21 Chapter 4 considers it in greater detail.

Further Reading

Civilizational Ideas and Geocultural Epistemologies

Avant, D., ed. 2020. Exclusion and Inclusion in Global Security Studies. *Journal of Global Security Studies* 5, 1.

Buzan, B. and A. Acharya. 2021. *Re-Imagining International Relations*. Cambridge University Press.

Cha. T. 2019. Competing visions of a postmodern world order: the Philadelphian system vs. the Tianxia system. *Cambridge Review of International Affairs* 31, 5.

Grovogui, S. 2006. *Beyond Eurocentrism and Anarchy*. Palgrave.

Hamati-Ataya, I. 2011. The "Problem of Values" and international relations scholarship. *International Studies Review* 13.

Hobson, J. M. 2012. *The Eurocentric Conception of World Politics: Western International Theory, 1760–2010*. Cambridge: Cambridge University Press.

Inayatullah N. and D. L. Blaney. 2004. *International Relations and the Problem of Difference*. Routledge.

Neumann, I. 1999. *Uses of the Other: The "East" in European Identity Formation*. University of Minnesota Press.

O'Hagan J. 2002. *Conceptualizing the West in International Relations*. Palgrave.

Reus-Smit, C. 2018. *On Cultural Diversity: International Theory in a World of Difference*. Cambridge University Press.

Spruyt, H. 2020. *The World Imagined: Collective Beliefs and Political Order in the Sinocentric, Islamic and Southeast Asian International Societies*. Cambridge University Press.

Taylor P. 1996. *The Way the Modern World Works*. New York.

Tickner, A. B. and D. L. Blaney. 2012. *Thinking International Relations Differently*. Abingdon: Routledge.

Zarakol, A. 2010. *After Defeat: How the East Learned to Live with the West*. Cambridge: Cambridge University Press.

Russia as a Civilization

Chebankova, E and P. Dutkiewicz, eds. 2021. *Civilizations and World Order*. Routledge.

Curanovic, A. 2020. *The Sense of Mission in Russian Foreign Policy*. Routledge.

Diesen, G. 2018. *The Decay of Western Civilization and Resurgence of Russia*. London: Routledge.

Kazharski, A. 2019. Civilizations as Ontological Security? *Problems of Post-Communism*.

Mjør, K. and S. Turoma, eds. 2020. *Russia as Civilization*. Routledge.

Poe, M. 1997. *Moscow, the Third Rome*. Washington, DC: The National Council for Soviet and East European Research.

Tsygankov, A. P. 2016. Crafting the State-Civilization. *Problems of Post-Communism*.

Voskressenski, A. D. 2017. *Non-Western theories of International relations*. Palgrave.

Russia's Contemporary Civilizational Discussions

Engström, M. 2014. Contemporary Russian Messianism and New Russian Foreign Policy. *Contemporary Security Policy* 35, 3.

Kozlovsky, V., ed. 2021. *Rossiyskoiye obshchestvo: arkhitektonika tsivilizatsionnogo razvitiya*. Moscow: FNIST RAN.

Laruelle, M. 2016. The Izborsky Club, or the New Conservative AvantGarde in Russia. *Russian Review* 75, 4.

Linde, F. 2016. The Civilizational Turn in Russian Political Discourse. *Russian Review* 74, 4.

Morozov, V. 2015. *Russia's Postcolonial Identity*. Basingstoke: Palgrave Macmillan

Neumann, I. 2016. Russia's Europe, 1991–2016: inferiority to superiority. *International Affairs*. 92, 6.

Oskanian, K. 2021. *Russian Exceptionalism between East and West*. Palgrave.

Pain, E., ed. 2010. *Ideologiya "osobogo puti" v Rossiyi i Germaniyi*. Moscow: Tri kvadrata.

Suslov, M. 2020. *Geopolitical Imagination: Ideology and Utopia in Post-Soviet Russia*. New York: Ibidem, Columbia University Press.

Suslov, M. and D. Uzlaner, eds. 2019. *Contemporary Russian Conservatism*. Leiden: Brill.

Tsygankov, A. 2004. *Whose World Order?* University of Notre Dame Press.

———. 2008. Self and Other in International Relations Theory. *International Studies Review*.

———. 2017. In the Shadow of Nikolai Danilevski. *Europe-Asia Studies*.

References

Akopov, Sergei V. 2013. *Развитие идеи транснационализма в российской политической философии XX века*. St. Petersburg: IPTs.

Anderl, F. and A. Witt. 2020. Problematizing the Global in Global IR. *Millennium*, 49, 1.

Anikin, Aleksei V. *Путь исканий. Социально-экономические идеи в России до марксизма*. Москва, 1990.

Arnason, Johan P. 2001. "Civilizational Patterns and Civilizing Processes." *International Sociology* 16.

———. 2003. *Civilizations in Dispute: Historical Questions and Theoretical Traditions*. Leiden: Brill.

Aris, Ben. 2022. Nine out of 10 Russians oppose concessions in exchange for end of sanctions. *Intellinews*, May 27

Averintsev, Sergei S. 1990. *Крещение Руси и путь русской культуры*. Москва.

Bakurkov, A. and I. Tyapin. 2021. Постлиберальный коммунитаризм для современной России. *Tetradi po konservatizmu*

Barry, David. 2019. Ethnodoxy, national exceptionalism, and xenophobia: a case study of contemporary Russia. *National Identities* 21, 3

Bassin, Mark. 2016. *The Gumilev Mystique*. Cambridge University Press

Berdyayev, Nikolai. 1995. *Tsarstvo dukkha i tsarstvo kesarya*. Moscow http://krotov.info/library/02_b/berdyaev/1947_40_00.html

Berenskoetter, Felix. 2014. Parameters of a National Biography. *European Journal of International Relations* 20, 1.

Bettiza, G. 2014. Civilizational Analysis in International Relations. *International Studies Review* 20, 4.

Blakkisrud, Helge. 2022. *Russkii* as the New *Rossiiskii*? Nation-Building in Russia After 1991 *Nationalities Papers*.

Blankley, Toney. 2005. *The West's Last Chance: Will We Win the Clash of Civilizations?* New York: Regnery Publishing.

Braslavskiy, R. and V. Kozlovskiy. 2021. Цивилизационное измерение структурирования обществ. *Sotsiologicheskoye obozreniye* 20, 1

Brudny Y. M. *Reinventing Russia: Russian Nationalism and the Soviet State, 1953–1991.* Cambridge University Press, 1999.

Buchanan, Patrick. J. 2002. *The Death of the West.* New York: St. Martin's Press.

Bull, Hedley and Adam Watson, eds. 1984. *The Expansion of International Society.* Oxford: University Press.

Buzan, Barry and Amitav Acharya. 2021. *Re-Imagining International Relations.* Cambridge University Press.

Bykova, Maria F., M. N. Forster, and L. Steiner, eds. 2021. *The Palgrave Handbook of Russian Thought.* London: Palgrave.

Chaadayev, Pyotr. 1991. Апология сумасшедшего. *Россия глазами русского*, под ред. А. Ф. Замалеева. Санкт-Петербург.

Charap, Samuel and Timothy J. Colton. 2017. *Everyone Loses: The Ukraine Crisis and the Ruinous Contest for Post-Soviet Eurasia.* London: Routledge.

Chebankova, Elena and Pyotr Dutkiewicz, eds. 2022. *Civilizations and World Order.* Routledge.

Danilevskii, Nikolai. 1990 [1884]. *Rossiia i Evropa* (Russia and Europe). Moscow: Kniga.

Dostoyevsky, Fyodor. 2006. *Politicheskoye zaveshchaniye. Sbornik statei za 1861–1881.* Moscow: Eksmo.

Drobnitsky, Dmitri. 2017. Mezhdu realizmom i real'nostyu, June 28 www.politanalitika. ru/v-polose-mnenij/mezhdu-realizmom-i-realnostyu/.

Dugin, Alaksandr. 2002. *Osnovy Geopolitiki.* Moscow Arktogeia.

———. 2013. Mezhdunarodnye otnosheniia: paradigmy, teorii, sotsiologiia (International Relations; Paradigms, Theories, Sociology). Moscow: Akademicheskii proekt.

———. 2022. Rossiya protiv anti-Rossyiyi: interesy i tsennosti. *Katehon*, March 28.

Emerson, C., G. Pattison, and R. A. Poole, eds. 2020. *The Oxford Handbook of Russian Religious Thought.* New York: Oxford University Press.

Fedotov, Georgiy. 1991. *Sud'ba i grekhi Rossiyi.* Moscow.

Finnemore, Martha. 1996. *National Interest in International Society.* Ithaca, NY: Cornell University Press.

Florovsky, Georgy. 1983. *Пути русского богословия.* Paris: IMCA-Press.

Gadzhiyev, Kamaludin. 2007. *Geopoliticheskiye gorizonty Rossiyi.* Moskva: Ekonomika.

Glinchikova, Alla. 2008. *Раскол или срыв «русской Реформации»?* Москва.

Gorbachev, Mikhail. 1987. *Perestroika: New Thinking for Our Country and the World* (New York: Harper & Row.

———. ed. 2003. *Grani globalizatsiyi.* Moscow: Al'pina.

Götz, Elias and Jørgen Staun. 2022. Why Russia attacked Ukraine: Strategic culture and radicalized narratives, *Contemporary Security Policy*.

Gress, D. 1998. *From Plato to NATO.* New York: Free Press.

Gumilev, Lev. 1990. *Etnogenez i biosfera zemli.* Moscow: Gidrometeoizdat.

Guzzini, Stefano, ed. 2012. *The Return of Geopolitics in Europe?* Cambridge: Cambridge University Press.

Hahn, Gordon. 2018. *Ukraine Over the Edge: Russia, the West and the "New Cold War."* Cherry Hill, NJ: McFarland & Co.

Hale, Henry and Marlene Laruelle. 2020. Rethinking Civilizational Identity from the Bottom Up. *Nationalities Papers* 48, 3.

Held, David. 1995. *Democracy and the Global Order*. Stanford University Press.

———. 2000. The Changing Contours of Political Community. In *Global Democracy*, edited by Barry Holden. London: Routledge.

Hughes, Chris. 1997. Globalization and Nationalism: Squaring the Circle in Chinese International Relations Theory. *Millennium* 26, 1.

Huntington, Samuel. 1997. *The Clash of Civilizations and the Remaking of World Order*. New York: Simon & Shuster.

Hwang, Y. 2021. Reappraising the Chinese School of International Relations: A postcolonial perspective. *Review of International Studies* 47, 3.

Hall, Martin and Patrick. T. Jackson, eds. 2010. *Civilizational Identity*. London: Palgrave.

Hauner, Milan. 1990. *What Is Asia to Us? Russia's Asian Heartland Yesterday and Today*. Boston: Unwin Hyman.

Ilyin, Ivan. 1992. O russkoi ideye. In: his *Nashi zadachi*. Vol. 1. Moscow: Papor.

Ivannikov, Sergei I. 2022. *Rossiya i Zapad. Russkaya tsivilizatsiya v usloviyakh global'noi voiny*. Moscow: Goryachaya liniya.

Jackson, Patrick. T. 2007. Civilizations as Actors. In: *Civilizational Identity*, edited by Martin Hall and Patrick Thaddeus Jackson. London: Palgrave.

Kagarlitskiy, Boris. 2003. *Периферийная империя: Россия и миросистема*. Москва.

———. 2010. *От империй — к империализму. Государство и возникновение буржуазной цивилизации*. Москва.

Kara-Murza, Sergei. 2002. *Sovetskaya tsivilizatsiya*. Moskva: Algoritm.

Katzenstein, Peter, ed. 2009. *Civilizations in World Politics: Plural and Pluralist Perspectives*. London: Routledge.

Kholmogorov, Yegor. 2006a. *Русский националист*. Москва: Yevropa.

———. 2006b. На своем глобусе, 22 декабря. www.apn.ru/index.php?newsid=35831,

———. 2019. "Pochemu Rossiya –Yevropa, a Yevrosoyuz … ne ochen." August 28 https://tsargrad.tv/articles/pochemu-rossija-evropa-a-evrosojuz-ne-ochen_213564.

Kinnvall, Catarina. 2004. Globalization and Religious Nationalism: Self, Identity, and the Search for Ontological Security. *Political Psychology* 25.

Kirillov, Igor'. 1914. *Третий Рим. Очерк исторического развития идеи русского мессианизма*. Москва.

Kotkin, Stephen. 1990. *Magnetic Mountain. Stalinism as Civilization*. Princeton: Princeton University Press.

Kotz, David and Fred Weir. 1997. *Revolution from Above: The Demise of the Soviet System*. London: Routledge.

Kozlovsky, Vladimir V., ed. 2021. *Российское общество: архитектоника цивилизационного развития*. St. Petersburg: FNISTS RAN.

Larson, Deborah W. and Aleksei Shevchenko. 2003. Shortcut to Greatness: The New Thinking and the Revolution in Soviet Foreign Policy. *International Organization* 57.

Laruelle, Marlene. 2008. *Russian Eurasianism: An Ideology of Empire*. Washington, DC, Johns Hopkins University Press.

Lavrov, Sergei. 2008. Russia and the World in the 21st Century. *Russia in Global Affairs* 3.

Lebedeva, Marina and Maksim Kharkevich. 2016. Teoriya mezhdunarodnykh otshoniy v zerkale sovremennykh rossiyskikh issledovaniy. *Vestnik MGIMO*.

Linde, Fabian. 2016. The Civilizational Turn in Russian Political Discourse. *Russian Review* 75, October.

Linklater, Andrew. 2013. *Transformation of Political Community*. Polity.

————. 2020. *The Idea of Civilization and the Making of the Global Order*. Bristol University Press.

Malia, Martin. 1999. *Russia Under Western Eyes*. Cambridge, MA: Harvard University Press.

Marcetic, Branko. 2022. Ignoring Gorbachev's Warnings. *Current Affairs*, September 7.

Marchenko, Gennadiy. 2020. Richard Kosolapov: sovetskiye politiki ikh sovetniki. *Svobodnaya mysl'* 1, March.

Maslovskiy, Mikhail. 2020. Contemporary Civilizational Analysis and Russian Sociology. In: *Russia as Civilization*, edited by K. J. Mjør and S. Turoma. L.: Routledge.

Mearsheimer, John J. 2018. *The Great Delusion: Liberal Dreams and International Realities*. New Haven: Yale University Press.

Medvedev, Dmitry. 2009. Go Russia! Kremlin.ru, September 10.

Mezhuyev, Boris. 2012. *Политическая критика Вадима Цымбурского*. Moscow.

————. 2015. In Memoriam. В.Л. Цымбурский. *Тетради по консерватизму*, № 1.

————. 2019. 'Ostrov Rossiya' i rossiyskaya politika identichnosti. *Rossiya v global'noi politike* 6.

Milov, Leonid V. 2006. О причинах возникновения крепостничества в России. *По следам ушедших эпох: статьи и заметки*.- Москва.http://scepsis.ru/library/id_1 588.html.

Mitzen, Jennifer. 2006. Ontological Security in World Politics. *European Journal of International Relations* 12 (3).

Narochnitskaya, Natalya. 2004. *Rossiya I russkiye v mirovoi istoriyi*. Moskva: mezhdunarodnyye otnosheniya.

Nazarov, Mikhail. 2005. *Вождю Третьего Рима*. Москва.

Nikolskiy, Sergei. 2022. Chto neset s soboi "filosofiya Pobedy". *Nezavisimaya gazeta*, June 1.

Norris, Pippa and Ronald Inglehart. 2019. Cultural Backlash: Trump, Brexit, and Authoritarian Populism. Cambridge University Press.

Neumann, Iver B. 1999. *Uses of the Other*. Minneapolis: University of Minnesota Press.

————. 2015. *Russia and the Idea of Europe*, 2nd ed. London: Routledge.

Omelicheva, Mariya Y. and Lidiya Zubytska. 2016. An Unending Quest for Russia's Place in the World. *New Perspectives* 24, 1.

Otunbayeva, Roza. 1991. V preddveriyi novogo miroporyadka. *Mezhdunarodnaya zhizn'* 3.

Panarin, Aleksandr. 2002. *Православная цивилизация в глобальном мире*, Moscow: Arktogeya.

————. 2006. Стратегическая нестабильность. Moscow: Arktogeya.

Panarin, A. S. 2014. *Православная цивилизация*. Москва: Institut russkoi tsyvilizatsiyi.

Pomerants, Grigory. 1990. *Открытость бездне*. М.: Советский писатель.

Pomerants, G. 2004. *The Spiritual Movement from the West*. Caux: Caux Books.

Putin, Vladimir. 2012a. Samoopredelenie russkogo naroda – eto polietnicheskaia tsivilizatsiia, skreplennaia russkim kul'turnym iadrom. *Nezavisimaia gazeta*, January 23.

————. 2013. Speech at the Valdai International Discussion Club, September 19 http://en.kremlin.ru/events/president/news/19243.

————. 2014. Address by President of the Russian Federation, Kremlin. Moscow, March 18.

————. 2022. Obrashcheniye Prezidenta Rossiyskoi Federatsiyi. Moscow, Kremlin, February 24 http://kremlin.ru/events/president/news/67843.

Remizov, Mikhail. 2016. *Русские и государство. Национальная идея до и после «крымской весны»*. Москва.

Robinson, Paul. 2019. *Russian Conservatism*. Ithaca, NY: Cornell University Press.

Russkaya doktrina 2007, edited by A. Averyanov. Москва: Yauza.

Sadykova, Elena L. 2014. *Mezhtsivilizatsionnyi dialog v sovremennykh mezhdunarodnykh otnosheniyakh*. Doctoral Diss.

Sakharov, Andrei D. 1990. Trevoga i nadezhda. Moskva: Progress.

Sakwa, Richard. 2015. *Frontline Ukraine*. London: Tauris.

Shestopal, Alexei V., ed. 2020. *Философия культуры в системе изучения международных отношений*. 2 vol. Moscow: MGIMO University.

Shih, Chih-Yu. 2014. China Rises Syndromes? Drafting National Schools of International Relations in Asia. *Сравнительная политика* 3 (17).

Simpson, G. 2008. The Ethics of New Liberalism. In: *The Oxford Handbook of International Relations*, edited by Christian Reus-Smit and Duncan Snidal. Oxford University Press.

Sinyavski, Andrei. 2001. *Osnovy sovetskoi tsivilizatsiyi*. Moskva: Agraf.

Smirnov, A. V., ed. 2018–2024. *Rossiyski proyekt tsivilizatsionnogo razvitiya*. Moscow: IFAN https://iphras.ru/page25149611.htm.

Smith, Mark. 2019. *The Russia Anxiety*. New York: Penguin.

Solovei, Valery. D. 2005. *Русская история: новое прочтение*, Москва

————. 2008. *Кровь и почва русской истории*. Москва.

Sorokin, Pitirim. 1957. *Social and Cultural Dynamics*. Boston: Extending Horizons Books.

————, ed. 1959. *Social and Cultural Mobility*. Boston: Free Press.

Stalin, I. V. 2002. *Slovo tovarishchu Stalinu*, edited by Richard Kosolapov. Moscow: Rodina.

Steele, Brent J. 2007. Liberal-Idealism: A Constructivist Critique. *International Studies Review* 9.

Steele, Brent J. and A. Homolar. 2019. Ontological insecurities and the politics of contemporary populism. *Cambridge Review of International Affairs*, 32, 3.

Toal, Gerard. 2017. *Near Abroad: Putin, the West and the Contest over Ukraine and the Caucasus*. New York: Oxford University Press.

Toynbee, Arnold J. 1948. *Civilization on Trial*. Oxford: Oxford University Press.

Tsipko, Aleksandr. 2022. Vo vlasti mutnoi intuitsiyi. *Nezavisimaya gazeta*, June 6.

Tsygankov, Andrei P. 2004. *Whose World Order?* University of Notre Dame Press.

————. 2016a. Crafting the State-Civilization. *Problems of Post-Communism* 63, 3.

————. 2016b. Uses of Eurasia: the Kremlin, the Eurasian Union, and the Izborsky Club. In *Digital Eurasia: Post-Soviet Geopolitics in the Age of New Media*, edited by Mark Bassin and Mikhail Suslov. Lexington.

————. 2017. In the Shadow of Nikolai Danilevski. *Europe-Asia Studies*.

————. 2019. *Russia's Foreign Policy*. 5th ed. Rowman & Littlefield.

————. 2022. *Russian Realism*. Routledge.

Tsygankov, Andrei and Pavel Tsygankov. 2014. Russian IR Theory. *European Review of International Studies* 1, 2.

————. 2021. Constructing National Values. *Foreign Policy Analysis*.

Tsymbursky, Vadim. 2007. *Ostrov Rossiya*. Moscow: Rosspen.

Wallerstein, Immanuel. 2004. *World-Systems Analysis: An Introduction*. The Duke University Press.

Yerasov, Boris S. 2002. *Tsivilizatsii: universalii i samobytnost'*. Moscow: Nauka

Zhaba, Sergei P., ed. 1954. *Русские мыслители о России и человечестве*. Paris: IMCA-Press.

Zarakol, Ayse. 2011. *After Defeat: How the East Learned to Live with the West*. Cambirdge: Cambridge University Press.

Zyuganov, Gennadi. 1999. *Geografiya pobedy*. Moskva: an unknown publisher.

———. 2002. *Globalizatsiya i sud'ba chelovechestva*. Moskva: Molodaya gvardiya.

3

SLAVOPHILES

Russia is an entirely original land, completely unlike European countries and states.

Konstantin Aksakov (1861, 7)

The mission of Russia is to show that ... it is the *third* Rome, not excluding the first and the second, but reconciling both.

Vladimir Solovyev (1989, 278)

Slavophiles have reflected on Russia's special spiritual conditions associated with Orthodox Christianity and its social extension, the commune-based free peasant labor. While influenced by Western European historical experience and ideas, Slavophiles attempted to break the European spell following the continent's revolutions during the 1840s. In their view, the revolutions signified the bankruptcy of the Western departure from Christian ideas and the triumph of immoral rationalism. Some Slavophiles aspired to engage in dialogue with the increasingly "decadent" Europe, while others found such dialogue superfluous, calling Russia instead to acquire isolation from the continent's developments.

The early Slavophiles, such as Aleksei Khomyakov and Ivan Kireevsky, were critical of Europe while locating Russia within it and arguing for Russia's special spiritual and social conditions. At the same time, they were critical of Russia's strong state system, especially the one established following Peter the Great's reforms. The early Slavophiles defended the spiritual autonomy of the Church and the freedom of peasant communes from state interference. In the late nineteenth century, Vladimir Solovyov took yet another step to engage in dialogue with Europe by explaining Russia's spiritual role and proposing the vision of reunification with the European continent based on new theocratic principles. His disciples, including Nikolai Berdyaev, also emphasized Russia's cultural ties

DOI: 10.4324/9781003377573-3

to Christian Europe while defending individual spiritual freedom from the state authorities' encroachments.

Other Slavophiles promoted various ideas of the Russia-fortress by arguing the virtues of isolation from European developments. Konstantin Aksakov was among the first to question the notion of Russia as a bridge to Europe. The late Slavophiles or Pan-Slavists introduced the principle of Russia–European cultural incompatibility except within the areas populated by people of Slavic origins. Ivan Ilyin and Alexander Solzhenitsyn wanted Russia to develop alongside separate cultural, geopolitical, and social paths. The influential post-Soviet thinker Alexander Panarin evolved from a Westernizer to an advocate of "civilizational" dialogue with the West and, then, to a defender of an anti-Western empire. Therefore, he expressed the full spectrum of perspectives on relations with the West, including dialogue and exceptionalism.

The Spiritual of the Russian Idea: Aleksei Khomyakov and Konstantin Aksakov

Russia's Orthodox identity has defined the divergence of the country's path from Europe. Political developments further deepened the two sides' spiritual and intellectual differences. Having accepted the national absolutism of European states, Russia did not accept the continent's movement toward democratization and secularization. The state increasingly followed the Byzantine practice of subordinating the church to its interests. In contrast, church circles continued to favor the idea of the harmonious unity (*simfoniya*) of the state and the church. The growing geopolitical differences between Russia and Europe, which became especially acute during the Crimean War, in the middle of the nineteenth century, also played an important role. Thus, the European influence on Russia was weakening spiritually, politically, and internationally.

Culturally and intellectually, Russia needed to redefine itself to the European continent. Without breaking all the spiritual relations with Europe, the Slavophile movement aimed to explain Russia's special historical, spiritual, and global path in the world. Reacting to the tendencies of secularization, Slavophiles wished to show Europe how to revive Christian ideals in spiritual and public life. Some of them have seen a revival in creating a theocratic system. Others believed that the church could only regain its influence by avoiding unnecessary involvement in public affairs and focusing on the salvation of souls. Without taking a direct part in politics and economic life, the church was supposed to contribute to the formation of a just social order by influencing the moral world of the individual.

Aleksei Khomyakov: Reuniting with Europe

Aleksei Khomyakov (1804–1860) was the recognized leader of the Slavophile movement. He formulated all the main ideas of the movement – *sobornost'* or a collective personality combining freedom and unity of the people, the superiority of Orthodox over Catholic Christianity, the development of Russia based on a communal economy, and the autocracy that does not interfere with issues of faith and economy. Khomyakov was a military officer and a thinker. He participated in the Turkish campaign of 1829 as a guard officer but spent the rest of his life as a theologian, philosopher, scholar, and poet.

Khomyakov's attitude to Europe was complex. Fascinated, he called the West the "land of holy miracles." He admired England and even dreamed of the reunification of its Church. He praised the West for "great and glorious deeds" based on Christianity (Zhaba 1954, 40). He also recognized the importance of science and education by crediting Peter the Great for his search for the "awakening of the Russian mind" (Ibid., 37). Khomyakov wanted not so much to isolate itself from the West but reunite with it based on the moral principles of true Christianity and the free peasant commune. He viewed Russia's spiritual separation from the West as an "historical accident."

> The separation that suppresses our spiritual power is a matter of historical accident and partly a consequence of a misunderstanding: it does not underlie either our spiritual principles or the character of our composition, as in Romano-Germanic Europe; it has resulted from, so to speak, an involuntary temptation when meeting with riches of knowledge, which until then was alien to us; [the separation] must disappear with a full acquaintance with this knowledge.
>
> *Ibid., 38*

Khomyakov considered it possible to bridge Russia and the West by mutual spiritual work and strengthening "pure Christianity" free from all hierarchy and authority. For its part, Russia had to repent for the attempts to subject the faith to political power associated with Peter the Great.

In assuming possible spiritual rapprochement with the West and stressing the importance of repentance for Russia's sins, Khomyakov resembled Vladimir Solovyov, although the latter's attitude was more radical.[1] Like Solovyev, Khomyakov had complex relations with the political authorities and the official church. He opposed censorship and published his major theological works abroad rather than in Russia.

Khomyakov was convinced of the moral strength of Russian ideals rooted in love, not power or political necessity. This faith-love recognized "no one else's power but its own, no one's judgment, except the judgment of Faith ... the reasonable freedom does not know any external authority over itself" (Zhaba 1954, 34). Khomyakov laid the foundations of this faith-love in the Orthodox Christianity of ordinary people while remaining critical of any hierarchical organization.

Khomyakov's social ideal was a free-peasant commune:

> The commune is the only surviving civic institution throughout Russian history. Take it away, and nothing will remain: a whole civil world can develop from it. ... It maintains in [the Russian peasant] a sense of freedom, the consciousness of his moral dignity, and all the high motives from which we expect his revival.
>
> *Ibid.., 41*

The thinker was a staunch opponent of serfdom and of any state interference in the affairs of the economy. He also opposed private property, viewing it as a break from Russian customs and the moral right of everyone to own land. To Khomyakov, the commune and the Russian people were the sources of "life basics" (*zhiznennyye nachala*) of any development (Ibid., 37).

Khomyakov also viewed Orthodox Christianity and the commune as the foundation of Russia's world mission. At the same time, he opposed the imposition of this mission on other people, praising the internal development and the force of example instead. He was highly critical of national pride and geopolitical power. For example, this thinker called Russia to repent for its expansionist foreign policy, which he considered the reason for the defeat in the Crimean War.

> The just war against Turkey to alleviate the fate of our eastern brothers served us as a punishment: God did not allow unclean hands to perform such a pure deed ... woe to those who want to defend the power of Christ with the impotence of a human instrument! Faith is a matter of spiritual freedom, which does not tolerate coercion.
>
> *Ibid., 44*

Therefore, the dissemination of Christian ideals was noble and necessary, but only while maintaining loyalty to these ideals at home.

Konstantin Aksakov: Isolating from Europe

Among Slavophiles, Konstantin Aksakov (1817–1860) was particularly well regarded for developing the theory of Russian commune and state-society relations. Having matured as a thinker under the stable period of Nikolai I, he concentrated on studying the country's historical, cultural, and ethnographic foundations. During the 1830s, Aksakov participated in the circle of Western-minded intellectuals led by Nikolai Stankevich. Following the death of Stankevich in 1840 and the rise of the group's new leader. Vissarion Belinsky, Aksakov broke with the circle. Soon, he became close to Khomyakov, Kireevsky, Samarin, and other Slavophiles alienated from Europe because of the revolutions of the 1840s. The manifesto of March 14, 1848, by Nicholas I, condemned the revolutions and resonated with Aksakov, strengthening his desire to substantiate the Russian path in its principal difference from the European one.

At the time, Aksakov was firmly on the intellectual path of separation from European developments. He even sent a letter to Nicholas expressing his solidarity with the manifesto's ideas of the immaturity and corrupt nature of revolutions and their leaders (Tsymbayev 1986, 155). In the letter, Aksakov called for destroying the "Western" or "revolutionary" tendency that had penetrated Russia from Peter the Great. Instead, the thinker advocated the strengthening of the "anti-revolutionary," that is, "Russian" intellectual and political developments (Ibid.). In a private letter, Aksakov expressed himself with the utmost certainty:

> The West is collapsing, the lies of the West are exposed, and it is clear to what illness his chosen path leads. ... You know how I was constantly against the western direction; I am even more against it now. To isolate from the West of Europe is all we need.
>
> *Ibid.*

Along with other Slavophiles, Aksakov supported Russia's participation in the Crimean War, hoping for the Slavs' liberation from the Ottoman Empire's rule.

While accepting and developing Khomyakov's views, Aksakov adopted a more radically defensive or isolationist perspective on relations with Europe. He did not live to see another formative event in the development of Slavophilism – the Polish uprising of 1863 – remaining in Russian memory primarily as a theoretician of relations between the people and the state. According to Aksakov, the foundations of Russia's internal freedom are the Orthodox religious tradition and the communal economy free of state interference and coercion. Rejecting the theory of patriarchal relations developed by the historian Sergei Solovyov, Aksakov (1852, 139) insisted that "the Russian land from the beginning has been the least patriarchal, the most family-oriented, and the most social (namely, communal) land." Consequently, the tasks of the state should include strengthening the commune and not encouraging its disintegration, which would contribute to the development of society based on the principles of "Christian humanism" (Aksakov 1861, 9–11).

These reflections formed Aksakov's perspective on the state. Associating Russian freedom with Orthodox Christianity and the peasant commune, the philosopher considered the state a necessary yet culturally foreign institution. Earlier than other Slavophiles, he endorsed the so-called Norman theory, according to which the Russians voluntarily called on the Scandinavian rulers, or Varangians, to govern Russia (Ibid., 4). Aksakov viewed this fact as confirming that Russian Slavs regarded the state "as a necessary, inevitable evil" and external to their needs (Zhaba 1954, 48). Political governance and the state did not constitute "the ideal of [Slav] existence":

> The Earth needed the state, but the Earth did not want to be the state[,] not to betray its high human task. ... The beginning of freedom is the Earth; the beginning of bondage is the state.
>
> *Ibid.*

The division had to be respected as one between political governance executed by the state, on the one hand, and the society-centered Christian faith and the free economy, on the other. From the spiritual standpoint, Aksakov (1861, 3–4) argued autocracy, like any other state, is a dead external form that does not contribute to the search for truth and morality. The thinker argued for a return to the principle of separation between the outer and the inner, which he considered to be observed in Muscovy, but completely violated during the Romanov period, especially Peter's rule.[2]

Aksakov's attitude to Peter the Great was typical of the early Slavophiles, separating them from their successors. Condemning the governance of Peter, the thinker was critical of not only the historical perspective of Russian Westernizers such as Solovyev but also the state-minded intellectuals such as Nikolai Karamzin. The latter wrote a history of Russia from the perspective of those governing the country. For example, Aksakov took issue with Mikhail Pogodin's praise for Karamzin's work as reflecting popular aspirations. According to Aksakov (2006), Karamzin wrote the history of the Russian state not noticing the Earth or the people and, therefore, failed to identify the historic harm inflicted by what Aksakov called Peter's "coup."

Aksakov's vision of Fortress Russia did not exclude, but assumed the importance of, internal reforms. Such reforms were to be conducted according to Russia's needs rather than to the changing Europe. Despite harsh criticism of Russia's historically state-serving autocracy, the thinker associated the country's future with the monarchy and pinned his hopes on Alexander II, who was crowned the new tsar in 1855. Using the patronage of Count Bludov, Aksakov handed Alexander a specially written "Note on the internal state of Russia." In the note, he advocated restoring the division of the responsibilities between the state and society by granting the people the broadest freedoms – speech, labor, and popular regional councils (*Zemsky Sobors*). Aksakov was convinced that European revolutions did not apply to Russia were it to reject the oppression by the state and recognize social needs and the support from below. He maintained that the tsar had nothing to fear from Western ideas. He believed there was no place in Russia for liberalism or conservatism, let alone revolutionary movements, given that even Yemelyan Pugachev – the leader of the rebellious Cossack movement in the eighteenth century – sought to present himself as a "legitimate tsar." The note ended by stressing Aksakov's motto: "The government should have the unlimited and exclusive freedom of *government*, while the people should be allowed the full freedom of *life* ... protected by the government" (Novikova and Sizemskaya 1997, 88). To a certain extent, the note turned out to be consonant with the thinking of Alexander. He soon initiated a series of reforms by abolishing serfdom and introducing glasnost and regional councils. Aksakov did not live to this time, having died from illness in 1860.

The early Slavophile ideas did not inspire considerable support for the oppressive state and the increasingly Westernizing intelligentsia. Westernizers such as Boris Chicherin asserted that the Slavophiles did not express "anything sensible about the so-called Russian ideas" (Ibid., 104).[3] The new advocates of Russia's indigenous path, including Konstantin Leontyev, criticized the Slavophile movement as "an ordinary, dull, bourgeois liberalism not differing in any significant respect from the Western, egalitarian priesthood" (Tsymbayev 1986, 110). The space for arguing Russia, both as the fortress and as the bridge, was to widen considerably.

The Fortresses of Ivan Aksakov and Nikolai Danilevsky

During the next period of Slavophil development, those favoring the idea of Russia's unique path went in radically different directions. Europe itself grew more divided between the liberal and conservative parts. Those supportive of Konstantin Aksakov's line of argument prioritized the protection of Slavs and presented a new defense of separating Russia from Europe (Pan-Slavists). Those sympathetic to the notion of Russia's European roots searched for ways to bring the two sides together, albeit on spiritual rather than social grounds (Vladimir Solovyev and his followers). The following two sections elaborate on these visions of Russia.

Ivan Aksakov: The Assertive Defense of a Slavic Fortress

Konstantin's younger brother, Ivan Aksakov (1823–1886), was best known for his activism in the area of international promotion of Slavic and Slavophil ideals. While broadly sharing his brother's views, Ivan matured intellectually under Nicholas I and during the Great Reforms of Alexander II, the new Polish revolt of 1863, and the development of Russian national consciousness in the period following the Crimean War.

In the Slavophile spirit, Ivan Aksakov viewed Russia's internal reforms – those related to peasant, judicial, regional governance, Constitution, and the Polish question – as principally linked to the issue of Russian identity and relation to Europe. Like Konstantin, Ivan proceeded from the idea of humankind's diversity and the particular path of Russia's development based on Christianity and peasant commune ideals. An admirer of Hegel's philosophy, he was convinced of the need for a dialectical combination of the general and the particular on a global and Russian scale. Ivan also assumed the importance of the common Christian roots in Europe.

At the same time as other Slavophiles, Ivan believed in the moral super-iority of the Russians over the Europeans. He was imbued with an awareness of Russia's religious and missionary role as the savior of a sinful and increasingly secular European civilization. He believed Russia's role was to consolidate its Christian roots and free itself spiritually, thereby showing the way to Western European peoples. Living in the reformist period, Aksakov continued to believe in the ideals of Muscovy Rus' rejecting the need for a constitution for Russia and any privileges for the nobility. Relative to the state-minded members of the Slavophile movement, such as Yuri Samarin, Aksakov was skeptical of the government and promoted the development of social relations, a radical conver-gence of estates, and the self-abolition of the noble stratum (Tsymbayev 1986, 187, 212–214).

Unlike Konstantin, the younger Aksakov became politically active and aimed to save Europe by promoting the values of Orthodox Christianity as practiced by the Slavic people worldwide. A participant in the Crimean War, he devoted him-self to journalism and editorial work, rallying the best Slavophil forces around the magazines *Russkaya Beseda*, *Parus* and, subsequently, despite the authorities' persecution, the newspapers *Den*, *Moskva,* and *Rus'*. Ivan was also involved with the activities of the Moscow Slavic Committee, established in 1858 and chaired by Mikhail Pogodin. Until the committee's closure in 1878, Aksakov played a crucial role in expressing and promoting the Slavic sympathies of the Russians. Responding to the Polish uprising of 1863, he rejected the possibility of using force to keep Poles within the Russian Empire while formulating the inter-national Slavophile platform for all those sympathetic to a new Slav cause. This cause was to form a confederation of all Slavic peoples in Russia and the Ottoman and Austro-Hungarian empires by forces of spiritual and moral influence. He took issue with those Pan-Slavists favoring the capture of Constantinople and the unification of the Slavs into a single state – Mikhail Pogodin, Rostislav Fadeyev, Aleksandr Kireyev, and others. "The unification of all Slavs into a single state is unimaginable, even in our dreams," wrote Aksakov (Khevrolina 1996, 306).[4]

Ivan Aksakov advocated a strict and assertive policy for European states out-side the Slavic area. He feared the revival of the Russian state's solidarity with European powers, similar to the Holy Alliance in the post-Napoleonic period, as directed against the Slavic peoples. Aksakov was also a staunch opponent of any rapprochement with Austria and Prussia. Hawkish in foreign policy, he even insisted on declaring the Balkan Peninsula a zone of Russian interests, not believing in the possibility of a war with Austria-Hungary. In February 1882, Aksakov argued,

> by excessive patience, we do not avert war, but only seduce and tempt our opponents to declare war on us … the dull growl of the beast, reminding others that he is alive and not so sick, is more likely to make others reckon with him than the assumption that he is completely dead.[5]

At the same time, he opposed the establishment of allied relations with France and England, arguing against involvement in European affairs and believing that "Russia will always be alien to the West" (Khevrolina 1996, 307).

The Defensive Fortress of Nikolai Danilevsky

Nikolai Danilevsky (1822–1885) was a member of the Pan-Slavist movement, yet quite distinct from Ivan Aksakov. A towering figure in Russian intellectual developments since the late nineteenth century,[6] Danilevsky was a radical critic of Russia's pro-Western leanings, one who advocated recognizing and cultivating indigenous national institutions and the ability to progress separately from European civilization. In many respects, he was the first to challenge the West-centered universalist – thinking systematically and advocating a defensive particularistic alternative. His main book, *Russia and Europe* (Danilevsky 1990), was published in 1869,[7] while its central ideas have anticipated those expressed by Oswald Spengler, Arnold Toynbee, Samuel Huntington, and others.

Danilevsky formulated his ideas in the context of increased political competition in Europe, as Russia was trying to recover its losses following defeat in the Crimean War. The new international context changed from the traditional Christian values that united the continent before the war to secular nationalist politics, and the struggle for political and military power. In part, Danilevsky's critique of the Western, liberal Enlightenment ideals echoed the eastern European and Prussian themes of anti-Westernism, Romanticism, and nationalism, emphasizing language, culture, and spirit (Knutsen 1997, 181–182). Danilevsky championed the idea of breaking away from Europe and completed Russia's transition from the country's Slavophile thinkers. The latter thought of Russia as a genuinely religious and social community and a better part of Europe.[8] As different as they were from Westernizers, Slavophiles saw Europe as Russia's only significant other by viewing the development of one in terms of another.

Danilevsky sought to break with Slavophiles in two ways. First, he designated Russia as a principally non-European culture. In his view, the critically important features of Russia were not a social community or its peasant equivalent, the commune, and not even Christianity, but an ability to develop independently from European and other civilizations as a separate economic, political, and cultural entity. Although he shared Slavophiles' criticism of Peter the Great's attempts to impose Western European cultural traditions on Russia, Danilevsky strongly defended Peter's state-building priorities.

> In Peter's activities, we must strictly separate two sides: on the one hand, his state role includes military, navy, administrative, and industrial initiatives, and on the other hand, his reforms devoted to changing lifestyle, mentality, habits, and ideas of Russian people. He deserves our eternal recognition

and cherished memory for his state role. ... However, the second side [of Peter] brought Russia the greatest harm.

Danilevsky 1990, 265–266

Secondly, Danilevsky refused to equate Slavic with Eastern Christian religion. Humiliated by defeat in the Crimean War, Russia was then experiencing a revival of the ideas of Slavic unity. However, a biologist by training, he was closer to the agnostic and positivist outlook rather than the religious one. His foundations of cultural-historical types had more to do with linguistic and ethnographic characteristics than religion. Philosophical and religious reflections of early Slavophiles, beginning with Khomyakov and Kireyevsky, were quite alien to Danilevsky. Nikolay Berdyaev (1990a, 99) correctly identified Danilevsky as "a man of an entirely different origin."

Danilevsky's theory bears a resemblance to some foreign particularist thinkers. His radical critique of the liberal Enlightenment ideals echoed the eastern European and Prussian themes of anti-Westernism, Romanticism, and nationalism, emphasizing language, culture, and spirit (Knutsen 1997, 181–182). Partly under German influences,[9] Danilevsky proposed to rethink the accepted principles of analyzing world history as universal by rejecting the linear view of progress and identifying local "historic-cultural types." Anticipating the later theories of Spengler, Toynbee, and Huntington, Danilevsky (1990, 88) distinguished multiple civilizations in the past, of which Romano-Germanic or European was only one. Other historic-cultural types included Egyptian, Chinese, Assyrian-Babylonian-Phoenician, Indian, Iranian, Jewish, Greek, Roman, and Arabian.

These types are not evolutionary stages on the ladder of gradual perfectibility ... but entirely different plans – plans without any common denominator – in which each entity evolves in a specific and distinct fashion toward the multiformity and perfection within its reach.

Ibid., 8

As he did not view progress in unidirectional and universal terms, Danilevsky proposed to abandon the concept of "universal humanity" (*obshchechelovechestvo*) "not only because it does not exist, but also because to desire it means being satisfied with banality and absence of any color and originality" (Ibid., 123). Having rejected the notion of universal humanity, Danilevsky introduced the concept of "all-humanity" (*vsechelovechestvo*), which meant a richness of cross-cultural interactions across the world. He compared those interactions with those streets that form squares by crossing. For Russia, this perspective did not mean the need to "lead" Europe or "catch up" with it, as was emphasized by Slavophiles and Westernizers, respectively. Instead, it meant developing its own, Slavic, type that would progress based on its laws.

As a scientist, Danilevsky articulated "laws" in developing historic-cultural types (Ibid., 91–92). The first law posited the linguistic criteria for forming such types. The second linked political independence to their emergence and successful development.[10] The third stressed relativism in the development of historic-cultural types that "are influenced by preceding or contemporary alien civilizations", yet are not transferable to other people. The fourth law concerned the importance of ethnic and political (federation) diversity as preconditions for developing and strengthening various cultural types. Finally, the fifth law described the growth of civilization by positing a relatively long period of its formation and a relatively short period of "flourishing and bearing fruits."

These laws were intended to show a way to Russia's own new and eleventh cultural type that might yet prove to be the most developed and would not owe anything to Europe. Danilevsky's outlook was more optimistic than those of Western particularists like Spengler and Huntington. Rather than viewing his culture as one in decline or on defense, he thought of the Slavic type as young and capable of producing the political, social, and economic foundations required for its authentic development. In his assessment, Russia only completed its state-building in the second half of the nineteenth century when, by liberating peasants, it entered the stage of flourishing (Ibid., 508). However, the main struggle for Slavic independence was still ahead and would have to involve the assertiveness of Slavs' interests before the Roman-Germanic world. Here, the thinker insisted that Russia abandon Christian principles (since the enemy had already done so) and be guided exclusively by state interests. "An eye for an eye … is the law of foreign policy and state-to-state relations. Here, there is no room for love and self-sacrifice" (Ibid., 34). Danilevsky's practical recommendations included forming an all-Slav federation with its capital in Constantinople, pushing Turks and Austro-Hungarians from the Balkans, annexing territories populated by ethnic Russians, and gaining full control over the Black Sea and the Straits. The "Russo-Slavic egoism" also demanded pitting European nations against each other, and not seek that they balance each other. Only when Europe "is fighting, it can be secure to us" (Ibid., 443).[11]

Overall, Danilevsky produced a principally new version of Russian particularism that was more essentialist and anti-European than Slavophiles. His ideas have greatly influenced intellectual developments in Russia by providing a vocabulary for new nationalist thinking and paving the way for radical anti-European reactions. Although Danilevsky's theory contained some elements of dialogue by reflecting on the richness of global cross-cultural interactions, the general thrust revealed hostility toward the European West.

The idea of Russia as a particular historic-cultural type drew sharp criticism from Westernizers, who attacked Danilevsky for his anti-European stance. Westernizers reiterated their belief in Europe's future and presented the thinker's views as degrading Russian discourse. The prominent historian turned politician, and a leader of "Cadets," or constitutional democrats, Pavel Milyukov, saw Danilevsky's book as a dangerous utopia and hailed Danilevsky's views of a Pan-Slav federation headed by Russia as nothing but an ideology of "hatred toward Europe" (Novikova and Sizemskaya 1997, 174).

In the meantime, the European continent began to crumble by splitting into progressive and anti-revolutionary camps. Europe was increasingly entering the turmoil of war and revolution. Russia's alignment with France and Britain and, subsequently, the decision to go to war in 1914 strengthened socialist radicals at home at the expense of established liberals and conservatives. As Germany was increasingly challenging Russia's position in Europe, new pan-Slavist voices in Russia grew highly critical of what they described as the "Romano-Germanic cultural type's" encroachment on Balkan Slavs. In the increasingly militaristic context, even Danilevsky's ideas of tactically rebuilding relations with Germany to regain Russia's internal strength seemed too moderate. Many pan-Slavists now sympathized with the idea of fighting Germany to revive Russia (Tsygankov 2012, 87).

Those who remained committed to Russia's spiritual unity with Europe accused Danilevsky of wanting to create a Slav future on the ruins of European culture. Such was the belief of Vladimir Solovyev (2000a, 413), to whose views we are now turning.

The European Bridge of Vladimir Solovyev

Unlike the early Slavophiles who believed in the superiority of Orthodox Christian ideals, new Slavophiles and their intellectual leader Vladimir Solovyev (1853–1900) saw Russia's salvation in strengthening an ecumenical dialogue with European Catholicism. Solovyev, therefore, refused to engage Danilevsky on the issue of potentially progressive non-European developments. Along with Westernizers, Solovyev did not grant enlightenment to non-European cultures; his attitude toward the East remained deeply ethnocentric, which was soon noted by his critics (Strakhov 1990).[12] He reconciles the East with the West through coercive power and the imposition of Russian values.

Bridging the Two Europes into the True Third Rome

For all the uniqueness of his views, Solovyev was a member of the Slavophile movement, sharing its understanding of Russia's position and role in the world. Despite his criticism of Slavophiles for idealizing the Eastern Church and denying the positive role of Peter the Great, Solovyev remained a defender of ideas developed by the early Slavophiles. Like them, he was influenced by French and German classical philosophy and Western theological thought.[13] Like Pyotr Chaadayev, Solovyev sympathized with the Western Church. He did not convert to Catholicism but acted as a radical critic of the Russian Orthodox Church. Some scholars (Losev 1990, 17) even called him a "church-political revolutionary."

Born in the year the Crimean War began, Solovyev was determined to critically assess Russia's historical and Orthodox Christian experience under new conditions. In the conditions of post-reform Russia in the second half of the nineteenth century, European secularization resulted in the rise of nationalism and socialism. Solovyev witnessed growing social activism and polarization, and these anxieties of the time were reflected in the philosopher's worldview. Fear for Europe in the face of secular radicalism from within and the rise of the non-Christian East from without gave Solovyev's philosophy an almost apocalyptic sound, warning of the end of history and the coming collapse of all European ideals.[14]

Being critical of various views of Slavophiles and Pan-Slavists, Solovyev was also not a statist or a liberal Westernizer. He proceeded from Europe's unconditional moral and political authority while condemning all manifestations of nationalism and obscurantism. Like the Westernizers and Chaadayev, Solovyev denounced serfdom and the tsarist autocracy, yet he did not support the growing movement toward individualism in Europe. In his (Solovyev 1989, 262) view, "our urgent need, an essential practical condition for the fulfillment of our highest national calling, is the spiritual liberation of Russia – a matter incomparably more important than the civil liberties for the peasants." Solovyev could be perceived as a Westernizer only in comparison with the conservative defenders of the autocracy in Russia because he opposed nationalism in its various manifestations. At the same time, like Chaadayev and the Slavophiles, Solovyev did not see the future of Russia in the formation and development of liberal democratic institutions. He was a religious Westernizer, preaching the unification of the Orthodox and Roman Catholic Churches to form a single theocratic order.

In arguing Russia's spiritual unity with Europe, Solovyev went further than the early Slavophiles. His understanding of the Russian mission of serving as the Third Rome was to create conditions for a new reunification with the European continent on theocratic principles, which were close to Catholicism. To him, the Third Rome meant the ability, not to live in isolation from the outside world, but to act in the historical dispute between East and West as a conciliatory third force.

The Solovyev system of Christian universalism was a continuation of the efforts by the early Slavophiles, especially Aleksei Khomyakov, to demonstrate the unique mission of Russia in the world. In the treatises "Spiritual Foundations of Life" (1884) and "The History and Future of Theocracy" (1885), Solovyev formulated the theory of free theocracy as an ideal system of government for Russia and Europe. The philosopher accepted the Catholic ideal of the supremacy of the Church over the state, rejecting both the Russian and the Western types of political systems. He condemned the Russian system of subordinating the Church's activities to the state. However, in the Western system, Solovyev rejected what he viewed as the tendency of the secular, law-enforcing state to suppress the spiritual freedom of the individual. According to him, only Christianity could save the state as a potentially important institution.

The Christian state combines the features of the eastern and western states. Eastern Christianity relegates state life to a secondary place while prioritizing spiritual or religious life. On the other hand, together with the West, Christianity recognizes the state's positive and active progressive nature. Not only does Christianity call on the state to fight against evil forces under the banner of the church, but it also requires that the state introduce moral principles into political and international life, as well as gradually raise the secular society to the height of the church ideal.

Zamaleyev 2002, 131

Solovyev's ideal world system was ecumenical Christianity. In his view, such Christianity should result from the reunification of the Orthodox and Catholic churches, spreading confidently beyond the borders of the European continent. Rejecting the accusations of wanting to catholicize Russia, the philosopher insisted that unification was essential for the Russians. Like many of his contemporaries, he sympathized with the liberation of the fraternal Slavic peoples of the Balkans from Turkish rule. However, unlike Nikolai Danilevsky, Mikhail Katkov, Nikolai Strakhov, and other late Slavophiles, Solovyev spoke not about one but two Slavic types.

These two Slavic types differ not only in ethnographic features, but, most importantly, in their spiritual principles: The Western Slavic people were formed under the spiritual influence of Rome, whereas the Eastern Slavs – under the spiritual influence of Byzantium.... [T]he spiritual unity of the Eastern and Western Slavs (as well as universal unity) is possible only if Orthodox Christianity and Catholicism do not exclude each other, if it will be possible, while remaining Orthodox, to be at the same time Catholic, and remaining Catholic, to be Orthodox.

Solovyev 1989, 319–320

Consequently, the Europe of the future is Christian Europe. In Solovyev's view, such a Europe was only being reborn and by no means had to give way to the pan-Slavic state, as argued by the philosopher's opponents (Ibid., 318). While insisting on such a unification of churches, Solovyev spoke in favor of Russia's "feat of national self-sacrifice," linking Russianness with adherence to the universal cause of God. "A people ready to devote themselves to this cause is a *theo-cratic* people by vocation and duty" (Ibid., 327).

Thus, Solovyev's response to the Pan-Slavists was not to reject Slavic unity but to call for its implementation based on love and voluntary sacrifice of their national interests. He believed that without creating a Christian community in the space of the entire European continent, a true solution to the Slavic question in the Balkans or Poland was not possible. The philosopher, therefore, called the Russian people to be inspired by the Christian idea of "Holy Rus" and to remember two other significant acts of national self-sacrifice – the appeal to the

Varangians to govern Russia and the European reform by Peter the Great (Ibid., 285). Both actions contributed to the movement of Russia toward the implementation of her conciliatory mission and, now, the philosopher believed Russia again faced the need for such an act. Solovyev thought such action should come precisely from Russia, guided by moral motives.

At the end of his life, Solovyev lost faith in the possibility of realizing his idea of theocracy. However, he did not abandon his efforts to preach the philosophy of goodness and love. By the end of his life, he published an extensive theoretical work, *Justification of Good. Moral Philosophy* (1899). By this time, the philosopher was full of apocalyptic forebodings and predictions about the world, which he expressed in his poem *Pan-Mongolism* (1894) and the philosophical essay *Three Conversations* (1900). The part of the latter work, *A Brief Story about the Antichrist*, painted an impressive picture of the rise, domination, and subsequent fall of the Antichrist, which resulted in the extermination of most of humanity. Shortly before his death, the philosopher again warned the world against the temptations of power and materiality, prioritizing spiritual and Christian ideals and values.

Critique of Russian Nationalism

Solovyev's critique of nationalism is the other side of his desire to assert Christian moral principles in international life and to defend "national self-sacrifice" in the interests of unification with Europe. His response to those supporting the national priorities was similar to the ideas of the early Slavophiles, yet more thoughtful. After all, Solovyev lived when discussions about the national and the European relationship shifted to the center of public attention. Following the efforts of Chancellor Alexander Gorchakov after the Crimean War, Russia entered a period of moderate isolation from European affairs and focused on addressing issues of internal development. The state's moderately nationalist or isolationist course drew criticism from both pan-Slavists and those supportive of active participation in European politics.

Solovyev's vision, developed in the book "The National Question in Russia," was closer to Europeanists but also sought to answer pan-Slavist concerns. The philosopher did not abandon the values of spirituality and state but sought to integrate them into the system of Russia's universal service to humanity. He defended European ideals and the need for Russia to "accept and actively assimilate those universal (*obchshechelovecheskiye*) forms of life and knowledge that have been developed by Western Europe" (Solovyev 1989, 262). The philosopher unequivocally presented these actions by his country as a means of "fulfilling the highest national vocation … of the *spiritual liberation of Russia*" (Ibid.). Solovyev (1990, 557) also partially accepted the arguments in favor of strengthening the state yet warned against deifying it or viewing it as being above the law.

Like Chaadayev and the early Westernizers, Solovyev opposed not the principle of the monarchy but its Russian version – autocracy. The thinker was convinced that the latter was responsible for imposing serfdom on Russia and placing the ideals of the Christian Church at the service of his interests. He believed the state could not embody the unconditional principle of morality or stand above the law, as in pagan Rome or Byzantium (Ibid., 557, 562). Inside the country, this leads to the suppression of the natural human right to a *"dignified existence"* (Solovyev 1989, 260) and, in foreign policy, such prioritization of the state inevitably entails the awakening of pagan instincts, expressed in the policy of nationalism and national interests (Ibid., 272). In addition to serfdom, or the enslavement of the peasantry, Solovyev viewed the prioritization of the state interest among the most important sins of Russia. "If Sevastopol was a just punishment for Serfdom, then what for was the Berlin Congress and its consequences?" asked the philosopher, referring to Russia's loss of the authority of European power (Solovyev 1990, 210). *"The idea of a nation,"* he insisted, *"is not what it thinks of itself in time, but what God thinks of it in eternity"* (Solovyev 1989, 220).

Solovyev's criticism of the Russian Orthodox Church and non-Western civilizations results from his conviction in the Euro-Christian vocation of Russia. The thinker was especially critical of Byzantine-originated Orthodox Christianity, which he considered subordinate to official power and, therefore, devoid of thought and spiritual freedom. The philosopher wrote in an open letter to one of the companions of the procurator of the Holy Synod, Konstantin Pobedonostsev,

> The state tutelage spares us from the struggle for Orthodox Christianity. On the other hand, Orthodox Christianity itself, instead of being the all-embracing universal banner of peoples, is becoming a simple attribute or appendage of Russian statehood.
>
> *Solovyev 1990, 187*

As in the case of the *Philosophical Letters* by Chaadayev (1991), the criticism by Solovyev was so sharp that it led to his conflict with the state and the official Christian Orthodox Church. The authorities banned Solovyev from publishing anything concerning questions of religion, and the philosopher had to publish his leading treatise on Russia and the universal church in France in French. Responding to the prohibition of publishing in Russia, the thinker wrote indignantly about the Orthodox Church as a "police institution" and "a servant of the secular authorities." "I fight with all my might against this anti-Christian and godless system, and in due time, with God's help, I hope to do something to destroy the system." (Solovyev 1990, 216). The philosopher's comparisons of Orthodox Christianity and Catholicism were not in favor of the former (Ibid., 218). Soloviev agreed with the thesis by Ivan Aksakov – another outcast of state and spiritual censorship – about the replacement of "internal truth" with "formal truth." He also agreed that "the abomination of desolation" reigns in the Russian church and that there are no guardian angels standing at the church fence but "gendarmes and district overseers." Soloviev's verdict was as harsh as possible: the national Russian "Church was *abandoned by the Spirit of Truth and Love*, and it is, therefore, not the true Church of God" (Losev 1990, 17).

Solovyev's adherence to Euro-Christianity often resulted in arrogance towards people of other cultures and religions. Like Russian Westernizers, he assumed European civilization's moral and spiritual superiority. At the same time, the philosopher was guided by fear of the people of the East. For example, in one of the early works, written on the eve of the Russian-Turkish war of 1877–1878, "Three Forces" Solovyev (1989, 28) characterized the "Muslim East" as a civilization that "destroys man and asserts only an *inhuman God*." Later, the philosopher demonstrated fear of the possible rise of Asia, anticipating the Mongol invasion and losing faith in the mission of Russia (Zhaba 1954, 239). Critics of the philosopher did not fail to point out his Eurocentrism and inability to recognize Eastern civilizations as equals to Christian cultures (Strakhov 1990).

Solovyev's Renaissance and Nikolai Berdyaev

Religious Westernizers ceased to progress in Russia in the twentieth century, as the Revolution completed the process of secularization that had already begun in the first half of the nineteenth century. Europe found itself at the mercy of the ideas of liberalism and socialism, rooted in the Enlightenment and the practice of the French Revolution. The herald of a new era was Friedrich Nietzsche, who announced the death of God and the birth of the *Superman*. Solovyev, who sought to defend the idea of Euro-Christianity, viewed the development of nationalism, nihilism, and socialism in the context of the growing secularization of the European world, yet he was essentially fighting a defensive battle. A longtime critic of positivism,[15] he denied socialism the ability to offer society a meaningful moral idea. Solovyev (2000b, 7–12) recognized the truth of the equality of rights, including economic rights, while at the same time rejecting the ambition of the new socialist movement to offer the people a worthy moral philosophy. The philosopher described Nietzscheism as "a pagan view of strength and beauty", testifying to "a man's forgetfulness of his true, high destiny" (Solovyev 2000b, 612–618). "Hearts were aflame with a new faith," the philosopher wrote, "but the minds did not work, for there were already ready-made and unconditional answers to all questions" (Florovsky 1991, 289). With the dying of Euro-Christian ideals in Europe, their lives in Russia also ended.

However, Solovyev's cause of ecumenical Christianity did not die intellectually. He had followers – Nikolai Berdyaev, Sergei Bulgakov, Fyodor Stepun, Georgy Fedotov, Semyon Frank, and others. Following the Bolshevik revolution, they had to immigrate and continue thinking about Russia and future Christian revival outside their homeland. Like Solovyev, they aimed to stress in their work the deep cultural connection of Russia with Christian Europe by defending the spiritual freedom of the individual from the encroachments of power. Like Solovyev, they associated Russianness with the ability to conduct a complex spiritual dialogue with European peoples. To illustrate the continuation of Christian universalism, let us briefly consider the views of Berdyaev.

Nikolai Berdyaev (1874–1948) was developing ideas of Christian universalism in a new era. Berdyaev lived during a growing violence, expressed in several revolutions in Russia, the Bolshevik dictatorship, the rise of Nazism in Germany, and two world wars. Having renounced his original Marxist beliefs, the philosopher switched to Christian idealism. In 1901, he first published the article "The Struggle for Idealism" and remained a consistent defender of the priority of spiritual and ethical principles alongside others. Berdyaev (1991, 38) further called for creating a national philosophical tradition based on the ideas of Solovyov.

Having been exiled from Russia in 1922, Berdyaev found refuge on the outskirts of Paris and devoted himself to affirming the ideals of spiritual freedom. He distinguished such an idea from political freedom, which he associated with Western individualism. Following the principle of collective personality or collegiality (*sobornost'*) formulated by Khomyakov, Berdyaev promoted the idea of "ontological unity" between I and You and defended the religious or sacred foundations of spiritual freedom. He considered political, national, and economic equality to be God's law, not subject to rationalization. In particular, in "The Philosophy of Inequality" (1918), he rejected the importance of the principles of the rule of law and national self-determination. In his view, "historical differentiations and inequalities, which formed the historical cosmos, could not be erased and eliminated by any social intervention." (Berdyaev 1990c, 354). In this matter, Berdyaev was incomparably more conservative than Solovyev, who recognized in the "Readings on God-manhood" the truth of socialism, including regarding the question of economic equality (Solovyev 1989, 7–12). However, later, Berdyaev evolved towards social liberalism and defended a democratic, not elitist social order.[16] In his autobiographical work "Self-knowledge" (1940), he admitted that he viewed himself as "an aristocratic thinker who recognized the truth of socialism" (Berdyaev 1990d, 9).

Despite his changeable views on the internal structure of society, Berdyaev all his life defended the principles of global Christian humanism. Not sharing Solovyev's ideas of theocratic utopia and the hierarchical unification of the Christian Orthodox and Catholic churches,[17] Berdyaev was consistent in his defense of Christian universalism. He was advancing the Slavophile themes of collegiality, God-manhood, and the kingdom of spirituality in the process of thinking through Western, mainly German philosophers such as Karl Marx, George Hegel, Arthur Schopenhauer, Immanuel Kant, Max Stirner, Friedrich Nietzsche, Martin Heidegger, and others (Berdyaev 1993, 1995). Berdyaev also professed the principles of active Christian humanism, often speaking with journalistic essays and public lectures and participating in social movements. In particular, he played an essential role in the Russian student Christian movement (RSKhD), founded in 1923 and striving for the Orthodox churching of culture and life. For example, in his discussion with Bishop Veniamin Fedchenkov,

Berdyaev defended the understanding of Christianity as an active religious trans-formation of the world and not as an ascetic path of personal salvation.[18]

With all his work, Berdyaev strove to establish a particular type of philoso-phizing and a unique understanding of Russia's mission in the world. He carried this understanding throughout his life and, in one of his final works, wrote

> the path of Russia is special. Russia is the Great East-West, a world in itself, and the Russian people possess great forces. The Russian people are the people of the future. He will resolve the issues the West can no longer resolve, which he does not even raise in their entire depth.
>
> *Berdyaev 1990a, 105*

Berdyaev's critique of Western life reflects the basic ideas of Slavophile thinking, including the assertion of the priority of spirituality and the condemnation of material limitations. Because of his criticism of the West, many considered Berdyaev pro-Soviet, especially since the thinker was not as critical of the Soviet system and did not believe in its rapid destruction. The philosopher formulated his view in the book *The Origins and Meaning of Russian Communism* (1937), in which he identified the phenomenon as growing from "national roots" determined by Russian history (Berdyaev 1990b, 7). Acknowledging the discontinuity of Russian history, Berdyaev nevertheless saw in the Soviet system a connection with the Moscow doctrine of the Third Rome. In his opinion, the Soviet and Moscow systems were examples of the messianic search for the "true kingdom" characteristic of the Russian people throughout its history (Ibid., 9).

However, Berdyaev was far from sympathetic to the USSR. True to Christian humanism, he condemned the practice of nationalism, ideological hostility, and suppression of personal freedoms. Recognizing that communism was correct in criticizing capitalism, he passionately argued the predominance of hatred over love in communism and the inability of the communist system to turn to the future, becoming "a source of creativity for a new, better life" (Ibid., 150). The thinker's ideal was close to the Slavophile model of free commonality, which he defined as "personalistic socialism that combines the principle of personality as the supreme value with the principle of the fraternal community of people" (Ibid., 152). In defining the "Russian idea," Berdyaev followed Solovyev, Dostoevsky, and other thinkers by stressing not nationally limited but universal and human dimensions.

From the point of view of international theory, the contribution of Solovyev's direction to the development of Slavophile thought is significant, reflecting Russia's special mission in the world. Thinkers in the tradition of the Russian religious renaissance saw Russia as sinful, yet also showed world humanity the way by constant struggle with the temptations of the material and by resist-ance to substituting spiritual freedom for a political one. In practice, the virtues of Christian universalism have often turned into weaknesses. A lacking understanding of the geopolitical foundations of the international system and a reluctance to analyze the nature of power resulted in naïve and impractical ideas. In terms of their implementation, Solovyev's theocratic utopia, or Christian universalism, was hardly better suited for strengthening Russia's influence in Europe or resolving the Slavic and Polish questions than the Pan-Slavist projects of seizing Constantinople. Somebody had to seriously consider the power conditions underlying the development of the international system. Another significant flaw concerned the Eurocentrism of Solovyev's thought, which at times was reminiscent of racism concerning the peoples of Asia and the East. Christian universalism, by itself, could hardly serve as a reliable guide to understanding and changing the world.

The Anti-Soviet Fortresses of Ivan Ilyin and Alexander Solzhenitsyn

The views of Ivan Ilyin and his followers are an essential and independent direction of Slavophil thought. Compared to the early Slavophiles and representatives of the Russian religious renaissance, this trend treated the state and state-initiated ideas with much greater respect, considering them an indispensable condition for the development of Russia. Compared to Pan-Slavism, Ivan Ilyin and Alexander Solzhenitsyn strove for isolation, not an expansion of their supported values. Their mission was of self-contained and self-affirming nature. In their work, they postulated that Russia's contribution to the world is not to save other peoples spiritually but to survive and continue progressing as a unique culture and statehood. This program was ambitious because the Bolshevik regime was in power inside the country while the European powers continued their attempts to weaken it from the outside.

The anti-Soviet Fortress of Ivan Ilyin

The Russian philosopher and jurist Ivan Ilyin (1883–1954) formulated his theory of state and law through the critical rethinking of ideas of the German philosopher George Hegel. While an independent thinker, Ilyin's understanding of the relationship between the state and society was close to Hegel's.[19] In *Philosophy of Law*, Hegel did not oppose the former to the latter but linked them by proposing the notion of a "political society" that developed on state-determined legal foundations. Following this path, Ilyin sought to formulate the legal foundations of an autocratic state and, secondly, to identify the conditions accompanying establishing a viable government. He considered both an autocratic monarchy and a strong government essential for the development of Russia.

First, the thinker considered it necessary to demonstrate that the autocratic rule operated within the framework of the law and was not the antithesis of individual freedom. "An autocracy is a form of government and, consequently, a kind of law; therefore, all the axioms of law and legal consciousness are valid for the autocracy as well" (Ilyin 1979). Many in Russia held similar positions. Representatives of the Russian legal tradition, beginning with Boris Chicherin accepted the idea of an unconstitutional monarchical power. The early Slavophiles, in particular, Konstantin Aksakov and Yuri Samarin, advocated the separation of the functions of state government from those of management and faith as belonging to the society. However, there were also significant differences. Ilyin supported complete economic freedom and the development of national "religious experience," but he believed in the close internal relations between the state and society. The early Slavophiles argued that the state had long passed the boundaries of the law assigned to it by social groups. However, Ilyin insisted that the Russian state was always aware of the limitations of its power: "As a national-political phenomenon, Russia was a product of a strong state power, which, however, never (not even under Ivan the Terrible!) interfered with the conduct of life, culture, and economy" (Ilyin 1992a, 311).

The disagreement, therefore, concerned the conditions under which an autocratic state could be necessary and practical, that is, achieving its goals while acting within the framework of the law and not violating individual rights. Ilyin disagreed with the early Slavophiles, who objected to the state's interference in the affairs of the economy and faith. He also rejected the views of the followers of Solovyov, who viewed the state as a largely obsolete and discredited institution.[20] Ilyin's view of the state as the organizer of all social life did not allow any compromise with ideological opponents. In his view, at stake was a question of social unity and territorial integrity; undermining the state translated into weakening of all social life foundations, leading to Russia's potential dismemberment. He viewed Russia as a single organism that could live and develop only under a "strong" autocratic power. Among the necessary conditions that demanded such power, he listed the significant size of the territory and population, the relative weakness of the means of communication, ethnic diversity, the presence of social and class divisions, weak legal consciousness, and a high level of external military threat (Ilyin 1992a, 316). In Ilyin's assessment, the more historically difficult the national unity and the more critical it is in a given historical period, the stronger the state power must be. Explaining each of these conditions, Ilyin concluded that "weak state power" does not apply to Russia, and such power is "a kind of luxury that only a people living under extremely favorable conditions can afford" (Ibid.).

Ilyin perceived the revolution and the arrival of Bolshevism to power in Russia as the establishment of a totalitarian regime that trampled on individual rights and not as a strong, legally constrained power. He argued that a state based on violence could not be strong because it did not have the required "spiritual authority" and "religious trust" of the people. A patriot of the Tsarist power, Ilyin took an active part in the struggle against Bolshevism, advancing in emigration to the position of a leading ideologist of the White Army. He collaborated with General Wrangel in founding The Russian All-Military Union (ROVS) and was one of the organizers of the Russian Foreign Congress in 1926. He also actively published in monarchist and conservative outlets and served as a board member of the Parisian newspaper *Vozrozhdenie* (Revival), edited by Pyort Struve. From 1927 to 1930, Ilyin was the editor and publisher of the journal *Russki kolokol* (the Russian bell).

While his ideological opponents, such as Berdyaev, saw Bolshevism as payment for Russia's sins, Ilyin viewed the new political regime as an absolute evil with no precedents in Russian history. In the highly controversial book *On Resistance to Evil by Force*, he criticized Leo Tolstoy's theory of non-resistance to evil. He argued for the Christian obligation to fight against the Soviet system (Ilyin 1925).[21] Berdyaev reviewed the book by titling his review "A Nightmare of Evil Good" and calling its author a non-Christian and "non-Russian thinker ... a stranger, a foreigner, and a German." Berdyayev (1992, 471) referred not to Ilyin's ethnic origin (German by mother), but to his thinking "alien to the best traditions of our national thought" (Ibid.). Pointing to Ilyin's self-rightness and lack of self-reflection, he accused Ilyin of fluttering moralism, spiritual pride, and striving (along with Tolstoy) to take on the role of a prophet. According to Berdyayev, the genuinely Christian outlook assumed that "the entire human race is afflicted by original sin and therefore cannot disintegrate into a race of good people, specially designed to fight evil by force, and a race of evil" (Ibid., 463). Ilyin (1994) indignantly rejected Berdyayev's criticism. Ilyin (1992a,1992b) wrote his famous series of essays, *Our Tasks*, from the exact positions of radicalism and conviction in the final collapse of the Soviet system as "insane", thoroughly "false," and distorting the entire course of Russian history.[22]

Ilyin's view of the international system was inseparable from his convictions as a statist and an Orthodox Christian isolationist. He saw Russia as a unique religious and cultural organism held together by the autocracy. He regarded criticism of the country's political and cultural foundations as an attempt to dismember it (Ilyin 1992a, 232–237). His theory of Russophobia combined religious, sociocultural, and geopolitical dimensions. In particular, Ilyin considered attempts to adopt socialist ideas as a Western Russophobic plan for Russia's geopolitical weakening.[23] The thinker traced such Western programs to European countries' alien religious and cultural traditions and the resulting fear of Russia and the Russian people (Ilyin 1992a, 19–20, 58–61). He believed in a politically motivated unwillingness to understand and search for the truth by concluding with indignation: *"Europe does not need the truth about Russia: it needs a convenient lie."* (Ibid., 99).

On these grounds, Ilyin defended a firm foreign policy based on the principles of Orthodox Christianity, geopolitical interests, and national isolation.[24] Like Danilevsky, he believed that the principles of Christian morality applied only to Orthodox Christian allies but not to the rest of the outside world. Concerning the latter, one should be guided by the interest of preserving geopolitical power proceeding from the existing balance of power.

Reminiscent of the views of the late Slavophiles,[25] Ilyin's theory did not have goals other than Russia's geopolitical and cultural survival. He rejected as untenable all attempts by the outside world and the countries of the West to teach Russia:

> We are not students or teachers of the West. We are disciples of God and teachers to ourselves. Before us is the task: to create a Russian original spiritual culture – from the Russian heart, by Russian contemplation, in Russian freedom, and by revealing Russian objectivity. And this is the meaning of the Russian idea.
>
> *Ilyin 1992a, 328*

Ilyin's ideal was the policy of Russian Tsarism, which he considered as a whole, "peaceful and balanced," and not aimed at expansion beyond the borders of the indigenous Russian lands. In particular, he opposed the Soviet "acquisitions" in Eastern Europe, likening any attempts to "Russify" the West to the "wise" advice of a bankrupt master.

> We have not justified ourselves before the court of history: we have failed to defend our freedom, our statehood, our faith, and our culture. What would we 'teach' the West? The Russian people should think about their shortcomings and vices, about their spiritual rebirth, strengthening, and prosperity, and not about how to impose a distorted 'Russian-like' image on people that have already developed in a different culture and with a language and character alien to us.
>
> *Ibid., 106*

Alexander Solzhenitsyn: Authoritarian State and Slavic Isolationism

Similar ideas guided the writer and thinker Alexander Solzhenitsyn (1918–2008). By publishing his main work, *The Gulag Archipelago* in the West, Solzhenitsyn emerged as radically critical of the Soviet system as Ilyin. Solzhenitsyn's views on Russian history, his conviction in a unique Orthodox Christian way of the country's development, and his suspicion of the West also brought the writer closer to the views of the ideologist of the White Army.

Solzhenitsyn was initially devoted to the Soviet system but became critical of Josef Stalin during the Second World War. While a military officer, he was arrested and sent to labor camps. During Khrushchev's liberalization, Solzhenitsyn was rehabilitated and published a viral story about a prisoner, *One Day in the Life of Ivan Denisovich*. However, the political liberalization in the country was soon over, and his attempts to publish other works, such as the novel *In the First Circle*, were unsuccessful. Solzhenitsyn began to submit his writings to the unofficial press (*Samizdat*) and then to the West. His attempts to persuade the Soviet leadership to initiate a policy change were unsuccessful. In 1974, the writer made public his "Letter to the Leaders of the Soviet Union (September 5, 1973)", in which he warned the country's leadership of the dangers of war with

China and the dead ends of technological civilization. Solzhenitsyn proposed abandoning communist ideology in favor of an authoritarian nationalist state and focusing on internal development. At the same time, he opposed the Western-style political system. In Ilyin's spirit, Solzhenitsyn argued for the legitimacy of autocratic rule, perhaps hoping it would resonate with the Soviet leaders. "*Order* is not immoral … until it turns into arbitrariness and tyranny.… It is not so much authoritarianism that is intolerable but arbitrariness and lawlessness" (Solzhenitsyn 1973). The Soviet authorities responded with persecution. For the publication of *The Gulag Archipelago* in the West, they deprived Solzhenitsyn of his Soviet citizenship and expelled him from the country. While living abroad, and following his return to Russia in 1994, the writer continued to advocate (1990, 1998, 2007) statist and Orthodox Christian ideas.

In understanding the relationship between the state and freedom, Solzhenitsyn advocated the combination of autocratic power and an Orthodox Christian model idea that cements society. Like Ilyin, the writer argued that the Old Russian system was incomparably superior to the one that replaced it. Solzhenitsyn developed these ideas in his main historical novel, *The Red Wheel*. In his essays for the general public, he argued the same ideas. True to the Slavophil trad-ition, he defended internal (as opposed to external, that is, political) freedoms, by which he understood the freedom to practice the Christian Orthodox religion and the connection of the peasant with the land and economy.

> If Russia has habitually lived in authoritarian systems for centuries, and in a democratic one for 8 months of 1917 it suffered such a collapse, then perhaps … it should be admitted that the evolutionary development of our country from one authoritarian form to another will be more natural, smooth, and painless for it?
>
> *Solzhenitsyn 1992a, 20*

Solzhenitsyn assessed the 1917 Revolution in Russia as a tragedy precisely from the point of view of the destruction of the Christian Orthodox Church and communal and other forms of free peasant life. The writer associated the main flaw of the Soviet system with the absence of these fundamental freedoms for Russians, and it was in the restoration of these freedoms that he saw the future revival of Russia.

Solzhenitsyn's conviction in the virtue of the Orthodox Christian foundations for Russia was largely behind his suspicion of Western societies. For example, he publicly condemned ideas of a possible convergence of the capitalist and socialist systems prevalent in the second half of the 1960s. He attacked the views of his West-minded liberal opponent Andrei Sakharov (Solzhenitsyn 1992b). Solzhenitsyn repeated the words of Sergei Bulgakov that "Westernism is a spir-itual surrender to the culturally strongest" (Ibid.). The writer saw the recovery of Russia not in the borrowing of external forms but in the restoration of the national traditions of "repentance and self-sufficiency" (Solzhenitsyn 1992a).

Like Ilyin, Solzhenitsyn defended a foreign policy to improve the internal health and preservation of the people. He believed Russia could focus on restoring its physical and spiritual strength if it abandoned extensive international involvement. (Ibid., 115–116).[26] In his intransigence towards the Soviet system, Solzhenitsyn was passionate and often expressed extreme views. For instance, he defended Nazi collaborators, like General Andrei Vlasov, or called on Western countries to use force against the USSR.[27] Simultaneously, Solzhenitsyn mistrusted the West for what he viewed as flawed moral and social foundations. He also leaned towards Ilyin's reasoning that the weakening of Russia was in the political interests of Western countries (Solzhenitsyn 2007).

The development of theories of Orthodox Christian isolationism was a significant step in developing the Russian worldview. Ilyin and Solzhenitsyn bridged the early Slavophile ideas of Christian peasant commune with the concept of a powerful state. They further rejected Solovyev's Eurocentric thinking by insisting on Russia's cultural and geographical self-sufficiency and the geopolitical limitations of cooperation with European powers. Finally, they presented Russia's primary goals in the world as limited to those of internal development.

Bridges and Fortresses after the USSR: Alexander Panarin

After the collapse of the Soviet Union, Slavophile thought found itself in new conditions. Following the Soviet censorship's disappearance, the opposition between the Solovyov and Ilyin line of thinking about Europe received a further incentive for development. While the desire for dialogue with the West was strong in the 1990s, it began to weaken in the 2000s favoring ideas of new isolation. These contradictions were entirely on display in the works of Aleksandr Panarin. Due to his disappointment in the West and the Russian ruling elites, his worldview underwent a radical transformation from liberal Westernism to conservative Eurasianism and Slavophilism.

From Westernism to the Russia-Bridge idea

Aleksandr Panarin developed as a thinker and citizen in the post-Stalin era. While studying at the Department of Philosophy of Moscow State University, Panarin was part of a group of students who actively debated the political transformation of society and interpreted the ideas of early Karl Marx in a social-democratic spirit. These activities resulted in Panarin's expulsion from the Komsomol and the university. Later, he graduated, but the authorities banned him from studying and teaching philosophy.

Panarin resumed his role as a public thinker during Mikhail Gorbachev's Perestroika. In his book on French neo-conservatism (Panarin 1989), he formulated one of his central ideas – the need for a socio-cultural reformation based on market economic principles and broad public participation. Panarin shared the French neoconservatives' belief in fighting the state's excessive centralization and liberating entrepreneurial initiatives. Still, he unequivocally supported the liberals by insisting that reformation requires democratization. Supporting the notion of the world's cultural diversity advanced by French neoconservatives, the philosopher also defends a global vision of the world, preempting critique of future prophets of the "end of history" (Francis Fukuyama) and the "clash of civilizations" (Samuel Huntington).

Sharing the positions of Gorbachev's New Political Thinking and its support for the principle of "unity of the human race," Panarin also argued for the need to abandon the Marxist theory of formations. In 1991, he wrote the article "Revolution and Reformation," in which he called to learn from the West how to revitalize entrepreneurial energies and do away with liberal and socialist myths about the end of history. Instead of ideology, the philosopher argued for the need to learn to live by everyday human concerns.

> The people who have not survived the Reformation do not know how to live in everyday life. … We have much to learn from the West – without its direct help and support, we cannot get out of the quagmire into which the ideology of revolutionary messianism has led us.
>
> *Panarin 1991, 220*

Soon, however, he became disillusioned with Westernism as a philosophy of change.

The Soviet Union's disintegration, the establishment of a pro-Western regime in power, and the beginning of economic reforms based on the "shock therapy" model dramatically changed Panarin's attitude to liberalism and the West. A supporter of democratic transformations, he immediately sensed the elitism of the new ruling elite, which used liberalism only as a new ideology of domination with the support of the West itself. Panarin re-evaluated the importance of dialogue with the West from national interests and values standpoints. He tried to formulate a national reformist project while remaining within the framework of liberal philosophy. For the philosopher, liberalism prioritized the individual's political, economic, and social freedom. Such philosophy appeals to the people, not to the ruling and cultural-ideological elites as the guardians of tradition. At the same time, unlike socialism, liberalism supports a reformist, not revolutionary, change in society, and therefore advocates the social involvement of the masses through existing political institutions. Panarin's concept of the liberal reformation remained principally different from the "revolution from below," which included elements of mass violence.

At this point, Panarin no longer advocated following the West in establishing the necessary social and political prerequisites for development.[28] He now viewed the West as in a state of crisis and needed to reform its social order's main priorities and principles. In his analysis, Panarin followed the humanistic philosophy of Western thinkers such as Karl Jaspers, Hans-Georg Gadamer, Arnold Toynbee, Jurgen Habermas, and others. In Russia, humanism has lived through the work of Vladimir Solovyev, Nikolai Berdyayev, Vladimir Vernadsky, Nikolai Bibler, Nikita Moiseyev, and others. They strived to think globally and connect Russia's role in world history to the spiritual changes of the contemporary world. Like many other humanistic philosophers, Panarin argued for a planetary reformation based on spiritual development rather than material consumption, profits, and new technologies. Following the humanistic critique of modernity, the thinker insisted on intertwining economic, political, environmental, and spiritual crises, none of which can be resolved by following the West (Ilyin, Panarin, Akhiezer 1996; Panarin 1996a,b; Panarin 1996c). He was now critical of the philosophy of historicism with its linear perspective on human development while presenting cultural and civilizational dialogue as the necessary alternative. Ironically, Panarin repeated here his earlier critiqued position of the New Political Thinking, which had also diagnosed the "crisis" of modern civilization.

In the article published in 1992, Panarin diagnosed the defeat of Russia's transformation and tried to formulate the "cultural and geopolitical principles of Russian liberal-democratic thinking rooted in national culture and tradition" (Panarin 1992, 1993a). He challenged Russian reformers to acknowledge that democratization in the country increased instability and led to state disintegration. "Reforms that discredit the national tradition and suppress the impulses of the population ... quickly result in a crisis of statehood," Panarin (1992, 205) argued, proposing a constructive rethinking of the Russian idea and patriotism. Relying on Russian historians Nikolai Karamzin, Vassily Klyuchevsky, and Georgy Fedotov, Panarin advocated a new kind of patriotism, which had nothing to do with ethnic nationalism or the support of the new ruling elite. He proposed to define Russianness as a spiritual and civilizational type held together by a geopolitical idea, such as the Orthodox Christian faith in the past. Panarin viewed the necessity of a new geopolitical idea not in confronting the West but in consolidating the post-Soviet space and salvaging it from "the growing fundamentalism" of religious and ethnic groups. In 1993, he began to advocate the idea of "civilized Eurasianism."

At that time, Panarin (1993a, 1993b, 1993c, 1993d, 1994, 1995a, 1995b) recognized the problems with using the notion of "Eurasianism" and wanted to salvage it from conservative and radical Eurasianists favoring rebuilding an anti-Western (Soviet) empire. His Eurasianism was compatible with liberal principles. Panarin introduced Eurasianism to strengthen liberalism, not weaken it. The purpose of the Eurasian idea was to preserve the level of geopolitical stability and cultural balance required for the reforms' success. The philosopher saw it as a socio-cultural safeguard for continuing with the initiated reforms. Politically, the advancement of this idea was necessary for the self-realization of various nationalities and ethnic groups in the name of the common good. Panarin's Eurasianism was also liberal because it was compatible with his other principles of national reformation. Among these principles were the separation of power from the property, the activation of small and medium-sized businesses, and the preservation of sufficient executive power to consistently implement the reforms.

Winning back Eurasianism from radicals and conservatives was extremely difficult – conservative Eurasianism had already been rising in the second half of the 1980s and was increasingly adopted by influential political forces, such as the Communist Party of the Russian Federation (Zyuganov 1995, 1998, 2002). The other problem was that the West, by its behavior towards Russia, often strengthened the position of Russian ultra-conservatives. By supporting the destructive "shock therapy" and not recognizing Russia's foreign policy interests in Europe and Eurasia, Western leaders unwittingly contributed to the development of anti-Western sentiments.

Russia did not progress toward strengthening statehood, as Panarin wished. Instead of protecting entrepreneurial freedom and initiative from the encroachments of bureaucracy, the Yeltsin state essentially became a hostage to big business and bureaucracy. At this stage, Panarin's Eurasianism began to show anti-Western overtones. The thinker worked hard to justify Eurasianism through internal economic and political tasks. However, his growing irritation with the policy of the West, which supported the predatory policy of the new Russian regime, began to affect the philosopher's views. As a result, the need for Eurasianism under his pen was increasingly justified by the fact that the West or Europe did not accept Russia outside Yeltsin's regime (Panarin 1995a, p. 69).

Forging the Eastern Orthodox Fortress

Therefore, conditions for strengthening the Panarin-advocated liberal Eurasianism were missing. And the more aggressively the ruling regime imposed pro-Western reforms on society and the more devastating their social consequences were, the more difficult it was for the philosopher to hold his liberal positions. In the late 1990s, Panarin moved to a more radical-conservative part of the political spectrum. The end of the 1990s became his Rubicon associated with the dismissal of the moderate Yevgeny Primakov's government, the NATO bombing of Yugoslavia, and the considerably increased Western criticism of Russia for the war in Chechnya, and the more active foreign policy in the former Soviet region. At about the same time, Panarin began cooperating with a leading conservative magazine, *Moskva*.

To Panarin, the question "how to change?" – fundamental for liberals – had to be replaced by the more urgent question "how to survive?" The "geopolitical pessimism" the philosopher once criticized was increasingly becoming the core of his Eurasian outlook. The West became the center of Panarin's criticism. He now associated with Western nations the main problems and injustices in the world. His major works – *The Temptation by Globalism* (1998), *The Orthodox Civilization in the Global World* (2001), and *Strategic Instability in the 21st Century* (2003) – were devoted to criticism of the Western role in the world. Panarin now associated the survival of Russian civilization with its opposition to the West and the necessary restoration of Orthodox Christian spirituality and governance of the Stalinist type. From these positions, the thinker emerged as sharply critical of Vladimir Putin's rule as weak and inappropriate to the tasks of Russia.

Panarin (2002a) now stressed the priority of reviving the Orthodox Christian religion while condemning Jewish influence on Russia. In the book *The Temptation of Globalism*, the philosopher painted a semi-apocalyptic picture of the usurpation of globalization by intelligence services, Jews, and the United States. Linking together such figures as Karl Marx, Leon Trotsky, and Boris Berezovsky, the philosopher wanted to substantiate the idea that Jews, by their very nature, tend to destroy any national culture, including that of Russia. Elsewhere, he defined globalization as "the Jewishness of the world" and its "liberation from state honor and national responsibility" (Panarin 2000, pp. 72–86; Panarin 2003a).

The changed attitude to the West led Panarin to criticize liberalism and reforms. While earlier he had defended the idea of liberal and progressive West, he now viewed liberalism as the ideology of Western degradation. In the book *Global Political Forecasting*, he traced (1999a, 212–214) how liberalism "lost the motives of social solidarity and compassion" in its struggle with Keynesianism and Soviet socialism, having turned into the justification for American expansionism and global domination. He found liberalism to be more dangerous and destructive than communism and compared the policy of the West with apartheid on a worldwide scale (Ibid., 373).

> Today the social-Darwinian principle of the world race of the "chosen" versus the criminal mass of "sub-humans" seems to be asserted in the very center of victorious Atlanticism seized by the euphoria of unipolarity.
>
> *Ibid., 111; Panarin 2002b*

Panarin viewed the actions of the West as a world war against the rest of the world, which "reflected the spiritual program ... of the self-consciousness of the modern West (first of all, the United States)" (Panarin 2002a, 46).

In Eurasia, Panarin believed, the Western strategy consisted of fragmentation and destruction of the preserved integrity of the continent and Russia itself. He interpreted the terrorist attacks in the United States in September 2001 as a result of the intelligence agencies' aspirations to rule the world. This drive to dominate the world also requires that Russia disintegrate and lose nationally minded elites (Panarin 2001), as well as Orthodox Christianity entering into conflict with Islam and the Muslim world (Panarin 1999b, 1999c). In Panarin's view (1999b), the ideas of cultural conflict and regional decentralization expressed in Samuel Huntington's *Clash of Civilizations* and Zbigniew Brzezinski's *The Grand Chess Board* were dangerous. They emerged in the Russian discursive space for a reason. No less dangerous, in his opinion (2002a), were the ideas of postmodernity that served to undermine the country's cultural integrity.

Panarin's positive program now had to do not with reforms but with a confrontation with Western civilization and, above all, the United States. The West had to change and, for salvation, Russia had to turn to the East and Eastern wisdom, for which an unrestrained pursuit of profits and consumer hedonism was unusual (Panarin 1998, 163). Panarin now associated capitalism and its formation not with entrepreneurship and Protestant ethics but with financial speculations once stressed by George Simmel in his polemics with Max Weber (Panarin 2000, 171). Modern capitalism, in his opinion (2002b), was giving rise to the new poverty. It was ultimately interested only in new consumerism and "did not know the higher dimensions of being, and had no obligations to history and culture."

Instead of the previously stressed importance of addressing internal socio-economic problems, Panarin was now focused (1998, 348) on not allowing any concessions to the West and not becoming a "second Munich." As an essential task of confronting Western globalism, the philosopher insisted on recreating the identity of Russia as the Third Rome and an Orthodox Christian fortress (Panarin 1999d). He advised Russia to "reintegrate" the former USSR and build alliances with anyone interested in opposing the Western powers, especially China and the countries of the Muslim world (Panarin 1999c, pp. 216–17, 225, 275, 310).

Instead of advocating entrepreneurship, Panarin now favored the idea of state service or "service asceticism." In his speech on receiving the Solzhenitsyn Prize in 2002, Panarin was unequivocal that he wanted to "rehabilitate" the Russian people as not adaptable to the market conditions.

> We must have institutions not adaptable to the market … perhaps the Russian people themselves, not quite adaptable to the market, are such a mysterious historical institution in the world. Perhaps these people are destined to defend those values that cannot be profitable. … And perhaps someday history will reward them for this.
>
> *Panarin (2002c)*

Panarin also critiqued (2002d) Putin's course as serving narrow elites and the "social apartheid." Panarin's notion of a strong state was now associated not with ensuring equal conditions in the market and protecting citizens from any abuse based on the law. Instead, a strong state meant the restoration of the principles of patriarchy and the service of the whole society (Panarin 2003a). He justified Stalin's policies and repressions while arguing the need to return to "extremely tough, authoritarian–autocratic statehood" and discipline. If Putin's state was the path to a corrupt dictatorship, then Stalin's was "the restoration of the archetypal nature of Russian history" that expressed the interests of the "popular majority" (Ibid.).

Panarin evolved from Westernism and defense of a dialogue with the West for over ten years to an anti-Western, radically conservative attitude. The reasons for the transformation of the philosopher's views had to do with the revolutionary nature of Russia's changes. Panarin supported gradual, nationally oriented reforms but admitted the defeat of his efforts and – desperate to be heard – assumed an extreme and uncompromised position. The related reason concerned the role of the West, which supported all the "reforms" of the Yeltsin regime. Western media and politicians openly welcomed or tacitly supported shock therapy, an oligarchic economy, using force against parliament, rampant corruption, fraudulent elections, and defamation of national history. The policy of transforming the world in the West's image was not limited to the political and economic imposition of neoliberal reforms. Still, it was accompanied by military interventions in the world – in Africa, the Balkans, Central Asia, and the Middle East.

Conclusion

Primarily influenced by European philosophy, Slavophiles have formulated their original view of the world. This view stressed the centrality of faith, free communal labor, and the socio-cultural unity of Orthodox Christians. Like Westernizers, they were motivated by European values rather than political interests. However, unlike Westernizers, Slavophiles were convinced of the superiority of their values over Western ones. They openly proclaimed the holiness of the Russian Orthodox faith, often demonstrating an ethnocentric attitude towards other Christian confessions and considering Russia the last hope for the revival of Christianity jointly with Europeans. Such was the hope of the early Slavophiles beginning with Khomyakov and Kireyevsky. Soloviev and his supporters continued to be guided by the same hope. Supporters of the Russian religious renaissance expelled from the country by the Bolsheviks preserved their faith in Russia's ability to overcome the temptations of materiality and finally live by Christ. After the collapse of the Soviet state, Panarin also wrote about reunification with the West but soon became disillusioned and shifted to strengthening Russia as an anti-Western Orthodox empire.

The development of Russian thinking about the world results from the state of Western civilization and the conditions of Russia's existence. The emergence and growth of Europe and the West have been the constituent themes of the Russian discourse. Generally speaking, the Slavophiles wanted to reunify with Europe, albeit on their foundations of the Orthodox faith, communal economy, and an autocratic state capable of maintaining stability in the country. The decline of the reunification discourse became possible due to growing tensions between Russia and European nations, which Slavophiles associated with weakening Christian ideals in the continent.

The secularization and capitalism in the West weakened the Slavophile discourse of rapprochement with Europe. The early Slavophiles feared revolutionary changes, viewing social transformations in Europe as a principal threat to traditional values. European support for the Polish uprisings of 1830 and 1863, the Crimean War of the mid- nineteenth century, and the growing geopolitical rivalry of the great powers turned the Slavophiles away from Europe. Solovyov, who defended Russian-European unity on Christian and theocratic grounds, was an exception among the Slavophiles, but even he warned them against the temptations of materiality and private property. Supporters of this thinking, like Berdyaev, also insisted on spiritual freedom and argued against capitalism and individualism as paths to the "true kingdom." Unlike Solovyov, they no longer proposed specific ideas for rapprochement with Europe.

Instead of the ideas of rapprochement and the bridge, the views of Russia's isolation grew strong. The arguments by Konstantin Aksakov and the Pan-Slavists pursued the objective of not getting closer to Europe but fencing off from it and building solid ties only with the Slavic peoples. The conservative thinkers Ivan Ilyin and Alexander Solzhenitsyn denounced the West for its lack of spirituality, cynicism, and desire for power while defending the independent development of Russia based on faith, a culturally specific economy, and a powerful state. In the end, Panarin also arrived at similar ideas, refusing to accept Western support for capitalism in Russia and advocating the creation of an anti-Western Third Rome as Russia's world mission. The discourse of isolation remains strong in contemporary Russia, which insists on the self-sufficiency of traditional ideals and denies genuine values to Europe and the West.

Notes

1 I consider Solovyev's views later in the chapter.
2 Aksakov also condemned Ivan IV for interfering with the Earth by establishing the particular class of state servants known as *Oprichnina* (Ibid, p. 11).
3 Some Western scholars also find in Slavophiles enemies of democracy and liberalism (Devlin 1999; Engelstein 2009). Others, however, assess Slavophiles as original thinkers offering a worthy response to the challenges of Western civilization (Rabow-Edling 2006).
4 Here, Ivan Aksakov also followed his brother Konstantin, who already in 1846 wrote that each Slavophile must sympathize with people of Slav origins, while "declining all possible dreams of their political unity in one wholeness" (Tsymbayev 1986, 31).
5 The letter was addressed to the head of the Holy Synod of the Russian Orthodox Church, Konstantin Pobedonostsev (Khevrolina 1996, 307).
6 This section draws on Tsygankov 2017.
7 English translation is Danilevskii 2013.
8 The second thinker who broke with the Slavophile line of thinking was Konstantin Leontyev, who thought of himself as a student of Danilevsky, but went further than his teacher by embracing the East and predicting that Russia would establish a "neo-Byzantine", rather than Slavonic, cultural type. Chapter 5 returns to Leontyev.
9 Vladimir Solovyev (2000, 561–591) offered a detailed critique of such influences in his work "Nemetskiy podlinnik russkiy spisok" (The German original and the Russian list).
10 Others such as Huntington (1997, 310), too, argued that power precedes culture, not the other way around.
11 Following Feodor Tyutchev, Danilevsky wanted the Russian Empire to expand at the expense of some territories of Austria, Italy, and Prussia (Tsymbursky 2006, 110).
12 Solovyev, for instance, demonstrated his deep fear of the Muslim East, referred to Islam as an "inhuman God" and later became obsessed with the "yellow peril" (Duncan 2000, 44–45).

13 He even intended to travel to the Vatican at the personal invitation of Cardinal Rampolle. However, the visit did not take place (Losev 1990, 18).

14 See especially his "Three conversations" and "The brief history of Anti-Christ" (Solovyev 1990).

15 In 1874, Solovyev defended MA dissertation titled "The crisis of Western philosophy: against positivism" (2000b).

16 Berdyayev and his supporters published in the journal *Novyi grad*. On their social liberal ideas, see Rabotyazhev 2009.

17 Berdyayev (1911, 223) believed in "the Church of the future" and assessed as false Solovyev's argument about the importance of formal agreements between the Orthodox and Catholic Church or one between the Russian government and the Vatican.

18 The discussion was the main event at the movement's second congress (Русское студенческое христианское движение http://ru.wikipedia.org/wiki).

19 Ilyin's most important works were not completed and titled as "On the Essence of Legal Consciousness" and "On the Monarchy."

20 Some of Solovyev's followers spoke in favor of the European federation and of Russia as its part. As argued by Fedotov, "Contemporary state provides a bad protection for a national culture ... Therefore, the withering away of the nation-state is not catastrophic for the culture of a nation. On contrary, it liberates such culture" (Fedotov 1991, 250).

21 For a summary of the controversy around the book, see Poltoratsky 1975.

22 In 1933, Ilyin, who lived in Germany at that time, even supported Hitler, believing that he had done Europe "the greatest service" by stopping the process of spreading the Bolshevik influence (Ilyin 1933). However, Ilyin soon developed a conflict with the Nazis and had to leave the country.

23 For example, he considered the left-leaning Georgi Fedotov a hater of Russia because the latter was critical of Russia's pre-revolutionary past: "It is unforgivable for a Russian person, who knows the Soviet system, to say that the Russian people are responsible for their communist government. ... All this is *not true;* all this is *a temptation;* all this is a decay of emigration from the rear and a *propaganda against Russia,* so useful to our foreign enemies and communists" (Ilyin 1992a, 173–174).

24 For Ilyin's understanding of nationalism, see his essays "On Russian nationalism" "Dangers and tasks of Russian nationalism" (1992a, 279–289).

25 On Slavophile views of Russophobia, see Shirinyants 2008, 86–106.

26 He later argued against preservation of Slavic unity in the territorial space of Russia, Ukraine, Belarus, and northern Kazakhstan (Solzhenitsyn 1990).

27 In one of his articles, he accused the West of not supporting the White Army more in 1919 (Solzhenitsyn 1976). He also called to demonstrate force (1972) rather than try to "appease" the Soviet state.

28 Panarin also opposed ideas that denied Russia its unique cultural distinctiveness, such as the idea of the "second Europe" proposed by some of his colleagues (Panarin 1996a, 1996b).

Further Reading

Russian Thought and Religious Philosophy

Bykova, M. F., M. N. Forster, and L. Steiner, eds. 2021. *The Palgrave Handbook of Russian Thought.* London: Palgrave.

Diesen, G. 2020. *Russian Conservatism: Managing Change under Permanent Revolution.* Boulder, CO: Rowman & Littlefield.

Emerson, C., G. Pattison, and R. A. Poole, eds. 2020. *The Oxford Handbook of Russian Religious Thought*. New York: Oxford University Press.
Neumann, I. B. 2015. *Russia and the Idea of Europe,* 2nd ed. London: Routledge.
Robinson, P. 2019. *Russian Conservatism*. Ithaca, NY: Cornell University Press.
Walicki, A. 1979. *A History of Russian Thought from Enlightenment to Marxism*. Stanford.
Zamaleyev, A. 2002. *Uchebnik russkoi politilogiyi*. St. Petersburg: Letniy sad.

Slavophiles and Pan-Slavists

Christoff, P. 1991. *An Introduction to Nineteenth Century Russian Slavophilism. Iu. F. Samarin.* London: Routledge.
Danilevskii, N. Ia. 2013. *Russia and Europe.* Translation and introduction by Stephen M. Woodburn. Slavica, Indiana University Press.
Duncan, P. J. S. 2000. *Russian Messianism.* London: Routledge.
Engelstein, L. 2009. *Slavophile Empire: Imperial Russia's Illiberal Path*. Ithaca, NY: Cornell University Press.
Petrovich, M. B. 1956. *The Emergence of Russian Panslavism.* New York: Columbia University Press.
Rabow-Edling, S. 2006. *Slavophile Thought and the Politics of Cultural Nationalism.* New York.
Riasanovsky, N. 1952. *Russia and the West in the Teaching of the Slavophiles.* Cambridge, MA: Harvard University Press.
Аксаков, К. С. 1861. Объ основныхъ началахъ русской исторіи. // Полное собраніе сочиненій Константина Сергѣевича Аксакова. Т. 1. Москва.
Цымбаев Н. И. 1986. Славянофильство. Из истории русской общественно-политической мысли. Москва.

Vladimir Solovyev and Slavophiles in the Twentieth Century

Berdyayev, N. 1990. *Istoki i smysl russkogo kommunizma.* Moscow: Nauka.
Brudny Y. M. *Reinventing Russia: Russian Nationalism and the Soviet State.* Cambridge University Press, 1999.
Marchenkov, V. L. 2021. Nikolai Berdyaev's Philosophy of Creativity as a Revolt against the Modern Worldview. In: *The Palgrave Handbook of Russian Thought*, edited by M. F. Bykova, M. N. Forster, and L. Steiner. London: Palgrave.
Motroshilova, N. V. 2021. Vladimir Solovyov: Philosophy as Systemic Unity. In: *The Palgrave Handbook of Russian Thought,* edited by M. F. Bykova, M. N. Forster, and L. Steiner. London: Palgrave.

Slavophiles after the USSR

Chebankova, E. 2020. *Political Ideologies in Contemporary Russia.* McGill-Queen's University Press.
Chebankova, E and P. Dutkiewicz, eds. 2021. *Civilizations and World Order.* Routledge.
Curanovic, A. 2020. *The Sense of Mission in Russian Foreign Policy.* Routledge.
Diesen, G. 2018. *The Decay of Western Civilization and Resurgence of Russia.* London: Routledge.
Mjør, K. and S. Turoma, eds. 2020. *Russia as Civilization.* Routledge.

References

Aksakov, Konstantin S. 1852. О древнем быте у славян вообще и у русских в особенности. *Московский Сборник.* Vol. 1

———. 1861. Объ основныхъ началахъ русской исторіи. In: *Полное собраніе сочиненій Константина Сергѣевича Аксакова.* Vol. 1.

———. 2006. О Карамзине. Речь, написанная для произнесения пред симбирским дворянством (1848). In: *Карамзин: pro et contra,* сост. Л. А. Сапченко. Санкт-Петербург, http://az.lib.ru/a/aksakow_k_s/text_0270.shtml.

Berdyaev, Nikolai. 1911. Проблема Востока и Запада в религиозном сознании Вл. Соловьева. In: *О Владимире Соловьева.* Moscow.: Путь http://krotov.info/libr ary/02_b/berdyaev/1911_solo.html).

———. 1990a. Russkaya ideya. In: *O Rossiyi i russkoi filosofskoi kul'ture,* ed. by E. B. Chekharin. Moscow: Nauka.

———. 1990b. *Истоки и смысл русского коммунизма.* Moscow: Nauka.

———. 1990c. *Философия неравенства. Письма к недругам по социальной философии.* In: Бердяев Н. Собрание сочинений. Vol. 4. Paris http://krotov.info/library/02_b/ berdyaev/1918_20_01.html.

———. 1990d. *Самопознание (опыт философской автобиографии).* Moscow: Kniga.

———. 1991. Философская истина и интеллигентская правда. In: *Вехи. Интеллигенция в России.* Moscow.

———. 1992. Кошмар злого добра. *Путь. Орган русской религиозной мысли.* Vol. 1, 4. Moscow.

———. 1993. Экзистенциальная диалектика божественного и человеческого. In: *О назначении человека.* Moscow http://krotov.info/library/02_b/berdyaev/194 4_041_1.htm.

———. 1995. *Царство духа и царство кесаря.* Moscow http://krotov.info/library/02_b/ berdyaev/1947_40_00.html.

Chaadayev, Pyotr. 1991. Апология сумасшедшего. *Россия глазами русского,* под ред. А. Ф. Замалеева. Санкт-Петербург.

Danilevsky, Nikolai. 1990 [1885]. *Rossiya i Yevropa.* Moscow: Kniga.

Danilevskii, Nikolai Ia. 2013. *Russia and Europe: The Slavic World's Political and Cultural Relations with the Germanic-Roman West.* Translation and introduction by Stephen M. Woodburn. Slavica, Indiana University Press.

Devlin, Judith. 1999. *Slavophiles and Commissars: Enemies of Democracy in Modern Russia.* New York: Palgrave Macmillan.

Duncan, Peter J. S. 2000. *Russian Messianism.* London: Routledge.

Engelstein, Laura. 2009. *Slavophile Empire: Imperial Russia's Illiberal Path.* Ithaca, NY: Cornell University Press.

Fedotov, Georgy. 1991. Новое отечество. In: *Судьба и грехи России.* Vol. 2.

———. 1991. *Пути русского богословия.* Moscow.

Huntington, Samuel. 1997. *The Clash of Civilizations and the Remaking of World Order.* New York: Simon & Shuster.

Ilyin, Ivan A. 1925. О Сопротивлении злу силою. Берлин, 1925.

———. 1933. Национал-социализм. Новый дух. *Возрождение,* Paris, 17 мая. http://ilji nru.tsygankov.ru/works/vozr170533.html.

———. 1979. Понятия монархии и республики www.gumer.info/bogoslov_Buks/ Philos/Ilin/ponmonarh.php.

———. 1992a. *Наши задачи: Историческая судьба и будущее России. Статьи 1948–1954 годов.* Vol. 1. Moscow: Papor.

———. 1992b. *Наши задачи: Историческая судьба и будущее России. Статьи 1948–1954 годов*. Vol. 2. Moscow: Papor.

———. 1994. Кошмар Н. А. Бердяева. *Собрание сочинений*, vol. 5. Moscow.

Ilyin, Victor, Aleksandr Panarin, Aleksandr Akhiezer. 1996. *Реформы и контрреформы в России*. Moscow: Izdatel'stvo MGU.

Khevrolina, Viktoriya M. 1996. Проблемы внешней политики России в общественной мысли страны. In: *История внешней политики России. Вторая половина XIX века*, edited by V. M. Khevrolina. Moscow: Nauka.

Knutsen, Torbjorn. 1997. *A History of International Relations Theory*, 2nd ed. Manchester University Press.

Losev, Aleksei F. 1990. Творческий пути Владимира Соловьева. In: Solovyev 1989.

Novikova, Lidiya I., Irina N. Sizemskaya. 1997. *Русская философия истории*. Moscow: Rosspen.

Panarin, Aleksandr. 1989. *Stil' retro v ideologii i politike*. Moscow: Mysl'

———. 1991. Revolution and Reformation. *Znamya* 6.

———. 1992. Цивилизационный процесс в России: опыт поражения и уроки на завтра', *Знамя* 7.

———. 1993a. 'Проект для России: фундаментальный либерализм или либеральный фундаментализм', *Знамя*, 9.

———. 1993b. Россия в поисках идеи: варианты цивилизационного выбора', *Вестник Московского Университета: Социально-политические исследования*, 5.

———. 1993c. Западники и евразийцы', *Общественные науки и современность*, 6.

———. 1993d. Между атлантизмом и евразийством' *Свободная мысль*, 11.

———. 1994. Россия в Евразии: геополитические вызовы и цивилизационные ответы', *Вопросы философии*, 12.

———. 1995a. Евразийский проект в миросистемном контексте', *Восток*, 2

———. 1995b. *Россия в цивилизационном процессе (между атлантизмом и евразийством)*. Moscow: Institut Filosofiyi.

———. 1996a. '«Вторая Европа» или «Третий Рим»? Парадоксы европеизма в современной России', *Вопросы философии*, 10

———. 1996b. *«Вторая Европа» или «Третий Рим»? Избранная социально-философская публицистика*, Moscow: Institut Filosofiyi.

———. 1996c. О возможностях отечественной культуры' *Новый мир*, 9.

———. 1998. *Реванш истории*, Москва: Algoritm.

———. 1999a. *Глобальное политическое прогнозирование*, Москва: Algoritm.

———. 1999b. Перспективы возрождения Третьего Мира', *Москва*, 4

———. 1999c. Глобальное всесмешение или новая повесть об антихристе', *Москва*, 1

———. 1999d. Перспективы возрождения Третьего Мира', *Москва*, Номер 4

———. 2000. *Искушение глобализмом*, Москва: Algoritm.

———. 2001. Presentation. In: *Онтология террора*, edited by F. Girenok, A. Dugin. Moscow: Arktogeya.

———. 2002a. *Православная цивилизация в глобальном мире*, Moscow: Arktogeya.

———. 2002b. Стратегическая нестабильность XXI века', *Moskva*, 4

———. 2002c. Я на стороне народа', *Завтра*, Номер 21 (444), 21 мая

———. 2002d. О «новом курсе». Два года спустя', *Москва*, 2.

———. 2003a. О Державнике-Отце и либеральных носителях эдипова комплекса. К 50-летию со дня смерти И. В. Сталина', *Москва*, 3

Poltoratsky, Nikolai. 1975. *И. А. Ильин и полемика вокруг его идей о сопротивлении злу силой* http://krotov.info/library/04_g/ipp/ius3.htm

Русское студенческое христианское движение http://ru.wikipedia.org/wiki

Rabotyazhev, Nikolai V. 2009. Консервативная геополитическая мысль в России: преемственность и обновление. *Вестник МГУ. Сер. 12, Политические науки*, 5.

Rabow-Edling, Sarah. 2006. *Slavophile Thought and the Politics of Cultural Nationalism.* Albany, NY: SUNY Press.

Shirinyants, Aleksandr A. 2008. *Русский хранитель. Политический консерватизм М. П. Погодина.* Moscow.

Solovyev, Vladimir S. 1989. *Сочинения в двух томах.* Vol. 1. Moscow: Pravda.

———. 1990. *Сочинения в двух томах.* Vol. 2. Moscow: Pravda.

———. 2000a. *Sochineniya.* Vol. 1, Moskva: Nauka.

———. 2000b. *Sochineniya.* Vol. 2, Moskva: Nauka.

Solzhenitsyn, Aleksandr. 1972. Нобелевская лекция.

———. 1973. *Письмо вождям Советского Союза* (5 сентября 1973). www.solzhenitsyn.ru/proizvedeniya/publizistika/.

———. 1990. Как нам обустроить Россию. Посильные соображения. Moscow: Izvestiya.

———. 1992a. Раскаяние и самоограничение как категории национальной жизни. In: *Из-под глыб: сборник статей.* Moscow.

———. 1992b. На возврате дыхания и сознания. In: *Из-под глыб: сборник статей.* Moscow.

———. 1998. Россия в обвале. Moscow.

———. 2007. Интервью журналу «Шпигель». www.pravoslavie.ru/36903.html

———. 1976. Если не желать быть слепым. Выступление по английскому радио. Лондон, 26 февраля 1976 www.solzhenitsyn.ru/proizvedeniya/publizistika/.

Strakhov, Nikolai N. 1990. *Наша культура и всемирное единство.* In: Danilevsky 1990.

Tsygankov, Andrei P. 2012. *Russia and the West from Alexander to Putin.* Cambridge University Press.

———. 2017. In the Shadow of Nikolai Danilevskii. *Europe-Asia Studies*

Tsymbayev, Nikolai I. 1986. *Славянофильство: Из истории русской общественно-политической мысли XIX века.* Moscow: MGU.

Tsymbursky, Vadim. 2006. *Ostrov Rossiya.* Moscow: Rosspen.

Zamalyeyev, Aleksandr. 2002. *Учебник русской политологии.* St. Petersburg: Gnozis.

Zhaba, Sergei P. 1954. *Русские мыслители о России и человечестве.* Paris: Ymca-Press.

Zyuganov, Gennady. 1995. *Россия и современный мир.* Москва.

———. 1998. *Geografiya pobedy.* Moskva: an unknown publisher.

———. 2002. *Globalizatsiya i sud'ba chelovechestva.* Moskva: Molodaya gvardiya.

4

COMMUNISTS

The victorious proletariat of this country ... would stand up against the capitalist world, attracting to itself the oppressed classes of other countries, raising an uprising in them against the capitalists, and, if necessary, even with military force against the exploiting classes and their states.

Stalin (2002, 26)

For all the contradictions of the present-day world, for all the diversity of social and political systems in it ... this world is one whole. We are all passengers aboard one ship, the Earth, and we must not allow it to be wrecked

Gorbachev (1987, 12)

Communism is the second significant variety of original Russian international thinking. In this chapter, I consider some of the essential ideas of Russian communism, defining them as theories for establishing social equality. Despite the depth of the existing differences, the authors of these theories are united in viewing social and economic equality as the central value.

Arriving from Europe, the Communist idea underwent a great change on Russian national soil, giving rise to several significant theories. Since the middle of the nineteenth century, following the development of capitalism, these theories varied from Aleksandr Hertzen's defense of the peasant commune and its principles to Leon Trotsky's promotion of permanent revolution in the interests of the world proletariat and to Mikhail Gorbachev's argument for transforming the world based on his New Thinking. The theoreticians of Russian Communism

DOI: 10.4324/9781003377573-4

were not planning to repeat the traditional Western European pattern of bourgeois development. Instead, they advocated a unique path for Russia, believing
in its mission. Unlike Slavophiles, Communists prioritized social equality rather
than the Orthodox faith. At the same time, like Slavophiles, Communists
believed in the superiority of Russian conditions for global development and of
the ability of the Russians to show humanity the most progressive path to social
improvement.

Like Slavophiles, Communists developed under the influence of Europe
and the West. Some of them, such as Aleksandr Herzen, Russian Populists,
Anarchists, and Josef Stalin, considered European capitalism the main threat to
nationally isolated development. Like Slavophiles, Herzen and others feared the
European revolutions of the 1840s but drew from them different conclusions.
While Slavophiles denounced Europe for materialism and the rejection of
Christianity, Herzen and Populists denounced the European revolutions for
rejecting the peasant commune as the basis of social equality and economic well-
being. Following Herzen, Nikolai Mikhailovsky criticized the Western theory
of progress as incompatible with the ideals of a holistic, that is, free communal
personality. Herzen, Populists, and then Stalin believed that Russia or the USSR
was not strong enough to survive the pressure of global capitalism and had to
develop in isolation. Stalin based his theory of National Communism on the
ideas of his predecessors under new industrial conditions.

More confident in Russia's domestic abilities were those who, like Vladimir
Lenin and Leon Trotsky, considered it possible and necessary to lead the
movement toward a world revolution. Based on Herzen's idea of the "advantage
of backwardness," they believed in the need to stimulate revolutionary processes
in the outside world, arguing that the USSR would not survive without them.
Their intransigence toward the European order led them to assume the possibility of breaking through the "chain of imperialism" as its weakest link. The
collapse of the European system and First World War became conditions for
developing Trotskyist-Leninist views and their practical implementation. These
views survived within the Soviet Union and, after its collapse, among those who
considered Western capitalism internally fragile and moving toward instability
and disintegration.

Russian Communist ideas progressed while Europe was weakening. However,
Communism found itself stagnating under the conditions of European revival
after the Second World War. Under these new conditions, Russian Communists
developed new theories, arguing for actively interacting with and learning from
the capitalist West and the Left forces within Western societies. The advocates
for building such bridges did not renounce their conditions and possibilities.
Frequently, they still believed that Russia or the USSR would point the way to
global development based on social equality and the integration of all the best
the world had created.

The Social Fortresses of the Russian Idea: Aleksander Herzen, Populists, and Anarchists

Aleksander Herzen and Communal Socialism

Alexander Herzen (1812–1870) and Nikolai Mikhailovsky (1842–1904) were essential contributors to the Russian Communist outlook – they revived interest in the socio-economic foundations of the peasant commune. Like Anarchists, they criticized Russian statehood but became more conservative, supporting the traditional peasant principles already developed in Russian life. In the peasant commune rather than in the Anarchist ideal of a world federation of free associations, the thinkers saw the promise of the future liberation of the Russian people. Even before them, Chaadayev viewed the economic backwardness of the Russians as an opportunity not to repeat the mistakes of European development. Based on this idea, Herzen, Pyotr Lavrov, Pyotr Tkachev, Mikhailovsky, and others advocated the preservation of the Russian commune as central to their theories of social liberation.

Herzen's notion of the "advantage of backwardness" became his main contribution to Russian IR theory. In anticipation of future socialist ideas, the concept offered a socio-economic justification for Russian missionary identity, linking pro-Western and Slavophile thought provisions. Initially developing his thinking under the influence of European ideas and in the circles of Moscow Westernizers, Herzen did not become a Westernizer. The thinker never believed in passively transferring Western ideals to Russian soil. Having emigrated from Russia, he was shocked by the suppression of the revolution of 1848 and soon became disappointed in the European standards: "I see the inevitable death of old Europe and do not regret anything that exists" (Zhaba 1954, 92). Especially hated for the thinker was the establishment on European soil of what he viewed as the bourgeois averaging of life, philistinism, and development in the name of development.

> "Everything is heading toward mediocrity," he wrote at that time, "faces are lost in the crowd. … Everything shrinks and withers on the depleted soil; no talents, no power of thought, no power of will."
>
> *Ibid., 94*

As for progress, "if progress is the goal, then for whom are we working? Who is this Moloch who, as the workers approach him, moves back instead of rewarding them?" (Ibid., 93). Herzen's most important ideal of a free personality was forever trampled upon by the offensiveness of bourgeois civilization.[1]

Having gone through a deep crisis, the thinker did not return to his homeland. He remained in Europe where "the word did not die," hoping to promote his beliefs in Europe and – through journalism – in Russia. The basis of these beliefs was the missionary faith in the undiscovered potential of the Russian people, who secretly formed a state of sixty million, which grew so strong and surprisingly without losing its communal principles, and was the first to endure it through the initial upheavals of social development ... which somehow [the Russian people] miraculously knew how to save himself under the yoke of the Mongol hordes and German bureaucrats. ... [The Russian people] retained his stately features, lively mind, and the wide revelry of a rich nature under the yoke of serfdom, and to the tsar's order, he responded a hundred years later with the enormous appearance of Pushkin.

Zhaba 1954, 93

It is on this Russian communal foundation that Herzen continued to develop his concept of a free personality. In his opinion, such a personality could not emerge on European soil with new petty-bourgeois ideals but had to be formed within the Russian commune to protect against social inequality and the political arbitrariness of the state. The thinker believed that precisely "because [Russians] are farther than Europe and freer than it, and because they are so far behind it" (Novikova and Sizemskaya 1997, 116), they will be able to point the way to the future. "We are free because we start with ourselves ... we are independent because we own nothing" (Walicki 1979, 167). This formulation resembled Marx's (1848) *The Communist Manifesto*: "The proletarians have nothing to lose but their chains. They will gain the whole world." Herzen, like Marx, assumed that the revolution posed no danger to its organizers. The difference, however, was that Marx was referring to the world proletariat, which "has no fatherland," while Herzen spoke of the role of Russia and Russians in world history.

Some of the positions expressed by the thinker brought him closer to representatives of the Slavophile tradition. Herzen wrote in his work, "The Russian People and Socialism,"

What a happiness for Russia that the rural community did not perish, that personal property did not fragment communal property, what a happiness it is for the Russian people that it remained outside all political movements, outside the European civilization.

Zhaba 1954, 97

However, unlike the Slavophiles, the thinker focused on socio-economic rather than religious forms, trying to comprehend the commune as a precursor and guarantee of future socialist development. He did not share the Slavophile idea of collective personality (*sobornost'*), which united "I" and "we." In Herzen's view, "The commune is the brainchild of the earth – it lulls a person and forms his independence" (Novikova and Sizemskaya 1997, 115). Together with his friend Nikolai Ogarev he believed that the free development of the commune would further liberate individual peasants. In his desire to establish the individual's freedom, Herzen argued for the right of everyone to the land, communal ownership, and secular government. "On these principles, and only on them," he believed, "future Russia can develop" (Zhaba 1954, 98). Both his initial support for Alexander II's reforms to abolish serfdom and the thinker's subsequent disappointment in their bourgeois, insufficiently radical orientation was rooted in these convictions.

Herzen viewed the economic and political future of Russia in the peasant commune. He remained skeptical of the political system of European states and considered representative institutions an obstacle to the development of a free individual.

> "Representation," he wrote, "is also a monarchy, but a hypocritical one. ... [attorneys, delegates] ... do the will of those who sent them, they are not above the people, there is nothing above the head of free people, not even any participation of the people in public affairs"
>
> *Ibid., 99–100*

Nor did he share the belief in the priority of law and legitimacy, rhetorically asking the Europeans, "Can we honestly be content with your worn-out morality, neither Christian nor human, existing only in rhetorical exercises and prosecutorial reports? What respect can your Roman-barbarian legitimacy inspire in us?" (Ibid., 99)

With Chaadayev and the Slavophiles, the thinker believed in the universal vocation of the Russian people, which he associated with the universal dissemination of communal experience.

> The Russian people are more for us than our homeland. We see in it the soil on which a new state system will develop, a soil that is not only not stagnant, not depleted, but carries within itself all the conditions for development.
>
> *Ibid., 96*

Like Slavophiles and Anarchists, Herzen thought that "the Slavic peoples do not like either the state or centralization" (Ibid., 97). However, unlike Anarchists, the thinker associated future socialism and revolution not with popular rebellion but with the establishment of the commune as a positive principle: "Save the commune and give freedom to the individual, spread rural and regional self-government throughout the cities and the entire state ... this is the question of the future of Russia" (Ibid.).

The Organic Socialism of Nikolai Mikhailovsky

Nikolai Mikhailovsky (1842–1904) was another major theoretician of Russian socialism and a member of the Populist movement[2] who defended Herzen's ideas. If Herzen mainly engaged in polemics with Westernizers by critically borrowing from the Slavophiles, then Mikhailovsky fought the thoughts of organicist and Marxist sociology that were developing in Russia.

Fundamental for Mikhailovsky was the critique of the Western notion of progress. Following Herzen, he rejected progress if it meant social and economic development at the expense of the individual and his integral development. In his famous essay "What is Progress?" Mikhailovsky criticized Herbert Spencer's theory of the "organic evolution of society," popular among Russian intellectuals, as incompatible with the ideal of an integral or holistic personality. The division of labor, presented in Spencerian (and Marxist) sociology as an inevitable historical process, meant for Mikhailovsky the disintegration of reality and, with it, of the individual, into separate, self-existing spheres. "Society," he wrote, "by the very process of its development seeks to split the individual, define him by a special function, and ... turn him from an individual into an organ" (Novikova and Sizemskaya 1997, 189).

The thinker rejected such a development as unacceptable, instead offering his own "formula of progress" as "the gradual development of a holistic personality" (Walicki 1979, 256). This understanding was close to other representatives of the Populist thought. In particular, Lavrov, who repeatedly argued with Mikhailovsky, proposed to define the highest form of progress as "the conscious development of solidarity based on the critical attitude of individuals towards themselves and the reality around them" (Novikova and Sizemskaya 1997, 188). It was with the "organic" or industrial progress, compared by Herzen with Moloch, that Mikhailovsky connected Russia's European path of development, which he viewed as harmful and unusual for Russia: "[W]e are a people who ... own all the richest experience of Europe, its history, science, but at the same time we are only scratched by civilization" (Zhaba 1954, 168–169).

Following Herzen and other thinkers, Mikhailovsky contrasted the European path with the Russian path, at the center of which was the peasant commune and the personality of the free peasant. The thinker viewed such a character as morally integral and in harmonious relations within the commune. Instead of repeating the economic experience of Europe, he advocated the progressive development of the Russian rural experience – without taking away the land from the peasant and turning peasants into urban proletarians. Mikhailovsky admitted that such an experience was "unprecedented" but considered it possible, given the historically unusual period in Russia's development: "We, too, are in an unprecedented position" (Ibid.).

Politically, the thinker believed Russia also faced unusual circumstances. For the practical implementation of Russian socialism, Mikhailovsky argued for state measures for the liberation of the individual. Unlike some other Populists who were skeptical of constitutionalism, Mikhailovsky supported it. He considered it possible to ally with liberal-constitutional forces in politics, believing that "many liberals are ... closer [to us] than you think" (Ibid., 171). At the same time, the thinker did not refuse the importance of Populist ideals, considering them so attractive that the liberals themselves would be interested in supporting them. However, his model of constitutionalism differed significantly from bourgeois liberalism as based on a powerful, enlightened government.

> "In Europe," he wrote, "political freedom was proclaimed after forming a strong, organized, and mentally and materially strong third estate. In this grief of Europe, there is a lesson for us. Our country's political freedom must be proclaimed before the bourgeoisie is so united and strong that it does not need an autocratic tsar."
>
> *Ibid., 170*

Revolutionary and Moral Equality in Russian Anarchism

The nineteenth-century Anarchist movement is essential for understanding the adaptation of Communist ideas in Russia. Its most influential figures in Russia – Mikhail Bakunin and Pyotr Kropotkin – represented two opposite mental and political types within Anarchism. Although both rejected the state in favor of universal equality and the principle of "sociability," their proposed methods of achieving these goals were fundamentally different. While Kropotkin stressed the moral transformation of society, the politically rebellious Bakunin considered violence essential as the means of revolutionary reorganization of the world. As the British historian of Russian thought, Isaiah Berlin (1955, 497), once noted, Bakunin "wanted to set fire to as many and as quickly as possible, and any thought of chaos, violence, and upheaval gave him infinite pleasure."

Before committing to Anarchism, which he understood as an immediate revolt against the tsar, Bakunin (1814–1876) was a Westernizer and a member of the Nikolai Stankevich circle. Bakunin was then schooled as a Hegelian and an admirer of German romantic philosophy while actively participating in the First International. Bakunin constantly argued with someone in his life, urging him to adopt the most radical solutions. In Europe, he pleaded with Marx, accusing him of pandering to the goals of the German state. In Russia, Bakunin argued with those Populists, who, like Pyotr Lavrov, opposed an immediate revolt against the state and wanted to take time to prepare a revolution.

The struggle against the state and the advocacy of a popular revolt constituted the essence and the meaning of Bakunin's worldview and activities. "Whoever wants the complete liberation of the masses of the people," he wrote, "should want with us the destruction of all states" (Zhaba 1954, 116). He considered the state the basis of all problems, arguing for the need to abandon everything that could help strengthen it: faith in God, the ideology of patriotism, and the concept of state interest. In the spirit of Feodor Dostoevsky's characters, Ivan Shatov, who considered faith in God to be proof of man's slavery, Bakunin argued that "the idea of God equals to the renunciation of human reason and justice," viewing such ideas as "the most resolute denial of human freedom that inevitably leads to the slavery of people in theory and in practice" (Ibid., 114). The thinker also denounced patriotism as a "flagrant denial of humanity," and of the principle of state interest as entailing debauchery and robbery on the part of the ruling class.

> State interest, truly terrible word! ... As soon as this word is uttered, everything falls silent, everything disappears: conscientiousness, honor, justice, right ... and the vilest deceptions, the most terrible crimes become worthy deeds.
>
> *Ibid., 116*

Bakunin contrasted the state with a world federation of free associations (communes) of workers, peasants, and artisans. He asserted his vision in a polemic with the Marxian idea of the dictatorship of the proletariat, which Marx's followers considered necessary for the revolution's victory. "No dictatorship can have any other purpose than to perpetuate itself ... freedom can only be created by freedom, i.e., all-round revolt and free organization of the working masses from below upwards" (Ibid., 119).

At the same time, Bakunin was by no means a cosmopolitan, insisting on the liberation potential of Russia and the Slavs. German-phobic and Slavophile, he supported the Polish uprisings of 1830 and 1863. He further advocated the crushing of the Russian empire, Austria and Germany, convinced that such crushing would become the basis for the future liberation of other peoples. In the struggle between statist and anarchist tendencies, the thinker saw the battle of ethnic principles – German and Slavic. "On the Pan-German banner it is written: to keep and strengthen the state at all costs; ... on our banner, on the contrary, it is inscribed in fiery, bloody letters: the destruction of all states" (Ibid., 121). Calling for a fraternal union of the Slavs, Bakunin warned that it was necessary "not to form a closed world among themselves, but [to conclude] a necessary close alliance with the peoples of the Latin tribe, who, like the Slavs, are threatened by the aggressive policy of the Germans" (Ibid.).

The thinking of Kropotkin (1842–1921) developed differently. Originating from a family close to the imperial court, a descendant of the Rurik dynasty, he was never inclined to Bakunin's radicalism. A good example is Kropotkin's reaction to the Polish uprising of 1863, which led to the uprising of Polish convicts in Siberia in 1866. At that time, in military service in Siberia, Kropotkin decided to leave the service, enrolling the following year at the Faculty of Physics and Mathematics of St. Petersburg University. Instead of taking the rebels' side and surrendering to the struggle, as Bakunin did, Kropotkin chose the path of moral condemnation of state violence and violence as a principle. Soon he also abandoned the field of science, engaging in the "cause of the liberation of the working people" (Gridchin 1991, 11). However, Bakunin's preparedness for a "sea of blood and fire" to liberate mankind did not inspire Kropotkin. Instead, he searched for a non-violent moral and ethical ideal of justice.

Kropotkin's main ideas aim to substantiate the moral ideal of Anarchism as social "sociability" (общительность). Having condemned, together with Bakunin, Marx's theory of the dictatorship of the proletariat, Kropotkin went further. He blamed the idea of class struggle as rooted in species' struggle in nature. In the book "Mutual Aid as a Factor of Evolution," the thinker established mutual aid's practical and ethical significance in social development. Based on the work of Pierre-Joseph Proudhon and other philosophers, Kropotkin sought to reframe the teachings of Darwin, which many commonly used to justify the "natural cause" of struggle in nature. At the same time, the author of "Mutual Aid" wanted to affirm the significance of the moral and ethical ideal of justice in society, contrasting it with ideas about the unlimited freedom of the individual. Advocating justice as the basic concept of morality, he argued for "recognition of the political and social equality of people" as the primary condition for "abolishing class divisions" (Kropotkin 1990, 273).

Kropotkin's revolution was, therefore, above all, a moral process. Proclaiming universal equality, the thinker sought to establish it not by force of arms but by gradually transforming ideas. Unlike Bakunin, who wanted nothing to do with the concept of God, Kropotkin was sympathetic to Christianity, albeit in its non-Orthodox interpretation by Leo Tolstoy. In his *Ethics*, Kropotkin analyzed in detail Tolstoy's views on Christianity, considering the writer's assertion of the moral dimension of Christianity to be a "wonderful attempt" (Ibid., 325–326).

Bolsheviks between Fortress and Expansion

In Russia, industrial civilization significantly progressed only following the Great Reforms of 1861. As a result, the ideas of social equality here had different roots than in Europe. Aleksandr Radishchev, the Populists, and even the Revolutionary Democrats prioritized the social liberation of the peasantry from serfdom or forced labor. Only the development of capitalism in Russia in the last third of the nineteenth century created the conditions for the formation of theories of the emancipation of the working class. Only then did the supporters of the traditional, non-capitalist path of development begin to lose influence.

The dispute between the Westernizers and the Slavophiles became about the rationale of borrowing the experience of capitalist development. As Russian intelligentsia grew radicalized, Russian Marxists experienced pro-Western and Russian influences. Legal Marxists, Socialist-Revolutionaries, and Mensheviks considered classical European Marxism fully applicable to Russian conditions. The other school was represented primarily by the Bolshevik group of Vladimir Ulyanov (Lenin), which argued for a "creative" application of Marxism in a country where essential prerequisites for the development of capitalism and bourgeois democracy were missing. Over time, supporters of the national-isolationist development of socialism also emerged among the Bolsheviks.

Vladimir Lenin, Lev Trotsky, and the Revolutionary Liberation from Global Capitalism

The Trotskyist-Leninist theory of the world revolution ideologically grew from the Anarchist critique of the state and the Herzen-Populist conviction in Russia's socio-economic uniqueness (advantage). The gradual weakening of the autocratic system and the spread of Marx's ideas made it possible to form a new ideological complex of anti-state messianism.

Of particular interest in this respect is the theory of permanent revolution by Leon Trotsky (1879–1940), one of the leaders of the Bolshevik movement. As a result of communication with German Social Democratic theoretician Alexander Parvus,[3] Trotsky posed the question of the readiness of the world system for revolution. He did so before other Bolsheviks – already by the time of the Revolution of 1905 and ten years before the First World War and the publication of Lenin's famous pamphlet *Imperialism*. In the manner typical of Trotsky as a publicist, he argued the need to discuss the issue without taking the trouble to support his reasoning with facts and figures. Later, in his book *Permanent Revolution*, published in 1926, Trotsky provided more detail and answered his critics. The object of his criticism was Social Democrats Georgy Plekhanov, Yuli Martov, Mark Axelrod, and others, who viewed Russia as insufficiently prepared for a proletarian revolution. Due to what they saw as the weakness of Russian capitalism, they proposed to form tactical alliances with the liberal bourgeoisie to weaken the autocracy. Instead, Trotsky (1926) argued that while being internally unprepared for a revolution, Russia was ready for it externally since "the world economy as a whole, and above all the European economy, is fully ripe for a socialist revolution." He, therefore, insisted that under such international conditions, one must raise the question not only of a bourgeois but also of a proletarian revolution.

The theory of permanent revolution assumed direct relations between the development of world capitalism and the revolutionary processes inside the country. Trotsky believed that without the growth of the revolutionary movement abroad, the transformations within the country after the Bolsheviks came to power in October 1917 would choke, leading to the restoration of capitalism. The theorist of Bolshevism insisted on the need for a constant struggle for the victory of revolutionary ideals. In their definition,

> [A permanent revolution is] a revolution that does not accept any class domination, does not stop at the democratic stage, goes over to socialist measures and a war against external reaction. ... [It is] a revolution, each subsequent stage of which has roots in the previous one, and which can end only with the complete liquidation of class society.
>
> *Ibid.*

Based on Marx's analysis of the European revolutions of 1848, Trotsky formulated three components of the permanent revolution. First, he insisted on the possibility and necessity of a transition from a bourgeois-democratic to a socialist revolution and the establishment of the proletariat's dictatorship with the peasantry's support for this. Secondly, after the successful implementation of the transition, permanence had to be achieved by constantly restructuring social relations. "Society is constantly shedding ... Explosions of civil and foreign wars alternate with periods of peaceful reforms. Revolutions of economy, technology, knowledge, family, way of life, morals, unfold in complex interaction, preventing society from reaching equilibrium" (Ibid.). Finally, the socialist revolution could not survive alone.

> [U]nder an isolated proletarian dictatorship, external and internal contradictions inevitably grow along with successes. While in further isolation, the proletarian state would eventually fall victim to these contradictions. The only way out for [such a state] is the victory of the proletariat of the advanced countries. From this point of view, the national revolution is not a self-contained whole: it is only a link in the international chain.
>
> *Ibid.*

Lenin later substantiated the relationship between the development of world capitalism and the Russian revolution in his work *Imperialism*. Written on the eve of the First World War, the work was primarily devoted to substantiating Trotsky's statement about the crisis of world capitalism. Economists John Hobson, Rudolf Hilferding, and others had already used the concept of imperialism in their writings. Lenin gave the idea a new meaning, defining it not only as the latest stage in the development of capitalism but the stage responsible for its decay and collapse. He believed such a collapse would result from the deepening contradiction between the growing socialization of production and the private nature of the ownership of capitalist enterprises. In analyzing the growth of socialization, Lenin (1916, 90) identified five characteristics of imperialism that distinguish it from the era of free competition: the concentration of production and the emergence of monopolies; consolidation of banks with the merging of banking capital with industrial capital; the formation of a financial oligarchy; the export of money, along with the export of goods, to new world markets; and the resulting division of the world between the capitalists and the major capitalist powers.

> As the export of capital grew and foreign and colonial ties and the "spheres of influence" of the largest monopoly unions expanded in every possible way, the matter "naturally" approached a worldwide agreement between them, the formation of international cartels.
>
> *Ibid., 70*

The main object of Lenin's criticism was the theoreticians of the Second International, in particular Karl Kautsky. The latter associated imperialism with a new stage of industrial-capitalist development while not ruling out the possibility of a gradual resolution of capitalist contradictions on a global scale (the theory of "ultra-imperialism"). Lenin viewed such ideas as a break from Marxism. In his view, they indicated a failure to understand all the depth of the contradictions in the capitalist world and its aggravation at a new, financial, and exploitative stage:

> Kautsky's empty talk about ultra-imperialism encourages … the deeply erroneous and propagandist imperialist thought that the dominance of finance capital *weakens* the unevenness and contradictions within the world economy, while in fact, it *strengthens* them.
>
> *Ibid., 94*

Like Trotsky, Lenin believed that unevenness is the law of capitalist development, and contradictions and wars between capitalist powers are inevitable companions of such uneven development.

For Russia, the new theory of imperialism meant new opportunities for the development of the revolutionary movement. Unlike Plekhanov and other supporters of classical Marxism,[4] the leaders of Bolshevism did not associate the socialist revolution with the world of industrially and financially developed capitalism. They argued that this type of capitalism did not produce a working class but a "labor aristocracy" since capitalists could offer workers higher wages, depriving them of their revolutionary potential (Lenin 1916, 110). Another matter is Russia, which Trotsky and Lenin considered a "weak link" in the chain of uneven development of capitalism. Although Russia was on the path of capitalist development and the disintegration of the agricultural system, Lenin argued the weaknesses of Russian capitalism in his earlier work, *The Development of Capitalism in Russia* (1899). According to his analysis, based on the All-Russian census of 1897, only 10 per cent of the population was employed in industry, while 75 per cent were agricultural workers (Anikin 1990, 362). However, according to Lenin, it was precisely the underdevelopment of Russian capitalism that made Russia a country where a breakthrough of all the chains of imperialist contradictions would become most likely. In the preface to *Imperialism* in the French and German editions published in July 1920, Lenin (1967) wrote about the inevitability of a world imperialist war and insisted that the revolution of 1917 confirmed his belief that "imperialism is the time of the proletarian revolution."

Here, one can identify an apparent connection between the Trotskyist-Leninist theory of revolution and the missionary ideas of Bakunin and Herzen. Like Bakunin, the leaders of Bolshevism strived for a revolutionary transformation of capitalism resulting in the establishment of the commune on a world scale. While being critical of Herzen and the Populist praises of the peasant commune as the foundation of the new social order,[5] Trotsky and Lenin nevertheless accepted the theory of the "advantage of backwardness" in the sense of breaking away from the stronghold of the developed capitalism. The revolution, as they expected, took place on Russian, not Western European, soil. The ideologists of the world revolution have been vindicated. Until the introduction of the New Economic Policy in 1921, the vast majority of Bolsheviks proceeded from the notion of an inevitable and imminent world revolution as an indispensable condition for their success. After Lenin's death and until the end of his days, Trotsky continued to link the achievements and failures of transformations within the USSR with the peculiarities of the world revolutionary movement.

The Socialist Fortress of Josef Stalin

The Stalinist theory of national communism broke with the Trotskyist-Leninist idea of permanent and world revolution. In a broader sense, Stalinism meant rejecting the tradition of the Anarchist overthrow of the state. Remaining convinced of the country's unique mission and the advantage of its initial backwardness in overcoming the industrial and economic gap with the Western world, Stalin gradually abandoned the criticism of the state and statehood as incompatible with the ideals of the revolution and a classless society. Contrary to the ideas of Trotsky and Lenin, he concluded that it was possible to build communism in a hostile capitalist environment.

The basis of the Stalinist worldview was the concept of building socialism in one country. Stalin supported Lenin's rejection of the theory of world revolution after 1921. In this regard, Stalin emphasized the possibility of peaceful coexistence with capitalism and the need for economic cooperation with it to build socialism. Stalin also considered it necessary to focus on building socialism. In the preface to the book *On the Roads to October*, published after Lenin's death, Stalin substantiated (2002, 26) the possibility of the victory of socialism in one country based on Lenin's law of the uneven economic and political development of capitalism:

> The victorious proletariat of this country would stand up against the rest, the capitalist world, attracting to itself the oppressed classes of other countries, raising an uprising in them against the capitalists, and, if necessary, even with military force against the exploiting classes and their states.

At the same time, Stalin hardly shared Lenin's new conviction about the relative safety of the Soviet Union from outside threats. Stalin agreed with Lenin that a respite was not "a short period during which the imperialist powers have many times had the opportunity to renew a more serious attempt at war with us." Instead, it was a new period "when we won back our basic international existence in the network of capitalist states" (Zagladin 1990, 59). These ideas, under the influence of Lenin's New Economic Policy, were also supported by Nikolai Bukharin. He advocated a policy of peaceful coexistence with capitalist countries and a moderate revival of the private sector within the country under state control. Echoing Lenin, Bukharin (1925) believed that there could be no talk of the world's imminent collapse of capitalism, and it was necessary to look for opportunities for cooperation with it. In the 1930s, Bukharin supported Maxim Litvinov's line of extensive collaboration with peace-loving states and social democratic parties to create an anti-fascist front. Bukharin's theory of international relations allowed for peaceful development and moderate mutual learning between the two systems.

It soon became apparent that Stalin did not share Bukharin's views and remained close to the traditional Bolshevik ideas about the antagonism of socio-economic contradictions and the inevitability of armed confrontation with the world of capitalism. At the Party congress held in 1927, Stalin announced a new threat from Western countries and the need to realize that peaceful coexistence was coming to an end. He soon launched forced industrialization, collectiv-ization, and the creation of a robust military industry. After carrying out these internal transformations, accompanied by mass purges in the Party and terror against the intelligentsia, the peasantry, and the military, Stalin proclaimed at the 18th Congress held in 1939 "the complete and final victory of socialism."

Not accepting the argument of Lenin-Bukharin about the need to proceed from the thesis of the relative security of the USSR from external threats, Stalin (2002, 32) also rejected the position of Trotsky. The latter, also based on the Leninist law of the development of capitalism, considered it impossible to com-plete successfully the socialist revolution in conditions of capitalist encirclement. Stalin believed that Trotsky underestimated the strength of the alliance between the proletariat and the peasantry. In his view, the Soviet military and economic capabilities were comparable with those of the imperialist states: "Distrust in the strength and ability of our revolution, disbelief in the strength and ability of the Russian proletariat – such is the subsoil of the theory[,] permanent revolution." As for Trotsky himself, he was well aware that it was the Stalinist theory that posed the main threat to his positions:

> The theory of socialism in a separate country, which rose on the yeast of reaction against October, is the only theory that consistently and to the end opposes the theory of permanent revolution. Under the blows of criticism, the epigones' attempt to limit the applicability of the theory of socialism in a particular country to Russia alone, in view of its special properties (space and natural wealth), does not improve but worsens the situation. The break with the international position always and inevitably leads to national mes-sianism, i.e., to the recognition of special advantages and qualities for one's own country, allowing it to supposedly fulfill the role that other countries cannot rise to.
>
> *Trotsky 1930*

Over time, Stalin's confidence in the possibility of the complete construc-tion of socialism and communism in the conditions of a capitalist encirclement continued to grow. As the discussion on the political economy of socialism after the war showed, Stalin intended to move further along the road to the victory of national communism. During the debate and in the published work, *Economic Problems of Socialism in the USSR*, the leader rejected several market economy concepts, such as profitability and profits, and also spoke in favor of reducing the sphere of commodity circulation and turning cooperative-collective farm property into state property. According to Stalin (2002, 246), this kind of movement towards statehood and planning was driven by the need to resist imperialism. The latter had stabilized and still threatened the USSR with war. But the point was not only in the essentially defensive opposition to capitalism but also in new opportunities for the offensive of socialism, which Stalin saw in the victory in the war. Under certain conditions, the leader now considered it possible to build communism, despite the existence of world capitalism. He felt such conditions to be the provision of a continuous and expanded growth of all social production, a gradual transition from commodity circulation to a system of direct product exchange, as well as an increase in cultural change for the comprehensive physical and mental development of all members of society (Barsenkov and Vdovin 2010, 432).

Stalin's national communism was guided primarily by the need for the state's survival in the face of external threats and challenges. One scholar wrote, "Marxists sought to achieve an unprecedented level of development of productive forces, while Stalin sought to correlate their development with the nation's political sovereignty" (Yeliseyev 2007, 295). Toward the end of his life, the leader of the Soviet state considered the possibility of further strengthening nationalism as the ideology of the USSR, increasingly emphasizing the national liberation character of the communist movement: "Lenin, Lenin, what about Lenin? We coped without Lenin for so long, and we will continue to cope!" (Ibid., 299). This evolution of Stalin was predicated on his nationalistic worldview. An early dispute with Lenin about the conditions for including non-Russian nationalities in the Soviet Union revealed Stalin's nationalism. Even long before this dispute in 1922, Stalin – an ethnic Georgian and then still Dzhugashvili – decided to join the Bolsheviks for ethnic rather than socio-economic reasons. The Mensheviks, for him, represented a "Jewish faction," and the future leader of the USSR chose a "truly Russian faction," even suggesting carrying out a pogrom within the Party (Tucker 1973, 140).

Bridges of the Late Soviet Period

After Stalin's death, the struggle between national and international tendencies in Russian communism took a new turn, as Nikita Khrushchev, in his characteristic decisive manner, announced in 1961 the possibility of entirely building communism as a classless society by 1980. Despite the leader's harsh criticism at the twentieth Congress, Khrushchev accepted some basic premises of Stalinist thought about enemies of socialist development. However, the new leadership of

Leonid Brezhnev revised the concept of building communism, replacing it with the theory of mature or developed socialism.

The new theory assumed the duration of the movement toward communism with the gradual improvement of production, socio-political, moral, and ideological relations (Barsenkov and Vdovin 2010, 515). At the same time, there was an official rejection of the concept of the dictatorship of the proletariat, and the new Constitution of the USSR of 1977 consolidated the nature of the Soviet state nationwide, that is, expressing the will of all social strata. One of the theory's leading advocates, the editor-in-chief of the central Party magazine *Kommunist*, Richard Kosolapov explained (1995) the approach by the need to "move away from Khrushchev's utopia about building communism by the beginning of the 80s" and by the tasks of substantiating the idea of a "classless socialist society." Arguing with the ideologists of reformist socialism, the theory of developed socialism continued the Stalinist tradition of thinking about the Western world as no longer representing the existential danger of capitalist restoration for the USSR.

The Social Reformism of Vladimir Zagladin

One of the prominent critics of the neo-Stalinist worldview during the Brezhnev era, especially in the field of international relations, was Vadim Zagladin (1927–2006). Zagladin's contribution to the Soviet IR theory was significant, especially if one remembers that even after Stalin's death, the political atmosphere for the development of independent thought was far from favorable. Although the official Soviet ideology could not fully control Marxist social theory – the conservative Stalinist and reformist Bukharinist approaches remained in competition – the discussions were quite limited due to the country's isolation from the world and its ideas. Soviet Marxism preserved such isolation and was not intellectually in the West, even among Marxists. While possessing some progressive characteristics, Soviet Marxism was a tool for maintaining the status quo and suppressing dissent. The hegemony of Soviet Marxism asserted rigid canons in studying international relations, suppressing the critical potential of authentic Marxist theory and imposing an ideological understanding of the processes taking place in the world. As a result, most of the international relations studies turned out to be interpretations of official documents and speeches of the leaders of the CPSU at its congresses.[6]

Under these conditions, a vital role in the development of social science belonged to a narrow circle of specialists who had authority in Party circles and privileged access to information.[7] In the post-Stalin era, a more favorable political climate emerged to develop creative thought. Following Nikita Khrushchev's revealing anti-Stalinist speech at the 20th Congress of the CPSU, a new search for the Soviet identity began in the country, and interaction with Western ideas became more intense. In his speech Khrushchev called for, among other things, a rapprochement with Europe.[8] The impact of de-Stalinization was irreversible. A significant part of the intellectual generation of the 1960s began to consider themselves "children of the 20th Congress." They joined the ranks of supporters of a rapprochement between the USSR and the West. Several scientific institutions emerged in which researchers carefully analyzed Western ideas concerning the development of international relations (Zimmerman 1969; Kubalkova and Cruickshank 1985; Hough 1986; Lynch 1987; Shenfield 1987; Light 1988; Simoniya 1990; Zagladin 1990; Wohlforth 1993). Within this vector of development, the intellectual formation of the future leader of the USSR, Mikhail Gorbachev, also took place (Arbatov 1991; English 2000; Shakhnazarov 2001; Zubok 2009).

Zagladin also belonged to the generation of "children of the 20th Congress." He was always moderate and cautious in their public expression. At the beginning of de-Stalinization, he was already thirty, remembering well the period of Stalin's dictatorship and the high human price paid for such a political system. Unlike some of his contemporaries and Party intellectuals such as Alexander Bovin or Fyodor Burlatsky, Zagladin never fell into disgrace and worked permanently in the International Department of the Communist Party Central Committee from 1964 to 1988. One of his most difficult responsibilities was maintaining relations with communist parties abroad. Before his work in the Central Committee, the graduate of the History Department at Moscow Institute of International Relations (MGIMO) was employed as a journalist by the magazines *Novoye Vremya* (*New Time*) and *Problems of Peace and Socialism* in Prague. During the Khrushchev era, both magazines were flagships of change and new thinking about socialism and international relations.

Along with journalistic and Party work, Zagladin was involved in research, gained a doctoral degree, and became a professor and a member of the Russian Academy of Natural Sciences. While at the Central Committee, he also chaired the department of the international labor movement at the Institute of Social Sciences under the Central Committee of the CPSU, which taught international students in foreign languages. Finally, Zagladin was elected a deputy of the Supreme Soviet of the RSFSR three times and worked for ten years as secretary of the Foreign Affairs Commission of the Council of the Union of the Supreme Soviet of the USSR.

Zagladin began his academic activity as an expert in the labor and national liberation movement. He published his first book in 1955 based on French materials (Zagladin 1955).[9] Well-educated and having access to foreign literature, he read widely. He was well aware of intellectual and political discussions outside the USSR. In particular, Zagladin was familiar with the debates among the European left, including those based on the ideas of the Italian communist Antonio Gramsci and French and German neo-Marxist thinkers. A number of these ideas favoring broad alliances of leftist forces, the expansion of the social support for Communist Parties, and the integration of humanistic approaches to socialism corresponded with the views of Zagladin and his reformist predecessors in Russia. Even more than the late Lenin and Bukharin, Zagladin believed in the stabilization and transformation of capitalism. He viewed these developments as requiring a new, more flexible policy of adaptation by the USSR. In his public work, he frequently defended the idea of internationalizing the world economy as responsible for changing the essence of contemporary international relations (Zagladin 1984).[10]

Holding these views, the thinker also tried to use his position to influence the direction of Soviet foreign policy. In particular, during his tenure in the International Department of the Central Committee of the CPSU, the functions of supporting relations with the communist parties of the world gradually expanded to the development of relations with socialist, social democratic, and liberal parties (Tolz 2006). One of a few, he had access to Leonid Brezhnev and contributed to preparing the foreign policy part of the General Secretary's speeches. On the other hand, Brezhnev was also influenced by those who fought against de-Stalinization. The Stalinists included, in particular, the influential secretary of the Party ideology Mikhail Suslov, the Central Committee supervisor of social science, Sergei Trapeznikov, and the editor-in-chief of the Communist Party magazine Richard Kosolapov.[11]

An essential area of Zagladin's research interests was problems and global significance issues. Since the late 1970s, mainly due to his efforts, the whole school of viewing the problems of humankind in their international or planetary dimension has developed in Russia, ultimately influencing Mikhail Gorbachev and his thinking. Following Party leader Georgy Malenkov's statement about the impossibility of fighting and winning a nuclear war, Zagladin and his associates developed the field of global security studies. They proposed to view problems of the international system – atomic weapons, environmental degradation of the planet, growing poverty, demographic, food crisis, and others – as uniting rather than separating capitalism and socialism and demanding urgent solutions (Zagladin and Frolov 1981; Shakhnazarov 1981; Leybin 1982; Arab-Ogly 1986). These ideas significantly expanded the horizons of Soviet Marxism. Many now viewed the world as increasingly global and interdependent, partly due to the influence of Western notions of global interdependence and their reception by leading Soviet intellectuals.[12] Along with ideas of democratization, reforms, and liberalization of relations with the countries of Eastern Europe, global studies greatly contributed to social change in the country.

Not surprisingly, during Perestroika, Zagladin became one of the leading advisers on Gorbachev's team, with whom he worked even after Gorbachev's resignation. During Perestroika, Soviet Marxism evolved toward European social democracy (Herman 1996; English 2000), aided by Zagladin and other advisers to Gorbachev. Both Gorbachev and Zagladin advocated a profound reform of the political system of society, not considering the dominance of Marxism and the Communist Party as a normal state of affairs. They argued for a continued rapprochement of the Soviet Union with the social democratic countries of Europe, which they viewed as containing key elements of socialism.

In the late period of his life, Zagladin became disillusioned with Soviet Marxism and the ability of the USSR to lead the world. In his view,

> We had official Marxism, which was not Marxism. Some people studied Marxism for real and understood it in their way, that is, in a way that was closer to the views of Marx himself. ... [W]e were forced to write one thing. Still, among ourselves, we discussed completely different problems and completely different approaches to these problems. And everything was left for the future, in reserve.
>
> *Tolz 2006*[13]

Zagladin also had no illusions about the possible preservation of the Soviet system. According to the memoirs of one of his colleagues Anatoly Chernyaev, Zagladin understood that the existing system was doomed and that "the whole system, this regime, should go somewhere and somehow be transformed" (Ibid.). In his assessment, the "dogmatic current in the communist movement" worldwide and within the country was too strong to save the movement itself (Ibid.).

The Global Dialogue of Mikhail Gorbachev

Gorbachev was a convinced socialist, yet his views radically differed from many of his political predecessors. He did not share isolationist and expansionist perspectives. Like Zagladin, Gorbachev viewed socialism as distinct yet compatible with Western ideals of democracy.[14]

By introducing his ideas of Perestroika and New Thinking, Gorbachev did not mean to replace the Soviet system with one similar to that of the West. He was a product of the system and a firm believer in the Soviet Union's principal viability. At the same time, Gorbachev was highly critical of how the system had performed in the past and wanted to renew it in some fundamental way. In particular, he dreamed of releasing human potential and social creativity that, in his opinion, were suppressed under the Stalinist regime. Eventually, Gorbachev meant to bring the system closer to the model of Scandinavian societies, which combined democracy with egalitarian principles in the economy.

Gorbachev's ideas proved particularly innovative in the area of world politics. He sought to break the Cold War hostilities and be accepted by the Western nations as equal members of the world. Gorbachev proposed a vision that required Cold War enemies to cooperate.[15] The new idea sought to present the old enemies with a common threat, leaving them little choice but to abandon their old hostilities. It was the vision of a global and principally non-divisive world, one which was in danger of destruction. With its arms races and power struggle, the Cold War put humankind on the verge of nuclear, ecological, and moral catastrophe. The New Thinking diagnosed the disaster as global, and it could only be resolved through global efforts. To quote the author of New Thinking,

For all the contradictions of the present-day world, for all the diversity of
social and political systems in it, and for all the different choices made by
the nations in different times, this world is nevertheless one whole. We are
all passengers aboard one ship, the Earth, and we must not allow it to be
wrecked. There will be no second Noah's Ark.

Gorbachev 1987, 12

It was, therefore, critical to acknowledge the importance of values "common
to all humankind" and to understand that security could only be mutual. The
reasons for this were the threat of mutual destruction in a nuclear war and
increased economic and ecological interdependence in the world.

The origins of New Thinking had little to do with the necessity of a strategic
retreat in the face of the West's growing economic and military strength – the
argument often advanced by realists (Brooks and Wohlforth 2000; Sushentsov
and Wohlforth 2020). To argue this is to neglect the domestic intellectual roots of
Gorbachev. The new leader did not make sense of the world regarding economic
or military capabilities. He was not a member of the Statist school, and his entire
thinking about international politics was shaped by the desire to reach out to the
liberal and social-democratic West. This thinking also had a distinct domestic
tradition stretching back to Nikolai Bukharin's and Nikita Khrushchev's foreign
policy liberalizations.

The legacy of the Cold War and the socioeconomic differences between
the Soviet Union and the West made it difficult to achieve the recognition of
Western nations Gorbachev sought. Such recognition was all the more difficult
since Gorbachev did not believe in the importance of Western values of political
democracy and market economy. Instead, he envisioned global unity from the
contributions of both capitalist and socialist systems. He was prepared to learn
from other systems and nations while remaining a socialist who believed that the
whole world would continue to be influenced by the socialist experience and
"socialist values." In his book *On My Country and the World*, Gorbachev (1999)
also discusses the global significance of the Russian 1917 revolution.

The new vision of world politics appealed to different groups within Soviet
society. Liberals were to be attracted to ideas of democratization, reform, and
rapprochement with the West. Gorbachev himself was influenced by the ideas
of European social democrats and liberal-minded scientists, such as Vladimir
Vernadsky, Pyotr Kapitsa, and Andrei Sakharov. Gorbachev's idea of a "Common
European home" also had its roots in Nikita Khrushchev's efforts to bring Soviet
Russia closer to Europe. Khrushchev saw Russia as culturally close to Europe,
and at one point, he even proposed the mutual disbandment of NATO and the
Warsaw Pact. New Thinking also initially appealed to at least some supporters
of a strong state, who understood the necessity to respond to Western military
pressures by reducing diplomatic tensions and moving in the direction of new
detente. Finally, Gorbachev's vision was that of a missionary, and he engaged
with some of those members of the intellectual and political class. The latter

wanted to capitalize on "socialist values" and lead the world to a socially egalitarian future. The leader of Perestroika traced his origins to the late Lenin's
notion of co-existence with capitalism, and he kept emphasizing that his project
was a development, not an abandonment, of socialism. As romantic as it was, the
vision had global ambitions and even elements of moral messianism.

The above-described vision left little room for the national interest as pursued
independently from the interests of other members of a global society. Gorbachev
did not expect the Soviet Union or any other nations to give up what they
perceived to be in their interests. Yet he called to acknowledge the futility of
narrowly viewed national gains and to develop a globally integrated approach
based on mutual responsibility and "balance of interests." Practically speaking,
he proposed compromises and multilateral negotiations to implement the new
vision.

For the Soviet Union, New Thinking implied the necessity to formulate its
national interest and foreign policy objectives in a way that would be respectful
to world opinion and non-threatening toward others. In particular, Gorbachev
proposed to rethink the nature of capitalism. The old ideological vision assumed
that the Soviet Union had to contain the influence of world capitalism because, at
its highest stage of development, imperialism, capitalism resulted from expansion
and war. Without stopping imperialism, the Soviet Union would be destroyed.
As Josef Stalin said in a slightly different context, "either we do it, or we shall
be crushed" (Sakwa 1999, 188). The Gorbachev vision posited something very
different. In February 1988, he criticized the very notion of imperialism as no
longer accurate. He argued that capitalism had developed domestic democratic
mechanisms of resisting expansion and war and was, therefore, self-containing.

Such criticism had its roots in the Soviet postwar debates. In the late 1940s,
Yevgeni Varga, director of the Moscow Institute of World Economy and World
Politics, began arguing that postwar capitalism could regulate its contradictions
and had relatively stabilized. After Stalin's death, those emphasizing the depth of
imperialist contradictions and the inevitability of the capitalist decline gathered
around the editor-in-chief of *Kommunist* and member of the Central Committee
of the Communist Party Richard Kosolapov (1975, 1979). Opposition to this
hardline view came from the Institute of World Economy and International
Relations.[16] Siding with supporters of the anti-imperialism view of capitalism
allowed Gorbachev to present the notion of military sufficiency in an entirely
different light and to call for a reevaluation of Soviet defense expenditures. It
provided the basis for terminating the arms race in which the Soviet Union had
been previously heavily involved. Clarifying the new approach, foreign minister
Eduard Shevardnadze argued that attempts to reach military parity with all the
potential enemies was, in fact, against Soviet national interest (Sestanovich 1990).

The introduction of the notion of "national interest" was partly strategic and
designed to preempt the possible critique that New Thinking was nothing but
a series of concessions to capitalism. Multiple withdrawals from Eastern Europe
and the Third World, as well as proposals to eliminate entire classes of nuclear

missiles, could now be presented as part of a long-term strategy. For example, the "loss" of Eastern Europe after the 1989 fall of the Berlin Wall could now be presented as a net "gain" in a general calculus of creating a favorable international environment. In February 1990, Shevardnadze insisted that "our national, as well as historical and everyday interest, is that our neighbors are stable and prosperous. We will only benefit from this" (Ibid., 10).

Despite Gorbachev's efforts to be a consensus-builder, opponents soon attacked his New Thinking from two different directions. Conservative forces charged that Gorbachev was "selling out" the Soviet interests to the West, whereas liberals saw him as indecisive in abandoning the "outdated" Soviet outlook. Revolutionary changes in the country further polarized foreign policy formation, making it impossible to sustain the originally devised plan with an appeal to all leading social groups. The original coalition of New Thinkers was reasonably broad, representing the industrial, military, Party, and academic establishment. Over time, however, that coalition began to fall apart, and the struggle of ideas around New Thinking suggested in which directions some future social and politico-economic groups were to emerge. In sum, progressive ideas cannot succeed without sufficient power. For success, they must also be able to shape the state to achieve their agenda.

Communists after the Soviet System

After the collapse of the Soviet system, the controversy between isolationist and global ideas on the left did not end. However, this controversy deepened in the context of the growing political polarization in Russia in the 1990s and the globalization policy pursued by Western states. Russia's theoretical discourse became fragmented, losing its national coherence. In Soviet times, isolationists and globalists still found some common ground, often working in the same departments and agreeing, for example, on the importance of developing ties with foreign parties and movements to strengthen the USSR. In post-Soviet times, "Stalinists" and "Trotskyists" had nothing in common, moving in opposite ideological and political directions.

The "Stalinists," who partly reproduced Herzen's idea of national salvation in isolation from European civilization, continued the movement towards nationalism and the geopolitics of opposing the West. The program of the left nationalism resembled conservative Soviet ideas, which were of little use for the new conditions. As for the Trotskyists, who traditionally stressed the importance of the international revolution, they responded to the defeat of the old communist idea by searching for a new subject in the global revolutionary process. At the end of the 1990s, such a subject was found in many respects in various informal movements advocating fair and socially responsible globalization, and not a rejection of it. Unlike the left nationalists, the left cosmopolitans accepted many European values (democracy, human rights), insisting that the Russian egalitarian idea should develop on their basis.

New Fortresses: Shielding Russia from Global Capitalism

In the first decade after the collapse of the Soviet Union, "Stalinist" thinking was represented primarily by those who were ideologically and politically close to the Communist Party of the Russian Federation (KPRF). Under their pen, Russia appeared economically, socially, and culturally self-sufficient as it was forced to survive in a hostile world (Zyuganov 1999, 2002; 2011). Many of the "Stalinist" themes and arguments resemble those of new Slavophiles. Fear of the West and its global aspirations became a central theme in the neo-Slavophile and the "Stalinist" discourse. In line with the traditional Bolshevik phobias of the world of capitalism, the neo-Stalinists demonstrated their conviction in the deep crisis of Western civilization, seeing in it considerable opportunities for Russia. Referring to the prophecies of the left-wing American sociologist Immanuel Wallerstein about the coming collapse of the Anglo-Saxon world order and the modern era itself, left-wing nationalists believed that "the greatest success will accompany those countries whose policies are characterized by the greatest firmness, rigidity, perseverance, and consistency."[17]

However, for the "Stalinists," the West had become not only an exploitative system of capitalism that suppresses the aspirations of the working people but also a civilization hostile to the very way of life in Russia.

Pointing to the significance of the cultural and civilizational features of Russia, the "Stalinists" brought it to a new level of existential opposition to the West, viewing its ethnic-geographical differences as a constant source of a threat to Russian culture and way of life. Such is the nature of traditional geopolitical thinking that it does not distinguish between the concepts of "difference" and "threat."

Such thinking assesses relations between Russian and Western cultures as a zero-sum game. The choice for Russia, therefore, is between becoming an independent Eurasian power and a de facto colony of the West.

The "Stalinists" extensively borrowed from Russian and Western geopolitical and late Slavophile theories. The influence of the Eurasian ideas associated with the names of Pyotr Savitsky, Nikolai Trubetskoy, and Lev Gumilyov was evident and significant. Gumilyov viewed Russia as an independent Eurasian civilization, capable of survival only by protecting itself from the "harmful" influences of the West.[18] Following the Pan-Slavist Nikolai Danilevsky, the "Stalinists" also announced that it was precisely the depth of civilizational differences that was responsible for "the fundamental alienation of Europe from Russia" (Zyuganov 1999, 13; Nartov 2000, 95; Zyuganov 2011).[19] Based on the views of Konstantin Leontyev, they further proclaimed the uniqueness of the ethnic composition of Russia and its geopolitical mission of pacifying the Eurasian region. Western theorists of the coming conflict of civilizations – Samuel Huntington and others – also made their contribution by strengthening the "Stalinist" presentation of Russia as a civilization with aspirations radically opposing those of the West.[20]

According to the new "Stalinists," only Russia could guarantee stability and balance to the world; without it, the world would most likely become a hostage to the predatory instincts of the West. Russia, therefore, must restore its self-sufficiency and imperial structure while offering the world an attractive global development model. As a great Eurasian power, Russia should build strategic alliances with non-European states to resist the West and strengthen Russian self-sufficiency. By drawing lessons from Russian history, the "Stalinists" pointed to the existence of mechanisms of reproducing the Russia-Eurasia from the Russian empire to the Stalinist USSR and the post-Soviet Eurasian empire (Zyuganov 1999, 130–131; Fursov 2001, 2010). Hoping for the West's decline and the US withdrawal from the Eurasian region, the "Stalinists" advocated the revival of a self-sufficient Russia-Eurasia. They saw Russia's future in restoring a geopolitically stable "union" in the space of the former USSR in partnership with China, India, Iran, and other non-Western countries (*Russkaya doktrina* 2007, 313). For example, for the KPRF leader Gennady Zyuganov (1999) and his supporters, the Soviet Union was a "natural" geopolitical form of "historic" Russia, while the country's new political borders were artificial and imposed by the West as a result of organized subversion.

Creative Learning from and Bridges to Globalization

Despite the collapse of the Soviet Union and the end of attempts to reform it, reformist socialism has survived in Russia as a tradition of thought. Both Western leftist theories and the practice of neo-liberal globalization have served as stimuli for Russian intellectual development. For many Russian theorists of global processes, taking advantage of the fruits of globalization while avoiding its blows and defeats is extremely difficult. It will require significant political, social, and intellectual mobilization. Globalization turned out to be far from harmonious and peaceful, creating new socio-economic and political divisions in the world. Security vacuums and violence spread across various regions, including the Middle East, Eurasia, and Europe. The Russian left is busy searching for a new alternative to global capitalism, in the absence of which a new wave of wars and conflicts awaits humanity (Kosolapov 2005, 2016; Kagarlitsky 2018).

One school of left thought is close to the ideas of Gorbachev, considering globalization as an objective process but in need of correction. This group of thinkers proceeds from the premise that it is impossible to reverse globalization. However, it is possible and necessary to make globalization more suitable and convenient for life, going beyond its narrow group interpretations and reformulating it in the interests of broad social strata and peoples, including Russia. Among Russian researchers of globalization, there has been an increased interest in the world-systems approach associated in the West with the name of Immanuel Wallerstein. Researchers in this group view the world-systems analysis as continuing with the Marxist tradition of "global thinking" and analyzing problems of the environment, population, and the arms race as requiring global solutions.

As we said earlier, this tradition associated with Zagladin and others greatly influenced Gorbachev's "new political thinking" (Gorbachev 2003; Ilyin 2005; Kosolapov 2016).

For example, the above-discussed Zagladin worked in the Gorbachev Foundation in the last years of his life, continuing with his studies of global problems and the possibilities of reforming socialism in the world. In the sphere of his interests a new civilization was forming, capable of overcoming the danger of humanity slipping into an emerging crisis, forming a greater Europe, and analyzing Russian national interests after the end of the Cold War. Unlike some of his colleagues, who quickly became supporters of liberal capitalism, Zagladin remained loyal to his socialist convictions. For example, speaking in 2002 at the event in memory of Ivan Frolov and delivering the talk "Globalization: World Order or World Disorder," Zagladin dissociated himself from theories linking world instability with globalization. Instead, he connected the emergence of new wars and the aggravation of human problems with the capitalist system, which did not live up to expectations. He viewed globalization as an objective process associated with "the stage of formation of a single material and spiritual being of the world human community" (Shul'man 2003, 72–80).

Leftist thought may yet experience revival because of the end of the monopoly of Soviet Marxism. Marxist and critical thinking have ontological and epistemological merits. First, Marxist thinking about the world has traditionally been critically reflexive and socially liberating. Secondly, the historically and structurally sensitive Marxist approaches are well-positioned to analyze the phenomena of global exploitation and social inequality and to reveal their social origins. Finally, Marxist analysis is often genuinely global in coverage, simultaneously viewing the world as unified and fragmented. In contrast to the three levels of analysis that dominate the IR theory – the individual, the state, and the international system – Marxism assumes that the struggle for human liberation is universal and limitless. All these features continue to contribute to developing the critical tradition in the IR theory, both in the former Soviet Russia and outside it.[21]

In the contemporary world, the leftist class analysis serves as a methodological basis for researching global processes (Ilyin and Inozemtsev 2001; Volodin and Shirokov 2002; Gorbachev 2003; Kosolapov 2016). Scholars have studied the degree and nature of the dependence of Russia and several other states on the centers of world capitalism and the possibility of preserving sovereignty for the implementation of nationally oriented reforms. National economic reforms can only succeed with a clear answer to this question. A class-based analysis can also offer a logically appealing explanation of Russia's flawed post-Soviet development. According to such an explanation, the USSR failed to sustain competition with the forces of world capitalism and the Western ideology of neoliberal economic development. These forces are responsible for destroying the Soviet middle class and the emergence of the type of Russian bourgeoisie with a mighty comprador group of raw material exporters. The merger of this

class with the state officials during the Yeltsin era assisted in the initial accumu-
lation of capital, clearing the way for young and aggressive big business while at
the same time integrating the country into the world economy on unequal terms
(Kagarlitsky 2003, 2018). Awareness and understanding of the new class divisions
after the end of the Cold War is an essential part of understanding the processes
of globalization.

Along with studying socio-economic processes, the global and social reformist
school also analyzes contemporary international socio-cultural and geopolitical
developments. Russian leftist thought today builds not only on Bukharin and
traditional Marxist thought but also on Russian and Western scholars of geopolitics and civilizations. This school's members assess knowledge of these processes
as essential for understanding the complexity and interconnectedness of relations
between the values and interests of the earth's inhabitants. In particular, the
foundation patronized by Gorbachev has for many years been concerned with
understanding the cultural diversity of the modern world (Gorbachev 2003;
Zdravomyslova 2015).

Indeed, Western-centric world-order projects often lack an understanding
of other cultures.[22] Socio-cultural divisions have accompanied globalization.
Contrary to the views of some Russian Westernizers, globalization does not
eliminate geopolitics but merely puts countries and regions in new geopolitical
conditions by creating new cultural and spatial boundaries. For example, the
Russian researcher Kamaludin Gadzhiyev (2000, 2007) wrote about the economic, cultural, civilizational, and informational dimensions of geopolitics,
arguing for stabilizing the international system through cooperative and collective security arrangements.

Transforming global Capitalism

The logic of neo-Trotskyist thinking after Soviet disintegration has differed from
"Stalinists" and advocates of reforming neoliberal globalization. Unlike the left
nationalists, the "Trotskyists," as before, remained convinced of the impossibility of breaking out of the Western capitalist system without revolutionary
support from outside. They also disagree with the supporters of the view that
globalization must be reformed but remains an "objective" process, that is, not
subject to fundamental revision (Gorbachev 2003). In contrast to the latter view,
the "Trotskyists" support transformation, not the reform of globalization. In
their opinion, what needs changing is not national policies but the world system
of capitalism itself. Such a system cannot be reformed because it is built on the
principles of exploitation of the periphery by the center.

A representative of the neo-Trotskyist trend, Boris Kagarlitsky demonstrated
in several of his books (2003, 2010) how capitalism arose and formed into a
"world system" in which the states of the center force the peripheral economies
to market relations. In this political and economic system, Russia managed to
secure the status of a "peripheral empire," claiming independence only within

limitations formed by the "world system." As a "semi-periphery," Russia has long been exploited by the center. The Western capitalist center exploited Russia through various types of non-equivalent exchange identified and studied by scholars such as Immanuel Wallerstein, Samir Amin, and Andre Gunder Frank. Never excluded from the capitalist world system, Russia has been its essential element and developed following global capitalist cycles. Following the Soviet disintegration, the non-equivalent exchange continued to operate and grow in Russia. As the countries of the former communist bloc were further drawn into the world system, the Western center of global capitalism controlled them through mechanisms of external debt by successfully redistributing capital in its favor. "Enormous money was transferred to Western currency, mainly to the US dollars, and taken out of the country" (Kagarlitsky 2003, 28). Therefore, even while experiencing a large-scale crisis during the 1990s, Russia served as an essential financial "donor" of the world economy.

What about Russia's alternatives in this world of global exploitation? According to the Trotskyist-Leninist school, the nature of the capitalist system and Russia's status as a semi-periphery in it require a transformation of the exploitative system as a whole of relations. There can be no success of socialism in a single country: "In the 21st century, Russia, like all mankind, has only one way out: to change the world system … [W]e are capable of fighting for a better future for ourselves, only trying to build a better world for all" (Ibid., 522).[23] Like the theorists of the world revolution, modern "Trotskyists" remain convinced that destruction of global capitalism must begin with revolutionary processes within its center. Therefore, Russia must prepare for a new global crisis and act, not in isolation, but with the forces of international opposition to the world capitalist system. Instead of trying to adapt to "objective" globalization, Russia must fight for its revolutionary reorganization.

Conclusion

Overall, the differences within Russian Communism result from their understanding of the relationship between changes within the country and outside. The disagreement began with the answer to the question: Should we fight for a better future for ourselves, showing the way to the rest of humanity, or creating a better world for everyone, ultimately helping ourselves? Both nationalists and internationalists have believed in Russia's unique mission, defined by Chaadayev (1991, 150) as the ability to "answer the most important questions that occupy humanity."

Nationalists stressed Russia's unique conditions – a country that remained outside European civilization (Herzen) or only "scratched by civilization" (Mikhailovsky) or was under capitalist encirclement (Stalin). They viewed these conditions as positioning Russia not to repeat Europe's problems and offer a new path of development. In practice, as the Soviet experience showed, such a path translated into the establishment of a powerful nationalist state exploitative of Russia's own human and material resources.

Internationalists recognized Russia's special conditions but stressed the larger context of its remaining dependence on Western global capitalism to advocate its transformation. They presented Russia as a weak link in the chain of imperialism (Lenin and Trotsky) or a semi-peripheral empire (Kagarlitsky), arguing the impossibility of successful independent development. To this group, Russia's unique mission is to be the first to break out of the global capitalist system and initiate the process of building a better system jointly with others. Judging by the Bolshevik Revolution's results, this school of thought proposed some progressive social ideas, but it too failed to solve the country's economic and social problems.

Finally, the third group within Russian Communism included those who, like Bukharin, Zagladin, and Gorbachev, were convinced that global change required recognition of objective economic and technological processes. Therefore, the change does not have to mean the destruction of capitalism or socialism but must result from their mutual learning and convergence. Russia's unique role here is to demonstrate its abilities and accomplishments and stimulate dialogue between different systems. Gorbachev's attempts to act on these ideas were not successful, in part due to the attractiveness of Western capitalism. It is still unknown whether this path of dialogue will have the opportunity to prove that it leads to global justice, democracy, and freedom from exploitation.

Notes

1 Even after almost twenty years, he defined philistinism as "the final form of Western civilization, is coming of age" (Ibid., 95).
2 Populists, or *Narodniki* in Russian, formed the nineteenth-century movement for changing Russia based on unique relations with the peasantry.
3 Parvus is often considered the first to transfer Marx's ideas of permanent revolution to Russian soil. With the outbreak of the Russo-Japanese War, he linked international and domestic conditions, predicting Russia's defeat and revolution.
4 Marx, however, did not view his theory of capitalist development as necessarily applicable to Russia. In his correspondence with Russian populists, he even acknowledged the possibility of Russia's socialist development based on a peasant community, believing, however, that for this a "proletarian revolution in the West" would have to take place (Anikin 1990, 383).
5 For example, see Lenin was critical of Mikhailovsky in books, "What are the friends of the people and how they fight against the Social Democrats," and "The Development of Capitalism in Russia."
6 The General Secretary of the Central Committee of the CPSU, Yury V. Andropov, stated in 1983: "We do not know the society in which we live," testifying that social scientists did not raise important questions about the country's development.
7 Only in special departments of the largest libraries in Moscow, which were closed to the general public, scholars had the opportunity to gain access to literature containing criticism of official Marxism-Leninism. To get such access, it was necessary not only to be a member of the Communist Party, but also to have permission from the "first department," which was responsible for the security of the state.

8 Khrushchev considered Russia culturally and politically close to Europe. In one of his speeches, he put forward a proposal for the mutual dissolution of NATO and the Warsaw Pact, with the simultaneous withdrawal of US military forces from Western European countries (Donaldson and Nogee 1998, 69).

9 For other works by Zagladin on the labor and socialist movement, see his 1970, 1975, 1982, 1987.

10 On this issue, Zagladin defended his position in arguments with more conservative opponents, who referred to Marx's statement that international relations are secondary and derived from social and economic ones. Among Zagladin's allies were representatives of several academic institutions, notably the Institute of World Economy and International Relations headed by Alexander Yakovlev (Yakovlev 1987). Later, during the years of Perestroika, this position became generally accepted.

11 Subsequently, in his stories about the past, Zagladin said that Brezhnev understood the danger of Stalin's rehabilitation and skillfully maneuvered between the Stalinists and the supporters of continued de-Stalinization, preventing the former from gaining the upper hand over the latter (Kolesnikov 2006a).

12 Even before coming to power, Gorbachev's team was influenced by ideas about the growing interdependence of the world. Gorbachev learned about these through Georgy Shakhnazarov, his future adviser. They first met in the early 1980s and had a lengthy conversation about the foundations of the new world order as described by Shakhnazarov (1981) in his unorthodox work (Shakhnazarov 2000, 277–282).

13 Zagladin later admitted to the weakness of his communist convictions: "If we talk specifically about the people who worked there (in the Central Committee), then they had a different degree of cynicism, a different degree of belief in this ultimate goal (building communism). I belonged to people who never believed that communism was possible. Nevertheless, life assigned me to this service, and I served conscientiously and honestly Also, work in the Central Committee was really interesting" (Kolesnikov 2006a). However, Zagladin was hardly in the category of complete cynics. Meeting with one of his acquaintances in 2004, Zagladin summed up the past and present in the following words: "I am very offended by what happened in the past, and I am ashamed of what is happening now" (Ibid.).

14 This section draws on parts of chapter 2 of my *Russia's Foreign Policy.*

15 On Gorbachev as a thinker who sought to improve the Soviet Union's world status through an innovative strategy of engaging the West, see Larson and Shevchenko 2003.

16 For a detailed analysis of debates between Old and New Thinkers, see English 2000.

17 Some left nationalists participated in a manifesto with other nationalist writers (*Russkaya doktrina* 2007, 11).

18 The next chapter considers Gumilyev's views in greater details.

19 It is ironic that the new "Stalinists" are often preoccupied not with socio-economic, but military-strategic issues. For instance, Zyuganov (1999, 13–21) lists military-strategic thinking as one of the three foundations of geopolitics, along with civilizational approaches and geographic determinism. His "three sources of geopolitics" are reminiscent of Lenin's "three sources and three components of Marxism." Zyuganov undoubtedly read the latter in the Soviet Party school. In his view, geopolitics has become what Marxism-Leninism was yesterday - "genuinely scientific" knowledge designed to prepare Russia for confrontation with the West.

20 According to Zyuganov (1999, 14), Huntington "proves quite convincingly that in the coming century, the main source of conflicts will not be economics or ideology, but civilizational differences." For the relations between Western geopolitical and Russian left-nationalist theories, see Tsygankov 2004.

21 The critical tradition in Western TMT continues to evolve (Rupert and Smith 2002, 2016; Briggs 2019).

22 According to some scholars, such projects contribute not to the promotion of the dialogue necessary for the formation of a new international system but to the further growth of isolationism and distrust between the subjects of world politics (Alker, Amin, Biersteker, and Inoguchi 1998; Inayatullah and Blaney 2004; Tickner and Blaney 2012; Colgan 2019).

23 In an afterword to the texts of the late Trotsky, Kagarlitsky concludes (2007, 607) by a call "for optimism" because "the predictions made by the Mexican exile came true," including concerning the capitalist counter-revolution in the USSR.

Further Reading

Alexander Hertzen, Populists, and Anarchists

Anikin, A. V. 1991. *Социально-экономические идеи в России до марксизма*. Москва: Мысль.

Bakunin, M. A. 1990. *Statism and Anarchy*. Revised ed. Cambridge University Press.

Billington, J. 1958. *Mikhailovsky and Russian Populism*. Oxford University Press.

Bykova, M. F., M. N. Forster, and L. Steiner, eds. 2021. *The Palgrave Handbook of Russian Thought*. London: Palgrave.

Herzen, A. I. 1979. *From the Other Shore* and *The Russian People and Socialism*. Oxford University Press.

Malia, M. 1965. *Alexander Herzen and the Birth of Russian Socialism*. New York: Grosset & Dunlap.

Pantin, I., L. Plimak, V. Khoros. 1986. *Революционная традиция в России*. Москва: Мысль.

Walicki, A. 1979. *A History of Russian Thought from Enlightenment to Marxism*. Stanford University Press.

Social Democrats and Bolsheviks

Agurski M. 1987. *The Third Rome: National Bolshevism in the USSR*. Boulder, CO.

Berdyayev, N. A. 1990. *Истоки и смысл русского коммунизма*. Москва: Наука.

Brewer, T. 1990. *Marxist Theories of Imperialism*. 2nd ed. London: Routledge.

Bykova, Marina. 2021. Lenin and His Controversy over Philosophy. In: *The Palgrave Handbook of Russian Thought*, edited by M. F. Bykova, M. N. Forster, and L. Steiner. London: Palgrave.

Cohen, Stephen. 1980. *Bukharin and the Bolshevik Revolution*. Oxford University Press.

Kagarlitsky, B. 2003. *Периферийная империя: Россия и миросистема*. Москва.

Kolakowski L. 1978. *Main Currents of Marxism*. 3 Vol. New York: Oxford University Press.

Lenin, V. 2021. *Imperialism: The Highest Stage of Capitalism*. Leftist Public Domain Project.

Plekhanov, V. 1990. *Fundamental Problems of Marxism*. 2nd Revised edition. Intl Pub Co.

Soboleva, Maja. 2021. Russian Marxism and Its Philosophy. In: *The Palgrave Handbook of Russian Thought*, edited by M. F. Bykova, M. N. Forster, and L. Steiner. London: Palgrave.

Late Soviet and Post-Soviet Communists

Fursov, A. I. 1996. *Колокола истории*. Москва: Инион.

Gorbachev, M. S. 1988. *Перестройка для нашей страны и для всего мира*. Москва: Политиздат.

Gorbachev, M. S., ed. 2003. *Грани глобализации*. Москва: Альпина.

Guseynov, A. A. 2021. The "Men of the Sixties": Philosophy as a Social Phenomenon. In: *The Palgrave Handbook of Russian Thought*, edited by M. F. Bykova, M. N. Forster, and L. Steiner. London: Palgrave.

Platonov, S. 1989. *После коммунизма*. Москва: Молодая гвардия.

Yeliseyev, A. 2007. *Социализм с русским лицом*. Москва: Арктогея.

Zyuganov, G. 2011. *Global'noye poraboshcheniye Rossiyi, ili globalizatsiya po-amerikanski*. Moscow: Eksmo.

References

Alker H. R., T. Amin, T. Biersteker, and T. Inoguchi. 1998. How Should We Theorize Contemporary Macro-Encounters: In Terms of Superstates, World Orders, or Civilizations? *Paper presented at the Third Pan-European International Relations Conference, SGIR-ISA*, Vienna, Austria, September 16–19.

Anikin, A. V. 1990. *Социально-экономические идеи в России до марксизма*. Москва: Политиздат.

Arab-Ogly, Eduard. 1986. *Обозримое будущее*. Москва: Политиздат.

Arbatov, Georgy A. 1991. *Затянувшееся выздоровление (1955–1985): свидетельство современника*. Москва: Мысль.

Barsenkov A. С., Vdovin A. И. 2010. *История России, 1917–2009*. Третье издание. Москва: Аспект Пресс.

Berlin, Isaiah. 1955. Herzen and Bakunin on Individual Liberty. In: *Continuity and Change in Russian and Soviet Thought*, edited by Ernest J. Simmons. Cambridge University Press.

Briggs, William. 2019. *Classical Marxism in an Age of Capitalist Crisis: The Past is Prologue*. London: Routledge.

Brooks, Stephen G., and William C. Wohlforth, "Power, Globalization, and the End of the Cold War: Reevaluating a Landmark Case for Ideas," *International Security* 25, 3, Winter 2000/01.

Bukharin, Nikolai I. 1925. О новой экономической политике и наших задачах. Доклад на собрании актива Московской организации 17 апреля. http://magister. msk.ru/library/politica/buharin/buhan008.htm.

Chaadayev, Pyotr Ya. 1991. Философические письма. In: *Россия глазами русского*, под ред. А. Ф. Замалеева. Санкт-Петербург: Letniy Sad.

Colgan, Jeffrey D. 2019. American Perspectives and Blind Spots on World Politics. *Journal of Global Security Studies* 4, 3.

Donaldson, Robert H. and Joseph L. Nogee. 1998. *The Foreign Policy of Russia*. Armonk, NY: M. E. Sharpe.

English, Robert D. 2000. *Russia and the Idea of the West. Gorbachev, Intellectuals, and the End of the Cold War*. New York: Columbia University Press.

Fursov, Andrei I. 2001. Русская власть, Россия и Евразия в больльших циклах истории. In: *Русский исторический журнал*, Том IV, № 1–4 www.zlev.ru/125/125_11.htm.

———. 2010. *Novaya oprichnina ili modernizatsiya po-russki*. Moscow. http://project03.ru/ PR/no.php#PART0.

Gadzhiyev, Kamaludin. 2000. *Введение в геополитику*. Москва: Логос.

———. 2007. *Геополитические горизонты России: контуры нового мирового порядка*. Москва: Экономика.

Gorbachev, Mikhail. 1987. *Perestroika: New Thinking for Our Country and the World.* New York: Harper & Row.

———, ed. 2003. *Grani globalizatsiyi.* Moscow: Alpina.

Gridchin, Yuri V. 1991. Этика человечности. In: Кропоткин П. А. *Этика: Избранные труды.* Москва.

Herman, Robert G. 1996. Identity, Norms, and National Security: The Soviet Foreign Policy Revolution and the End of Cold War. In: *The Culture of National Security,* edited by Peter J. Katzenstein. New York: Columbia University Press.

Hough, Jeffrey F. 1986. *The Struggle for the Third World: Soviet Debates and American Options.* Washington, DC: The Brookings Institute.

Ilyin, Mikhail V. 2005. Вопросы глобализации и равенства в российской политологии. In: *Российская наука международных отношений: новые направления,* под ред. А. П. Цыганкова и П. А. Цыганкова. Москва: Per Se.

Ilyin, Mikhail V., Vladislav L. Inozemstsev, eds. 2001. *Мегатренды мирового развития.* Москва.

Inayatullah, Naeem and David L. Blaney. 2004. *International Relations and the Problem of Difference.* London: Routledge.

Kagarlitsky, Boris. 2003. *Periferiynaya imperiya.* Moscow: Kul'tura.

———. 2007. Пророчества великого «неудачника». In: *Антология позднего Троцкого.* Москва.

———. 2010. *От империй — к империализму. Государство и возникновение буржуазной цивилизации.* Москва.

———. 2018. Marxism in the Post-Globalization Era. *Russia in Global Affairs,* March 20.

Kolesnikov, Andrei. 2006a. Слово и Дело Вадима Загладина. *VIPerson,* 21 ноября www.viperson.ru/wind.php?ID=265305&soch=1).

———. 2006b. Спичрайтеры. *Российская газета,* 21 декабря

Kosolapov, Nikolai A. 2005. Rossiya i novyi miroporyadok v otsutstviye levoi alternativy. In: *Rossiyaskaya nauka mezhdunarodnykh otnosheniy,* edited by A. P. Tsygankov and P. A. Tsygankov. Moscow: Per se.

———. 2016. Obshchesistemnyye interesy vmesto natsionalnykh. *Russia in Global Affairs,* March 6.

Kosolapov, Richard. 1975. *Socialism and International Relations.* Moscow: Politizdat.

———. 1979. *Socialism: Questions of Theory.* Moscow: Politizdat.

———. 1995. «Оставь, старина, старые грабли!» *Независимая газета,* 26 декабря.

Kropotkin, Pyotr. 1990. *Этика.* Moscow.

Kubalkova Vendulka and A. A. Cruickshank. 1985. *Marxism and International Relations.* Oxford University Press.

Larson, Deborah Welch and Alexei Shevchenko. 2003. Shortcut to Greatness: The New Thinking and the Revolution in Soviet Foreign Policy. *International Organization* 57, Winter.

Leibin, Valery. 1982. *«Модели мира» и образ человека.* Москва: Мысль.

Lenin, Vladimir I. 1916. *Империализм как высшая стадия капитализма.* Петроград www.gumer.info/bibliotek_Buks/Polit/Article/len_imper.php

———. 1967. Предисловие в французскому и немецкому изданию «Империализма». Ленин В. И. *Избранные произведения в трех томах.* Москва: Политиздат.

———. 1966. Что такое друзья народа и как они воюют против социал-демократов. В: *Избранные произведения в трех томах.* Москва: Политиздат.

———. 1966. Развитие капитализма в России. В: *Избранные произведения в трех томах.* Москва: Политиздат.

Light, Margo. 1988. *Marxism and Soviet International Relations*. London.

Lynch, Allen. 1987. *The Soviet Study of International Relations*. Cambridge University Press.

Marx, Karl. 1848. *Manifesto of the Communist Party* www.marxists.org/archive/marx/works/1848/communist-manifesto/index.htm

Nartov, Nikolai A. 2000. Геополитика. Москва.

Novikova, Lidiya and Irina Sizemskaya. 1997. *Русская философия истории*. Москва: Магистр.

Rupert, Mark and H. Smith, eds. 2002. *Historical Materialism and Globalization: Essays on Continuity and Change*. London: Routledge.

———. 2016. *Historical Materialism and Globalisation: Essays on Continuity and Change*. 2nd edition. London: Routledge.

Russkaya doktrina. 2007. Москва.

Sakwa, Richard. 1999. *The Rise and Fall of the Soviet Union, 1917–1991*. London: Routledge.

Sestanovich, Stephen. 1990. The Invention of Soviet National Interest. *National Interest* 20.

Shakhnazarov, Georgy. 1981. *Грядущий миропорядок*. Москва: Мысль.

———. 2001. *С вождями и без них*. Москва: Вагриус.

Shenfield Steven. 1987. *The Nuclear Predicament: Explorations in Soviet Ideology*. London: Routledge.

Shul'man, Olga I. 2003. Мера всех наук. Философия глобальных проблем. *Человек*, № 8.

Simoniya, Nodar A, ed. 1990. *СССР в мировом сообществе: от старого мышления к новому*. Москва: Прогресс.

Stalin, Iosif V. 2002. *Слово товарищу Сталину*. Составитель Р. Косолапов. Москва.

Sushenstov, Andrey A. and William C. Wohlforth. 2020. The tragedy of US–Russian relations: NATO centrality and the revisionists' spiral. *International Politics*.

Tickner, Arlene B. and David L. Blaney. 2012. *Thinking International Relations Differently*. London: Routledge.

Tolz, Victor. 2006. Понять перестройку. *Свобода*, 29 мая www.svobodanews.ru/content/Transcript/159253.html

Trotsky, Lev. 1930. *Перманентная революция*. Москва www.marxists.org/russkij/trotsky/1930/perm-rev/index.htm.

Tsygankov, Andrei P. 2004. *Whose World Order? Russia's Perception of American Ideas after the Cold War*. Notre Dame University Press.

Tsygankov, Andrei P. 2022. *Russia's Foreign Policy*. 6th ed. Lanham: Rowman & Littlefield.

Tucker, Robert C. 1973. *Stalin as a Revolutionary, 1879–1929: A Study in History and Personality*. New York: Norton.

Volodin, Aleksei and G. Shirokov. 2002. *Глобализация: начало, тенденции, перспективы*. Москва: Экономика.

Walicki, Andrzej. 1979. *A History of Russian Thought from the Enlightenment to Marxism*. Stanford University Press.

Wohlforth William C. 1993. *The Elusive Balance: Power and Perceptions During the Cold War*. Ithaca, NY: Cornell University Press.

Yakovlev, Aleksandr, ed. 1987. *Капитализм на исходе столетия*. Москва: Политиздат.

Yeliseyev, Aleksandr. 2007. *Социализм с русским лицом*. Москва.

Zagladin, Nikita V. 1990. *История успехов и неудач советской дипломатии*. Москва: Международные отношения.

Zagladin, Vadim V. 1955. *Борьба французского народа за мир и национальную независимость*, Москва.

———. 1970. *Закономерности рабочего движения и борьба за социализм*. Москва.

———. 1975. *Предпосылки социализма и борьба за социализм*. Москва.

———. 1982. *За права трудящихся, за мир и безопасность народов. Коммунистический авангард рабочего движения в начале 80-х годов.* Москва.

———. 1984. Марксизм-ленинизм о роли рабочего класса и международных отношениях. *Рабочий класс и современный мир*, № 4.

———. 1987. *Интернациональный характер Великой Октябрьской социалистической революции.* Москва.

Zagladin, Vadim V. and Ivan Frolov. 1981. *Глобальные проблемы современности: научный и социальный аспекты.* Москва.

Zdravomyslova, Ol'ga. 2015. Горбачевские чтения. Вып. 10. ВРЕМЯ ПЕРЕМЕН: ИДЕИ И ЛЮДИ. 1968–1988–2008. Moscow: Gorbachev-Fond.

Zhaba. 1954. *Русские мыслители о России и человечестве.* Paris: Imca-Press.

Zimmerman, William. 1969. *Soviet Perspectives on International Relations, 1956–67.* Princeton University Press.

Zubok, Vladislav M. 2009. *Zhivago's Children: The Last Russian Intelligentsia.* Cambridge University Press.

Zyuganov, Gennady. 1999. *География победы.* Москва.

———. 2002. *Globalizatsiya i sud'ba chelovechestva.* Moscow: Molodaya gvardiya.

———. 2011. *Global'noye poraboshcheniye Rossiyi, ili globalizatsiya po-amerikanski.* Moscow: Eksmo.

5

EURASIANISTS

Russia is "an exceptional, specific culture, which has no less intrinsic value and no less historical significance than European and Asian cultures."

Yevraziystvo (2002, 130)

Russia "opposes all local and provincially limited civilizations [and has] all the reasons to claim the role of the genuinely global world."

Malyavin (2022)

Relative to Slavophiles and Communists, the Eurasianist thinkers are preoccupied with geopolitical processes and the importance of preserving national independence from the encroachment of foreign powers – mainly Western. Eurasianism, again, appears relevant in Russia. The concepts central to Eurasianist thought, such as cultural "independence," "space for development" (*mestorazvitiye*), and a strong state, are again in demand today. Russian geographers, philosophers, and linguists associated with the Eurasianist movement are again calling for appreciation of the importance of geopolitics in stabilizing and developing the complex continent.

Scholars of Eurasianism often emphasize Russia's preoccupation with empire and security from perceived threats posed by the West and its geopolitical ambitions (Laruelle 2008; LeDonne 2020). However, like Slavophiles and Communists, Eurasianists are a diverse group. Not all of them focus on Russia's geopolitical expansion and confronting the West. Some Eurasianists are predominantly interested in regional stability and economic prosperity, viewing the notion of imperial autarchy as outdated and unable to address complex national interests. They believe Russia's unique role in the world must result from its particular geographic position and the ability to unite Slavic and Turkish people. In addition, not all Eurasianists are radically anti-European. Even classical Eurasianists

DOI: 10.4324/9781003377573-5

such as Pyotr Savitsky (1998 65) cautioned that from their worldview, "[I]t does not follow that we should withdraw from Europe into a hostile isolation and that we have no points of vital contact with it."

Globalization has created new political and social conditions to define Russia's national ideas and defend national and geopolitical interests. Understanding Russia's geopolitical and civilizational identity is a prerequisite for successful global and regional relations. Non-Western civilizations are actively participating in shaping the contemporary global world. The new international conditions are global and local, requiring a creative, strategic way of bridging them. The national, the regional, and the global must be harmonized and not developed at the expense of each other. The idea of Eurasia is also getting transformed under late modern conditions encouraging its new interpretation. Russians are rereading works of classical Eurasianists with new requirements in mind. Many insisted that Eurasia must be stabilized as a single entity and that Russia must play a key role. The new global conditions present the problem of cross–cultural interaction in a new way, and the new generation of Russian IR scholars must work hard to understand these developments.

The chapter shows Eurasianists' intellectual roots and political attitudes are diverse. Those fearful of European influences tend to advocate the establishment of Russia and Eurasia as a "special autarchic world" (Trubetskoi 2002a). Western pressures in the form of NATO expansion and global democracy promotion have revived the ideas of the Russia-fortress. These ideas have influenced political, religious, and policy circles and are not limited to Eurasianists. As the previous chapter showed, several Orthodox priests, including Patriarch Kirill, politicians from Communists to the ruling United Russia party, and intellectual clubs such as the Izborsky club and the Zinovyev's club have all promoted the idea of Russia's Eurasian uniqueness. Public intellectuals have worked to spread the image of Russia as the Eurasian fortress free of Western influences. Others, like Alexander Dugin, have advanced ideas of Eurasianist expansionism to defeat the West and the West-centered order. Still, others have supported various projects of Russia's dialogue within and outside the greater Eurasian region.

Eurasia in World History

As a landmass, the Eurasian region has traditionally prevented the Western world from a confrontation with non-Western civilizations. Occupying the vast space between Central and Northern Europe, the Middle East, and East Asia, Eurasia connects and helps to stabilize some of the most volatile territories – the Balkans, the Caucasus, Central Asia, and Afghanistan – from which instability tends to spread outward. Historically, these regions have been located between major cultural entities while not developing a sufficiently strong identification with any of them, producing a dense mixture of ethnic, religious, and linguistic affiliations. Under external tensions, these territories tend to be unstable, leading to violence of much greater scope.[1] Under more stable international conditions, they serve as cultural, political, and transportation bridges connecting significant ways of life and continents worldwide.

As a unified region, Eurasia has been held together by political, economic, and cultural layers. Politically, the area has consisted of principalities or empires but rarely with recognized fixed territorial boundaries, remaining relatively open to inside and outside influences. Since the eighteenth century, Eurasia has established itself as a Russia-centered empire that ultimately has stretched from the Baltics to Afghanistan. In 1943, the British geographer Halford Mackinder famously referred to Russia as the "Heartland" of Eurasia and "the greatest natural fortress on earth" (Mackinder 1943, 601). Economically, the region has been a wealth of resources that Russia extracted and transported from one continent to another, mainly from East to West. The Baltic Sea and the Black Sea have been vital for economic connections across continents. In addition, Eurasia has brought together diverse ethnicities and religions, teaching them how to communicate and preserve a measure of cultural openness. Politically, economically and culturally, the region has functioned as a unity in diversity, serving as a hub of various influences and providing stability for European nations to the north and the countries of Asia and the Middle East to the south.

Perhaps most significantly, Eurasia has historically solidified the great cultural peace between the Christian West and the Islamic world. After the decline of the Mongols, Europe emerged as the most powerful civilization. Still fearful of Muslims, it relied mainly on military and economic expansion to secure its position in the world. It was ultimately left to the Russians to learn to absorb influences from both East and West, thereby preserving the fragile cross-cultural equilibrium. While identifying with Eastern Christianity, the Russian empire developed tolerance towards other cultures. Tensions between the Russians and different nationalities were a part of the empire's existence. Yet, these tensions were not as pronounced as in overseas empires, partly because of the absence of an official distinction between the metropolitan center and the colonial periphery (Hosking 1997, 40). Over time, the Russian empire developed special ties with Islam. Russian tsars supported those Muslim authorities willing to submit to the empire's general directions. Russians even served as arbitrators in disputes between Muslims from the Volga River to Central Asia (Crews 2006).[2] Russian intellectuals, Westernizers, and Slavophiles had difficulties accepting Islam but were ultimately challenged in their Eurocentric assumptions (Tsygankov 2008).

More than anything else, this cultural experience made Russia the heartland of Eurasia.[3] With its access to vast resources, a large landmass, and a highly centralized state, the culturally open empire was able to provide the region with economic, political, and cultural cohesion. Although the system underwent a significant mutation under Soviet rule, it preserved some important ties across the region. In line with the old Russia, the Soviet Union did not become an empire in the traditional sense of the word. Instead, it became what one historian called an "affirmative-action empire" (Martin (2001). The center concentrated all decision-making power while granting nationalities multiple privileges, including the territorial status of republics and various affirmative-action programs to preserve local cultures and languages. In addition, the Soviet state provided citizens with significant social and economic rights.[4] An emergency system, rather than a natural state of the historic Russian statehood (McDaniel 1996), the Soviet Union has played its role in unifying Eurasia and preserving global peace.

While these realities have informed Russian geopolitical thinking, other powers too commonly think in terms of geopolitics to understand the global power and foreign policy. Modern globalization would also be impossible without the support of large states that promote private capital to world markets while protecting property rights and freedom of investment. Just as empires politically dominated previous globalizations and commercial expansions – the British in the nineteenth century and the Dutch in the seventeenth century – so the geo-political engine of modern globalization since the end of the Cold War has been the United States, the world's only superpower (Taylor 1996). The promotion of European and American values in the world, with its characteristic rhetoric of protecting the rights of the individual, has always accompanied a desire to strengthen power and control over resources.

Precursors of Fortress Eurasia

Pan-Slavists, especially Nikolai Danilevsky and Vladimir Lamansky, and after them, Konstantin Leontyev, became landmark figures in the development of isolationist Russian international thought. Danilevsky attributed the Slavs to a particular cultural-historical type abandoning the Eurocentric ideas of the early Slavophiles. Leontyev went even further by criticizing the very idea of Slavism and proclaiming the ideal of "Byzantism" and the closeness of Russians to the Turks. Few thinkers influenced the development of Eurasianist theories more than Danilevsky and Leontyev.[5]

The Pan-Slavist Break with Europe

Pan-Slavism contributed to Eurasian ideas, although it originated from Slavophile ideas of Russia's special mission in Europe. Politically, pan-Slavism arose in Russia in the second half of the nineteenth century. In 1867 – partly as a reaction to the Polish uprising of 1863 –the pan-Slavist movement held its congress in Moscow. The movement gained strength following Russia's victory in the 1877–1878 war with Turkey. As a result, Bulgaria and Serbia gained independence from the Ottoman Empire. Expanded territories populated by the Slavic peoples emerged in Serbia, Montenegro, Wallachia, and Moldavia. Turkey capitulated at Plevna and accepted the decisions of the 1884–1885 Congress of Berlin, which deprived Turkey of several territories in favor of Russia and Austria-Hungary. Under these political conditions, the positions of those advocating the unification of the Slavs under Russian rule grew strong.

The most prominent ideologists of Russian pan-Slavism were Mikhail Pogodin, Ivan Aksakov, Nikolai Danilevsky, and Vladimir Lamansky. I examined the views of Aksakov and Danilevsky in the chapter on the Slavophiles, and here I turn to Lamansky (1833–1914) as a forerunner of Eurasianism.

Like Danilevsky, Lamansky departed from the traditional Slavophile perspective that assessed global development in terms of the interaction between Russia and Europe. Lamansky's position was intermediate between Danilevsky and other pan-Slavist thinkers. Like the Slavophiles and Pan-Slavists, Lamansky believed in the backwardness of the non-Western world. He called the civilizations of Asia "the worlds of the past," comparing it to the European "world of the present" and the Greek-Slavic "world of the future" (Lamansky 1916). He considered the worlds of the past to be the future object of absorption by other parts of the world. This linear-chronological scheme closely resembled the views of other Slavophiles but not of Danilevsky. The latter, as we remember, abandoned the chronological division of ethnocultural formations, considering non-Western historic-cultural types such as Egyptian, Chinese, Indian, and others as equivalent to the Western European type (Danilevsky 1990, 88, 123).

At the same time, Lamansky did not consider all European worlds obsolete, separating West German Europe from the sea worlds of Spain, Britain, and the United States. Several years before the British geographer Halford Mackinder,[6] Lamansky wrote about the importance of resistance of large geographic regions to colonial-continental expansionism. He predicted the rise of the British Empire with its dominions (Canada, Australia) and the United States. Lamansky (1916) believed that Britain and the United States were to assimilate Latin America and form a superpower, thereby becoming the world's political center. Western Europe would become a provincial fringe relative to this newly formed empire. His prediction about the civilizational absorption of the Latin American peoples by the British Empire was erroneous, but Lamansky's attempt to break with linear thinking was significant. Danilevsky rejected the linear Slavophile vision, paving the way for Leontyev and the Eurasians.

The Neo-Byzantium of Konstantin Leontyev

Considering himself a student of Danilevsky, Leontyev made his original contribution to Russian IR theory. Viewing the development of humankind as a cyclical process, he singled out in it the stages of initial "simplicity," "flourishing complexity," and secondary "mixing simplicity" (Leontyev 1991, 242). He viewed the last stage not as absorbing the achievements of the previous stage – in the manner of Hegelian dialectical simplification – but as the decline and decay of civilization. Leontyev believed Europe passed the stage of its "flourishing complexity" during the Renaissance era. Following the end of that era, Europe entered the stage of decline.

On the other hand, Russia has entered the complexity stage since Peter the Great and remained in that stage. Leontyev argued that Russia could have developed this capacity if it had "persisted in its separateness" and did not submit to Europe (Ibid, 289). Like Danilevsky, Leontyev viewed Peter not so much as a Westernizer but as a ruler who strengthened the sovereign foundations of Russian statehood and the social stratification required for "flourishing complexity" (Ibid, 188).

The thinker viewed the "separation" from Europe as essential for breaking with the Slavic identity and establishing Byzantism as Russia's national and geopolitical identity. He considered such identity as rooted in Russian culture. In particular, Leontyev pointed to the historical significance of Orthodox Tsarism and the rural community as institutions not "corrupted" by Western ideas of individual freedom and human happiness. In the thinker's assessment, Byzantism survived and strengthened despite popular revolts such as those organized by Stepan Razin and Yemelyan Pugachev. Byzantism assisted Russia in uniting it ideologically and politically, thereby giving the country "all our strength in the fight against Poland, against the Swedes, against France and Turkey" (Ibid, 191).

As for the ideal of the Slavic identity, Leontyev considered it vague, non-specific, and incapable of uniting Russians. He rejected everything based on ethnic, tribal, and blood relations as unworthy of great nations: "What is a tribe without a system of religious and state ideas? ... And what is pure blood? Spiritual infertility!" (Ibid, 199). In addition, the Slavs historically demonstrated their inability to unite. Based on the detailed analysis of the ethnographic and political differences among the Czechs, Bulgarians, Slovaks, Serbs, Poles, and Russians, the thinker rejected the claims of Slavism. Leontyev viewed such claims as insufficient, at best. Byzantism, on the other hand, was "the only reliable anchor of our not only Russian but also pan-Slavic protection" (Ibid, 215).

Therefore, Leontyev considered it essential for Russia, the ideal of a state guided by a religious idea and capable of encouraging imperial social diversity. In his view, only such a state can protect the country from disintegration. Anticipating the arguments by Eurasianists, the thinker declared the perniciousness of the reproduction of European ideas on Russian soil while asserting the cultural closeness of Russians to the Turks rather than the Slavs. The former consul in Constantinople, Leontyev, developed the view of the two peoples' cultural similarities by comparing their social structures and state organization. He considered a strong power of the state necessary for successfully opposing not only the increasingly decrepit Europe but also dormant China. Leontyev insisted on "uniting Chinese state organization with Indian religiosity" to defeat the ideas of European socialism (Duncan 2000, 43). In the last quarter of the nineteenth century, he was one of the first to suggest that China would become the gravedigger of European, and possibly Russian, civilization. In 1891, he wrote that "Russia can only die in two ways ... either from the sword of awakened Chinese or by voluntary merging with the pan-European republican federation" (Leontyev (1991, 199). The scenario of Chinese expansion, the thinker believed, could come true in the next few centuries.[7]

Such were some of the ideas of pan-Slavism and Leontyev. Their contribution to Russian IR theory is contradictory. The hostile attitude towards Europe hardly strengthened the position of Russia, which historically not only competed but also cooperated with European countries in opposing common threats. For instance, militant pan-Slavism came into conflict with the interests of Russia by pushing it into an armed confrontation with Austria, Turkey, and Prussia. The rejection of the principle of political balancing contributed to the consolidation of European powers on an anti-Russian basis, as happened during the Crimean War. However, the assessment of Danilevsky and Leontyev should not be limited to criticism of pan-Slavist isolationist attitudes. By rejecting Eurocentrism, both thinkers significantly contributed to recognizing cultural pluralism in the world – the point frequently missed by their critics. For example, Pavel Milyukov assessed Danilevsky's work as nothing more than "a sermon of Russia's hatred of Europe" (Novikova and Sizemskaya 1997, 174), while Vladimir Solovyov (1990, 413) acused the author of the book *Russia and Europe* of trying to build a Slavic future on the ruins of European culture.[8] Speaking from the Eurocentric positions, these critics failed to appreciate the movement begun by the two thinkers toward a better understanding of non-European civilizations.[9]

Classical Eurasianism between the Fortress and the Expansion

Born in the twentieth century, classical Eurasianism has undergone many influences of the nineteenth century. In addition to the late Slavophiles, Danilevsky and Leontyev, diverse sources influenced Eurasianists. Such sources included geographical thought, Russian literature, poetry, and art,[10] German organicist sociology, and geopolitics.[11] During its rise in the mid-1920s, many well-known historians, philosophers, linguists, geographers, writers, and artists joined classical Eurasianism. The movement was conservative and produced advocates of the Russia-fortress and separation from European liberalism. However, some Eurasianists demonstrated commitment to socialist revolutionary ideas arguing for a global expansion.

The Conservative Eurasianism of Nikolai Trubetskoi

One of the founders of Eurasianism, Nikolai Trubetskoi (1890–1938), absorbed and reworked various ideological sources. Although the Slavophile conviction in the messianic destiny of the Russians was not very typical for the thinker, who rejected the notion of universal, he shared the late Slavophile desire to ethnically and politically isolate Russia from the Europeans. Trubetskoi combined that desire with the conviction in Russia's geographical and anthropological wholeness, characteristic of Russian geopolitical thought.

Following the late Slavophiles, Trubetskoi reproduced a culturally pluralistic and cyclical vision of the modern world in his works. Under the influence of Danilevsky, he criticized the Eurocentric perception, arguing that Europe is only a part of humanity and the rest are no less significant parts of it (Trubetskoi 1998, 2002c). From the author of *Russia and Europe*, Trubetskoi also borrowed the idea of the potential conflict between different cultures. Through one of his laws of cultural-historic types, Danilevsky postulated the relativism of social develop-ment and the human inability fully to transfer their influences to other peoples. Developing this idea, Trubetskoi asserted "an organic, and not at all a causal rela-tionship of culture, ethnography, and geography" (Yevraziystvo 2002, 128). He understood the culture of Russia as "an exceptional, specific culture, which has no less intrinsic value and no less historical significance than European and Asian cultures" (Ibid, 130). At the same time, Trubetskoi believed that Asian cultures were closer to Russian (Ibid, 134, 154). Such reasoning was only one step away from associating the identity of Russia with that of Eurasia.

No less obvious was the influence of Leontyev, with whom the authors of *Yevraziystvo* agreed in their critique of Slavophiles for attempting to "dissolve Russian culture in an abstract and romantic pan-Slavism" (Ibid, 129). But Trubetskoi went further than his predecessor, creating the theory of the Turanian element as the foundation of Russian culture.[12] Being a linguist and ethnog-rapher, he considered the Slavs primarily a linguistic community. He associated the sociocultural foundation of the Russians with a conglomerate of Turkic, Ugro-Finnish, "Manchurian," Mongolian, and other peoples (Trubetskoi 1993). The mentality of these peoples became the foundation of Russian statehood in the Muscovite period, only later superimposed on Orthodoxy and merged with it. According to Trubetskoi, the Russians were able to free themselves from the dominance of the Mongol influence by organically reworking this influence:

> For any nation, a foreign yoke is not only misfortune but also a school. …
> [T]he beneficence or harmfulness of the yoke as a school can be judged by
> the form in which the liberated nation will appear.
>
> *Ibid, 87*

Finally, of special importance was the influence of geographic and geopolitical thought on Eurasianism in general and Trubetskoi in particular. The works of Russian geographers Lev Mechnikov, Nikolai Przhevalsky, Veniamin Semenov-Tyan Shansky, and several other representatives of the Russian Geographical Society were essential in paving the way for Eurasianists to reason about the geo-graphical wholeness or integrity of the continent. As a result, Eurasianists argued that "from the point of view of climate and other geographical conditions, Eurasia represents an autarchic and coherent entity (Yevraziystvo 2002, 132). For example, the works of Mechnikov (2019) demonstrated such autarchy and coherence by establishing the geographic connection with the location of the great rivers, while Semenov-Tien-Shansky (1915) identified the space between Russia's greatest rivers, the Volga and the Yenisei, as the country's geographical center and the foundation of its political power. Subsequently, Trubetskoi and, especially, Savitsky cited the geographical self-sufficiency of the continent as the main reason for arguing the sociocultural, ethnic, economic, and political identity of Eurasia.[13]

Overall, Eurasianists wanted to isolate Russia from the "alien" and "hostile" European continent while assuming the position of self-sufficiency and refusing active geopolitical expansion. Trubetskoi's understanding of freedom and statehood was closely related to this position. The thinker and his associates unequivocally defined freedom in terms of the assertion of Russian-Eurasian self-sufficiency and non-Europeanism. The logic of opposing Europe made the emphasis by Eurasianists on building a powerful state almost synonymous with the idea of freedom. From the international standpoint, Russian freedom consisted of strengthening and defending the cultural values of Orthodox Christianity and ethnic diversity within the geopolitical area of the Russian Empire and the USSR.

The attitude of Trubetskoi and many of his supporters toward the Soviet system was highly critical. Eurasianists paid tribute to the restoration of the traditional imperial space by the Bolsheviks but did not consider such a restoration to be to their merit. Instead, Eurasianists viewed such a restoration as the result of the sociocultural and geographical forces embedded in the Eurasian continent. According to Trubetskoi, gathering the Eurasian lands did not mean that the Bolsheviks grasped the imperatives of Russian ideological and cultural identity. On the contrary, he considered the Bolsheviks' power established in Russia continuing the same Eurocentric development which Peter had imposed on the country several centuries ago.

In attempting to establish Russia's ideological self-sufficiency, Trubetskoi set the task of formulating a new ideology capable of competing with both Bolshevism and Western democracy. He considered the idea of sacrifice the basis of such an ideology and the ideocratic state formed on its grounds as essential. Such a state had to be created not in the name of a class or an individual people but of the totality of peoples inhabiting Eurasia as an "autarkic special world" (Trubetskoi 2002b, 197). Trubetskoi's interpretation of Russian history was also related to his views on preserving the Eurasian world's autarkic nature. In this world, the figures of Genghis Khan and Russian princes like Alexander Nevsky, who preferred cohabitation with the Tatars to subjugation to Europe, acquired special significance (Trubetskoi 2002a).[14] At the same time, the thinker viewed Soviet attempts to create an ideocracy of socialism as creating "perverse ideas about the essence of the considered historical period" (Trubetskoi 2002b, 198).[15]

The Revolutionary Expansion of Pyotr Suvchinsky

Not all Eurasians were irreconcilable critics of the Soviet system. Already in the second half of the 1920s, a Parisian group stood out within the Eurasian movement, arguing for dialogue with the Soviet system and striving for its gradual transformation. Unlike the Prague group (Nikolai Trubetskoi, Pyotr

Savitsky, Nikolai Alekseev, and others), the leaders of the Paris group (Pyotr Suvchinsky, Dmitry Svyatopolk-Mirsky, Lev Karsavin, Vladimir Nikitin, and others) demonstrated an openness to Marxist ideas. They called for the political organization of Eurasianism in the manner of the Bolshevik movement. The new print outlet of the Paris group was the weekly *Yevraziya*, financed from dubious sources and devoted a significant place to exposing the opponents of the USSR and trying to combine Eurasianism and communism ideologically. In protest, Pyotr Savitsky and Nikolai Alekseev announced in 1929 that the weekly was no longer a Eurasian publication. A year earlier, Trubetskoi had refused to partici- pate in all Eurasianist organizations, also refusing to recognize the new group. The latter, he believed, was alien to the Eurasian doctrine because it abandoned Orthodox Christian ideas and Russian traditions in favor of the views of Karl Marx and Nikolai Fedorov (Laruelle 2004, 39).[16] Subsequently, left-wing beliefs led several representatives of the Prague group to the decision to emigrate to the USSR, which, however, did not save them from repression by the Soviet authorities.

Pyotr Suvchinsky (1892–1985) was a philosopher, musicologist, and critic. As one of the founders of the Eurasianist movement, he sympathized with the idea of its radicalization. In the 1920s, he corresponded with the leading proletarian writer Maxim Gorky and kept in touch with Nikolai Ustryalov, the leader of the National Bolshevik movement *Smena vekh* (change of milestones). Ideologically, the difference between Suvchinsky's worldview and the views of Trubetskoi was on display concerning the Bolshevik Revolution. Eurasianism did not view the revolution as the end of Russia. However, Trubetskoi considered the post- revolutionary processes to be the result of highly traumatic sociocultural and geographical developments viewing Bolshevism as a destructive and harmful movement (Trubetskoi 2002c 191).

On the contrary, Suvchinsky viewed the revolution as a purifying and rejuvenating phenomenon of Russian statehood. He defended not so much the tradition and its re-creation under twentieth-century conditions but the rejection of the old ideological and sociocultural forms. The weekly *Yevraziya*, co-edited by Suvchinsky, viewed Eurasianism as an ontologically revolutionary movement. It defined "the Russian revolutionary process as a heroic attempt to overcome [old individualistic] forms and find new, adequate ones" (Laruelle 2004, 39). In this interpretation, Russia paved the way for humanity, showing it new forms of religiosity and social creativity. From the beginning of the 1920s, Suvchinsky intellectually evolved away from the traditional adherence to the ideals of the Russian church to the plans of Nikolai Fedorov's "all- unity.[17] The expansionist motive of Suvchinsky's thinking was also evident in the thinker's positioning of Russia in the system of international relations preceding the period of rivalry with the United States after the Second World War. Such positioning, he believed, could be "analogous only to the United States" (Suvchinsky 1929, 2). He considered the movement towards achieving such a status possible based on

awareness and consolidation of the three main points of the Russian historical and modern type ... the primary religious and cultural substance of
the Russian-Eurasian peoples; revolution as a set of ideas and processes that
led to the creation of modern Russia, and a system of consequences of the
revolution, formally expressed in Soviet federalism and economic etatism.

Ibid.[18]

Classical Eurasianists were initially united by their criticism of Europe, which
they associated with geopolitical aspirations to deprive Russian civilization of
its independence. With all the diversity of Eurasianism, it has contributed to the
awareness of the strong ties between Russia and the people bordering it and the
external perception of Russia as an ethnically and geographically unified region.
Eurasianists offered the Russian state a new set of ideological myths to cement its
economic, political, and cultural foundations.

The Anti-Soviet Fortress of Lev Gumilev

The shaping and growth of Lev Gumilev as a Eurasianist thinker took place in
the postwar and post–Stalin periods. As a successor to the work of the classical
Eurasianists, Gumilev was not recognized by official science. He was a semi-
marginalized researcher who published only one of his works in Soviet times,
moreover, in a small circulation for library use (Gumilev 1990).[19] Nevertheless, his
contribution to developing the ideas of geopolitical survival and self-sufficiency
turned out to be significant and deeply original.

Russia as a Distinctive Super-Ethnic Group

Because of the dominance of official Marxism, academic circles did not accept
a geopolitical analysis. Such analysis, however, was practiced in the military-
political circles of the Soviet state. Having defeated Nazi Germany, the Soviet
Union strengthened its authority worldwide and within the country. However,
the Cold War meant a confrontation with the United States, the most powerful
military and economic power, presenting the Soviet elite with new geopolitical
and ideological challenges. Despite the official ban on Eurasianist theories, analysts
of the General Staff of the Soviet Ministry of Defense continued to develop ideas
of Eurasianist expansion to achieve a final victory over the "Atlanticism" of the
West. For example, in the 1970s, the General Staff considered plans for a non-
nuclear war to drive Americans out of Euro-Asia (which included Europe itself)
and establish complete control over it (Tsymbursky 2007 18–19; McGwire 1991,
26–27). Such preparations were doomed to failure due to their extreme ambition. In addition, the Soviet elite lacked strategic unity. One manifestation of the
latter was the termination of the Strategic Intelligence unit created in 1938 by
Lavrenty Beria for coordinating the activities of the Chief Intelligence Service
(GRU) and the Internal Security Division (NKVD) (Potapov 2000). The Soviet

security services competed for influence and acted as bureaucratic agencies complicating the conduct of grand strategy.

While the planners of the General Staff were looking for ways to contain the Atlanticist plans of the United States globally, the loyal follower of classical Eurasianism was busy developing ideas of Russia's cultural identity and its incompatibility with the "alien" European "super-ethnic group." Gumilev read widely and relied in his analysis on works by historians of ancient and modern civilizations, biologists, ethnographers, scholars of cybernetics, and philosophers. However, he was exceptionally sympathetic to the analysis of Nikolai Trubetskoi and Pyotr Savitsky. Gumilev was personally acquainted with the latter and maintained relations with him all his life. He took Savitsky's concept of geographical "spatial development" (*mestorazvitiye*) as a point of departure and wanted to strengthen it with theories of ethnicity, including those of Trubetskoi. His concept of *passionarnost'* (passionate personality of unusual willpower) behind the development of an ethnic community became Gumilev's main contribution to the Eurasian theory of ethnic development or ethnogenesis (*etnogenez*). He considered his analysis of Russia as a particular super-ethnic group to be strictly scientific and consistent with the latest evidence in biochemical science. In Gumilev's (2002, 480) opinion, Eurasianists "really lacked natural science [even though] the Eurasian doctrine was conceived as a synthesis of the humanities and natural sciences, a synthesis of history and geography."

The Cyclical Theory of Ethnogenesis

Following Savitsky, Gumilev (1990, 186) considered the basis for the development of an ethnic group to be geographical location or exceptional landscapes of the Earth. Such landscapes require particular adaptations of people.[20] However, for Gumilev, the geographic location was only a starting point in creating a general theory of ethnic development or ethnogenesis. The thinker defined an ethnic community as "a stable, naturally formed group of people distinguished by a peculiar stereotype of behavior that changes in historical time" (Gumilev 1990, 135). He further stressed the combination of the social and the biogeographic in his understanding of ethnicity. Borrowing the biosphere concept from the founder of biogeochemistry, Vladimir Vernadsky, Gumilev (1990, 23) argued that an ethnic community is formed under social and natural influences. The thinker believed that, in addition to the effect of a particular landscape, ethnic groups experience the impact of biochemical energy. Speaking against the social understanding of ethnicity practiced by Soviet Marxist ethnographers, he argued that an ethnic community "can exist across several [socio-economic] formations" (Ibid, 35). Gumilev's concept of ethnicity is an essentialist or, in his definition, an "elementary" phenomenon. It combines various dimensions and is not reducible "to sociological, biological, or geographical phenomena" (Ibid, 56).

Gumilev's theory of ethnogenesis included a set of concepts, some traditional and some original for Russian and world ethnography. In understanding the cycles of ethnic development – emergence, rise, decline, and death – the thinker followed Danilevsky, Leontyev, Trubetskoi, and all those who did not share a linear understanding of the historical process of human development. Generally speaking, Gumilev's approach to the interaction among ethnic groups was common in the cyclical school and emphasized their qualitative differences and the dominance of competitive principles. Gumilev allowed coexistence and miscegenation, or partial borrowing of the characteristics of another ethnic group, but did not consider the possibility of mutually beneficial inter-ethnic interaction and cooperation. He assessed the absorption of small ethnic groups by larger ones to be more characteristic of the inter-ethnic interaction and, like Leontyev, favored the "separation" or relatively isolated development of super-ethnic groups.

Concerning the interaction of large or super-ethnic communities, Gumilev considered their values "mutually exclusive and, in any case, poorly compatible with each other" (Gumilev, Ermolaev 2002, 469). He rejected ideas of universal humanity with no less indignation than his predecessors.

> "Talking about the history of all mankind," he wrote, "does not make sense. The so-called universal history is only a mechanical totality of knowledge about the history of various super-ethnic groups. ... [F]rom an ethnic point of view, historical humanity does not represent any phenomenological community."
>
> *Ibid*[21]

Justifying the impossibility of the existence of a single humanity, Gumilev went further than his teachers, not limiting himself to criticizing the ethnocentrism of cosmopolitan theories. His main contribution to developing ethno-cyclical approaches was the theory of levels of *passionarnost'* (emotional or willpower drive) behind super-ethnic communities. The thinker assessed the emergence of highly driven people resulting from cosmic irradiation (Gumilev 1989, 595–596; Gumilev 1990, 485). He explained the difference in levels of *passionarnost'* by the differences in the geographic landscapes of the Earth, viewing such a difference as fundamental and unavoidable.

According to Gumilev, super-ethnic groups progress based on their internal laws and historical calendar, moving from rising to breakdown, inertia, and decline. Each super-ethnic group has a life of about 1500 years. The thinker associated the development of the Russian-Eurasian ethnic group with the rise of Moscow's *passionarnost'* at the beginning of the thirteenth century, giving it about 800 years. In his opinion, the post-Napoleonic period marked a phase of breakdown in the development of Russia, and Gorbachev's perestroika marked a transition to an inertial growth phase. Gumilev considered all attempts by Russia to copy Europe doomed to failure because Russians and Europeans live in different historical times and are at various stages of their ethnic development. The Europeans are five hundred years older than the Russians entering the inertial phase already in the fifteenth century, while the Russians have yet to prove their ability for further development (Gumilev and Ermolaev, 471–472).[22]

Overall, the IR theory of the last representative of classical Eurasianism assumed that the Russians constitute a super-ethnic group that unites Eurasian peoples and strives to defend their unity and independence in confrontation with other super-ethnic groups, in particular European ones. In creating the original theory of *passionarnost'*-based tension, Gumilev generally followed the Eurasianists. He shared their understanding of the course of human development, the emphasis on the principal role of geography in the formation of ethnicity, the importance of strengthening statehood, and the unique nature of Eurasian history. In his assessment, such a record created tensions in the relationship between Russians and Europeans. At the same time, it encouraged cooperation and unity among the peoples of Eurasia. His attitude toward the Bolshevik system was as critical as that of his teachers, Trubetskoi and Savitsky. Gumilev rejected the ambitions of Communist ideology to "teach" the Russians how to interact with other peoples of the Eurasian continent, considering the national policy of the USSR to be deeply flawed (Ibid, 473).

The Reemergence of Eurasianism

The Soviet dissolution and the regional instability that resulted from it created conditions for the revival of Eurasianism in the new Russia. The empire's disappearance in an historically unstable environment created a security vacuum and led to recent conflicts on Russia's periphery (Tsygankov 2012). Such disputes included those ethnically based in the Caucasus, Central Asia, Moldova, and Ukraine. Such conflicts have also been energy-based, resulting from the post-Soviet states' needs for energy for exports or domestic consumption. Other conflicts were related to domestic political instability, cross-regional immigration, and illegal activities.

Evidence of instability throughout the region included the August 2008 Russia–Georgia war, the ongoing Russia–Ukraine military conflict, terrorist attacks, the instability of Afghanistan, the inability of Central Asian rulers to rein in some local clans and drug lords, the weakness of legitimately elected bodies of power in Moldova and Ukraine. Russia and other states have had limited success in bringing stability to the region. Indeed, Russia has contributed significantly to the Eurasian meltdown by initially suffering from a state weakness and then securitizing the conflict with Ukraine. The interests of China and the Muslim world have been too peripheral to successfully fill the emerged security vacuum and compensate for the weakness of Russia in Eurasia. As to the West, its attempts to expand its economic and security institutions at Russia's expense have encouraged Russia's anti-Western thinking and the zero-sum competition for spheres of influence.

Russian thinkers have engaged in complex geopolitical discussions in response to these developments,[23] validating some of the old Eurasianist ideas and creating new ones. This section reviews Eurasianist schools of fortress, expansion, and dialogue that emerged under new post–Soviet conditions.[24]

The Rise of Fortress Thinking and Interest in Danilevsky

Danilevsky's ideas proved influential even before the Soviet dissolution. On the right, his influence was important to classical Eurasianism.[25] The movement's leader Nikolai Trubetskoi took the "laws" of historic-cultural types to his heart by identifying the linguistic and ethnic foundations of Russia–Eurasia and building on Danilevsky's points about the non-transferable nature of cultures' essential characteristics. Also influenced by Leontyev, Trubetskoi further developed the idea of cultural relativism by positing the "organic" connection of "culture, ethnicity, and geography" (Yevraziystvo 2002, 128). Danilevsky's ideas of cyclical cultural development also influenced Gumilev, who insisted that sufficiently strong cultures borrow from each other but never assimilate and rarely cooperate.

On the left, Danilevsky's ideas partly resonated even with socialists, Communists, and their sympathizers. One admirer of these ideas was émigré intellectual Nikolay Ustryalov who was sympathetic to the Bolshevik Revolution and worked to develop the particularistic ideology of National-Bolshevism for Soviet Russia.[26] The Paris group within Eurasianism also sympathized with the ideas of cultural anti-Westernism. Finally, in response to all these developments, some Soviet Communists entertained merging socialist ideas with those of nationalism and cultural isolationism. The fact that Stalin at times appealed to Russian, rather than Marxist, slogans and symbols encouraged, in his way, the indigenous tradition of nationalist thinking (Dunlop 1983, 15). After the end of Stalin's terrorist rule, the Soviet regime became more susceptible to nationalist ideas.[27] Many of Russia's new nationalists opposed the Soviet government but, following Danilevsky's tradition, continued to be highly critical of the West and visualized Russia as socially and culturally superior. Within Russian nationalism, the so-called National Bolsheviks were advocating a synthesis of the Bolshevik regime and Russia's indigenous tradition (Agurski 1987; Dunlop 1983, 254–265).

Following the Soviet dissolution, Danilevsky's ideas of a cultural fortress enjoyed even more tremendous popularity. The first edition of his book in 1991 sold 70,000 copies and became standard reading at military academies. At least seven other editions have been published since then (Woodburn 2013, xiv, xvii). The translator of Danilevsky in English wrote that "his book, which was only modestly successful in his lifetime, now enjoys the greatest fame and readership it has ever had – within Russia at least" (Ibid, xvii). He appropriately called Russia and Europe "the most important nineteenth-century book for the post-Soviet period and thus an object worthy of further study by specialists and non-specialists alike" (Ibid, xv).

Danilevsky strongly influenced the language and arguments of neo-Eurasianists in their newly revived debate with Westernizers. The latter continued to assert that Russia is an organic part of Western civilization and should develop in the same direction as the West. The dominance of pro-Western narratives associated with Mikhail Gorbachev and Boris Yeltsin soon met formidable opposition, which advanced a different civilizational identity for Russia. Initiated by presidential advisor Sergei Stankevich and then the Chief of Foreign Intelligence Yevgeny Primakov, this perspective advocated the notion of Russia standing in firm opposition to the West by advancing the familiar view of Russia's cultural self-sufficiency. Officials, such as Minister of Railroad Transportation Vladimir Yakunin (2012, 2013), promote the notion of Russia-civilization in their speeches and public writing. Orthodox priests, including Patriarch Kirill, endorse the idea of Russia's religion-centered civilizational distinctiveness.[28] Within political circles, Danilevsky also influenced the language of Russian Communists who insisted that, as a unique civilization, Russia must be isolated from the West to survive and preserve its uniqueness (Zyuganov 1999, 13; Nartov 1999, 95). Politicians from the relatively marginal to the well-established ones regularly speak on Russia's national interests as tied to its geopolitical and cultural self-sufficiency.

Outside political circles, most prominent Eurasianist, nationalist, and neo-Slavophile thinkers did not hide Danilevsky's influence on their theories and heavily relied on his arguments (Zyuganov 2002; Narochnitskaya 2004; Kortunov 2009; Dugin 2015). Russia's leading geopolitical thinker, Vadim Tsymbursky, even wrote his doctoral dissertation on Danilevsky's geopolitical theory. Tsymbursky praised Danilevsky's vision of Russia and Europe as "distinct yet partly interdependent and therefore competing for mastering their geocultural spaces."[29] Many within Russian academic and expert circles reference Danilevsky's work by adopting a highly positive tone. Some credit him as the founding father of the idea of the plurality of civilization in world politics (Dugin 2015). In the context of broken relations with the West, many assess such plurality as a precondition of Russia's cultural and political survival. The leading neo-Slavophile thinker, Natalya Narochnitskaya, called Danilevsky's "theory of historic-cultural types and especially his sociology of Western culture murderous" for West-centered ideas of Russia (Narochnitskaya 2004, 105). One survey of Russian IR theorists found that Danilevsky's influence in Russian academia is considerably more prominent than that of other Russian and Western thinkers. In response to a request to identify the three most important Russian thinkers of the nineteenth and twentieth centuries relevant to the development of Russian IR theory, 35 per cent identified Danilevsky, 18 per cent said Konstantin Leontyev, and 15 per cent identified Alexander Panarin. Around 15 per cent of respondents indicated their support for ideas of Eurasianism and Eurasian integration as especially significant for Russia.[30] Eurasianists, of course, were themselves influenced by Danilevsky.

The trauma of the Soviet breakup, accompanied by economic, social, and political instability in the region, was responsible for Russia's rise in the fortress discourse. The state collapse exacerbated the sense of vulnerability in the face of

Western pressures in the form of NATO expansion and global democracy promotion. In the context of domestic instability following Soviet disintegration, these pressures served to revive the ideas of the nationalist fortress. Nationalist ideas influenced the Kremlin, which provided a favorable environment for their further proliferation. Due to Russia's cultural distinctiveness, Western pressures helped to mobilize Russian elites for a counter-response, further alienating the country from its significant other.

Following the beginning of the war in Ukraine, the isolationist Eurasianist discourse grew stronger. Russian thinkers influenced by Danilevsky and Tsymbursky have argued that the country has completed its attempts to establish stable relations with Europe since Peter the Great and decisively turned to Asia and the Middle East. For example, Yury Solozobov (2022) of the Institute of Strategic Studies has assessed Putin's official trip to Iran in July 2022 as indicative of a "divorce" with Europe and a strategic "exit to Eurasia." Citing Tsymbursky's theory of Russia's cyclical relations with Europe, Solozobov concluded that the entire era of such cycles is now in the past, as Russia, Iran, and Turkey are building a "new civilizational alliance in continental Eurasia" to thwart the global ambitions of the West (Ibid.).

The Neo-Eurasianist Expansion of Alexander Dugin

The most radical response to the pressure of the West was the response of the new expansionism, which Alexander Dugin formulated. His theories differ from many fortress theories, including neo-Soviet and isolationist ones.

The son of a general of the Soviet Chief Intelligence Office (GRU), Dugin continued the line of geopolitical developments once associated with the General Staff and focused on creating a global Eurasian strategy. The primary ideological sources of Dugin's works were the theories of the European right. He took to the extreme Savitsky's geographical determinism while discarding the ethnographic developments of Trubetskoi and Gumilev as unnecessary. Under Dugin's pen, Russia appeared as a power capable of restoring and expanding the Soviet area of geopolitical influence in opposition to the "Atlantic" forces led by the United States.

Dugin formulated his Eurasian views in the voluminous book "Fundamentals of Geopolitics," which was positively received by the military-conservative circles of Russia and became a textbook for teaching geopolitics in the country's military academies. In understanding the geopolitical position of Russia, the thinker followed the European geographers of the late nineteenth and early twentieth centuries. They were confident in the certainty of competition between large geographic areas for world control. At the same time, they proceeded from the inescapable rivalry between sea and land powers and the centrality of the Eurasian continent in world confrontation. One of the theorems of British geographer Mackinder stated, in particular, that Eurasia is the "Heartland," or "core land" of the world. Therefore, whoever owns the heartland will own the world. The definition of Eurasia was much broader than that of Russian Eurasianists.

The latter identified it with the geographical space of Greater Russia, stretching from the European borders of the turn of the nineteenth and twentieth centuries to the Asian and Muslim worlds. For Dugin, Eurasia included Europe, much of Asia, and the Muslim world (Dugin 2000).[31] Dugin's idea of Russia's geopolitical position and role is built primarily on Mackinder's theorem. According to this view, Russia is placed at the center of the world confrontation with its middle Eurasian position and, therefore, cannot evade the struggle of the continents because modern world politics is still a sphere of rivalry between sea and land powers (Tsygankov 2003).

Thus, Dugin formulated the understanding of the international system not as a struggle between states or culturally separate civilizations but as a clash of two opposite geopolitical spaces defined by their power aspirations – the Eurasian Land and the Atlantic Sea. Dugin's thinking is the opposite to understanding civilization as a geopolitically, economically, and culturally self-sufficient spatial entity. The bipolar vision of the world does not exclude, but presupposes, building global alliances based on geopolitical orientations. Dugin identified a Eurasian orientation in Russia, Germany, Iran, and, to a lesser extent, Japan, while associating Atlanticism with the policies of the United States and the United Kingdom. In his opinion, Russia's position between West and East implies the need to expand far beyond what some see as Russia's traditional or historical borders. "The new Empire must be Eurasian, all-continental, and in the long run, global" (Ibid, 213).

On a regional scale, Dugin views the speedy integration of Eurasia with Russia as its center as necessary. Only such integration will become a genuine guarantee of Russian security and sovereignty and prepare the country for a global confrontation with Atlanticism. "Russia can act on behalf of the Heartland with full geopolitical justification. Its strategic interests are not only close to the continent's interests, but are strictly identical to them" (Ibid, 166). However, geopolitical self-sufficiency on the scale of the continent is illusory without the continuation of geopolitical expansion, Dugin wrote (2000, 6–7), referring to the example of the activities of Western countries:

> The intellectual elite of the West itself, without hesitation, follows the path of asserting its own geopolitical identity, direct military aggression, an impressive and cynical example of which we see in the NATO aggression against Yugoslavia. [...] Before such a demonstration of Atlanticist will, power and audacity, the only logical answer is to turn to one's civilizational potential, mobilize strategic, economic, social and cultural resources needed by Russia in order not to be erased from history by the iron fist of the builders of the "new world order."

In the thinker's mind, Eurasian geopolitics "is not an area of aggression but a last line of defense. It is always risky to assert one's civilizational 'I,' but to refuse it is tantamount to historical suicide" (Ibid).[32]

What Russian strategy could establish control over the Eurasian continent? Above all, Dugin insisted that Russia must rebuild the empire through a new type of reform and new geopolitical alliances. Inside the country, he proposed relying on the Russian ethnic group and Orthodox Church to recreate a multi-ethnic and multi-confessional empire (2000, 185–192). Russia's foreign policy should be oriented to Germany, Iran, and Japan (Dugin 2000, 220–245, 421). In developing these ideas, Dugin formulated three geopolitical projects – pan-European, pan-Asian, and pan-Arab – with the ultimate goal of gaining access to the seas and oceans in the north, south, and east, turning Eurasia into a self-sufficient geopolitical empire. As for China, Dugin perceived it as a severe threat to the future of the Eurasian empire, and he proposes a whole range of measures to weaken it (2000, 236, 359). The result of the Russian strategy was to be an empire of several empires – a European one organized around Germany and Mittleeuropa; the Pacific, based on the rule of Japan; Central Asia centered in Iran, and the Russian Empire at the center of the world.

Following the beginning of the war in Ukraine, Dugin (2022a, b) argued that Russia has finally implemented a global or expansionist Eurasianist strategy, and that such a strategy has begun to bring actual dividends. In his assessment, Ukrainian territory decided the fundamental conflict between Atlanticism and Eurasianism. Russia was rising by way of eliminating Ukraine as "anti-Russia." The West has been put on the defense, as Russia has also built sufficiently strong relations across the region and the world to deal the decisive blow to the US-centered unipolar world. Dugin now viewed China as an essential pillar of confronting the West, thereby revising his earlier skepticism regarding Beijing's intentions. He also never mentioned his earlier hope for converting Germany's foreign policy into a Eurasian one.

Despite the vast popularity of Dugin's geopolitical theories, especially in the circles of the military and intelligence communities, many Russian analysts were very skeptical of these theories, primarily due to Russia's material and economic weakness. The idea of global expansion did not have significant support within the country. Most experts and theorists of geopolitics leaned toward the ideas of classical Eurasianism or realism. The views of Fortress Eurasia remained popular and dominant here.

For comparison, let us recall the position of Tsymbursky. He considered himself a theorist of civilizational geopolitics but argued for the isolationist development of Russia. Unlike Dugin, Tsymbursky believed that after the Soviet collapse, the main threats to Russia did not come from the West or other civilizations but from the nearby peripheral territories. Relying mainly on the work of Russian thinkers – from the late Slavophiles to geographers, he formulated the theory of Russia as a geopolitical and civilizational island.[33]

Instead of annexing the former Soviet territories, Tsymbursky considered it necessary to maintain their independence as a protective belt between Russia and potentially aggressive civilizations. Instead of advocating a neo-Soviet fortress and expansion, he assumed the main task of the country to be the development of Russia's "internal Eurasia" in the Urals, Siberia, and the Far East. Despite the growing instability in the world, the thinker considered such internal develop-ment timely, necessary, and possible. In his assessment, such a strategy required moving the capital of Russia from Moscow to Siberia, attracting new investments and industrial energy there, and pursuing a foreign policy of balancing between the leading global centers of power. According to Tsymbursky, Russia has several decades to recover and develop. Attempts to expand or recreate the neo-Soviet empire, he warned, might result in overstrain and the subsequent collapse of the country.

There was a lot of realism in Tsymbursky's theories, although they lacked attention to Russia's relations with its neighbors in the Eurasian region – China, Iran, and other countries. An attempt to develop an understanding of such relations and Eurasia as an open space for dialogue was the theory of Eurasia as a place of exchange and interaction between different civilizations.

The Idea of the Eurasia Bridge

Under growing alienation from the West and the rise of theories of fortress and expansion, ideas of the Eurasia bridge turned out to be less influential. Nevertheless, these ideas have existed and had the opportunity to progress. One can identify several stages in their evolution. Their future development partly depends on the ability of Russia and Russian elites to overcome the anti-Western attitudes and end the confrontation with the Western world.

In the late Soviet period, the ideas of a Eurasian dialogue existed and could have progressed if Gorbachev's reforms had not failed. During that time, influ-ential thinkers viewed Eurasia as a community of destiny connecting Russia and the non-Russian people of the region. While supporting the reforms, they opposed both pro-Western "separatism" and ideas of Russia as a fortress. Gorbachev supported the new union of Eurasianist nature in place of the USSR. In his *Perestroika* book (1987 edition), he upgraded his "common European home" formula by adding the Asian dimension: "The Soviet Union is an Asian, as well as European country." (Hauner 1990, 11). In October 1988, in his wel-coming message to foreign guests attending the Asia-Pacific Region conference in Vladivostok, he stressed that "the Soviet Union was a Eurasian state ... to serve as a hopeful bridge bringing together two great continents" (Ibid, 249). Gorbachev's principal foreign policy advisor Georgi Shakhanazarov wrote later about his regret that the post-Soviet Commonwealth of Independent States was not named "the Commonwealth of the Euro-Asian States," which "would have emphasized the unique feature of our country that for centuries has served as a bridge between the two great continents and civilizations" (Shakhanazarov, 2001, 486). Gorbachev's liberal foreign minister Eduard Shevardnadze, too, referred to the Soviet Union as a "great Eurasian space" and a "world of worlds" (*mir mirov*). Citing the Russian philosopher Georgy Fedotov, Shevardnadze said

Russia had to politically live in a complex world of both European and Asian nations (Otunbayeva 1991, 186–187).[34]

The idea of a "world of worlds" was first proposed by the Soviet thinker Mikhail Gefter. Gefter, a liberal intellectual who used the notion of Eurasia to stress commonalities in historical legacy and development trajectory among the region's peoples. Eurasia was a "country of countries" and a group of diverse nations united by a common historical destiny (Gefter 1991, 460–467). The discussion took place during the years leading up to the Soviet breakup. With Gorbachev, Gefter defended the notion of Soviet path dependency and argued that "we cannot begin with how and by which means the European humanity emerged. We must not throw away everything that has been created through the suffering of our previous generations" (Gefter 1991, 37–63, 465). In the meantime, Russian intellectuals took issue with Western global dominance advocating the world's irredeemable diversity (Tsygankov 2004).

After the Soviet disintegration, Vadim Mezhuev, Aleksandr Panarin, and others have argued that Russia should continue to fulfill the mission of preserving a unique supranational community (Tolz 2001, 240). At the time, the general public supported the idea of a transnational community in the former USSR, showing support at sixty to seventy per cent. During the referendum of 17 March 1991, which took place in the context of Gorbachev's struggle for a renewed union in all of the Soviet republics except the three Baltics, Armenia, Georgia, and Moldavia, 147 million people voted, and 76.4 per cent approved the preservation of the union.[35] The president of Kazakhstan, Nursultan Nazarbayev, promoted the same idea of reviving the union of the republics as the integration of Eurasia while preserving the development of relations with the West (Suslov 2020, 205; Pantin 2022, 20).

The second birth of the Eurasia bridge idea took place after the Soviet dissolution, when Russia began to regain confidence as a prosperous economic power. Encouraged by economic prosperity and a growing political stabilization, scholars proposed connecting the region by stressing Russia's Eurasianist identity as an "intersection" of various economic and cultural influences in the area. They perceived the world as increasingly interdependent but also politically and culturally pluralist. They hoped that Russia would take advantage of its "intersection" position in Eurasia by implementing a coherent strategy of transregional economic development and preserving Eurasian political order and peace (Tsygankov 2003, 2022a). In the context of Russia's growing tensions with the West in the second half of the 1990s, and especially following the West-supported global democracy strategy, these ideas had run into difficulties finding support in the official circles and progressing to their practical implementation.

However, following Russia's officially proclaimed "turn to the East," the idea of the Eurasia bridge enjoyed a revitalization. For the first time, Eurasia was conceived as a system of Russia's unique relations with China, India, and other non-Western nations within the framework of the Shanghai Cooperation Organization and based on respect for commercial openness and political sovereignty. This ambitious idea also included the proposal to coordinate economic activities between China's One Belt and One Road project and the Russia-initiated Eurasian Economic Union. Russia's definition of itself as an "influential European and Asian power" in the official documents took on a new meaning.

Russia's "turn to the East" was proclaimed in 2012, when Putin wrote of the need to catch the "Chinese wind" in the "sails" of the Russian economy (*Valdai Club*, July 1, 2019).[36] In 2013, China introduced the One Belt and One Road project. The next push toward the new Eurasianism came following Russia's recent crisis in relations with the West following the 2014 annexation of Crimea. Russia had to rediscover the importance of non-European partners alongside geopolitics and civilizational self-awareness (Tsygankov 2022b). Behind the idea was the vision developed by experts associated with the Valdai Club, who presented the Eurasian space as the area from the Atlantic to the Pacific Ocean operating for the political and economic benefits of all the region's inhabitants. Goods and services are to flow from China, Russia, the Middle East, and other subregions. Europe, too, has been visualized as a potential contributor, while Russia's role is to facilitate the region's multilateralism and integration by preventing attempts by other powers to dominate Eurasia (Ibid).

Other Russian scholars specializing in Asia promoted the Eurasia bridge perspective. For instance, Vladimir Malyavin (2022) wrote the book *Evraziya i vsemirnost'* (Eurasia and the Integrated World), in which he advanced the notion of Eurasia as a meta-civilizational community. In his analysis, Eurasia incorporates Russia, Europe, and the larger northern Asian area. Eurasia functions as an economically, politically, and culturally diverse and open space on principles that differ from the nationalism of what the author defined as the "aggressive Western modernity" (Ibid.). In Malyavin's view, Russia proper "opposes all local and provincially limited civilizations" and has "all the reasons to claim the role of the genuinely global world" (Ibid).

Critics of the greater Eurasia idea include those skeptical of growing ties with China as potentially undermining Russia's sovereignty (Kortunov 2019) and those arguing for a closer alliance with non-Western nations. While the former advocate for the prioritization of relations with Europe, the latter are fearful of it as perpetuating Russia's political and economic dependence on the West.

Following the Russia–China declaration about reaching a new "level of strategic mutual trust" in January 2021, Russian experts favored further development of relations between the two countries, describing them as an "entente" and indicating all levels of military cooperation, except the NATO-like commitment to defending each other from an outside attack (For similar earlier views, see Lukin 2020; Trenin 2020). This view grew even more prominent in Russia following the 2022 war in Ukraine. The war has further isolated Moscow from the West due to the latter's support for Kyiv, as China, India, Iran, and other non-Western powers refused to support the West's sanctions against Russia. All three powers have been members of the Shanghai Cooperation Organization, alongside Russia – the central institution for organizing economic and political activities in Eurasia. The organization has not included any Western members. These developments suggest that, despite Russia's initial intent for the greater Eurasia to include Europe, the dialogue in Eurasia will remain confined mainly to non-Western powers.

Conclusion

Of all Russian civilizational theories, Eurasianism was the least inclined to hold a dialogue with Western nations. In some respects, the movement was created as anti-Western and focused on opposing Europe and the West. Even Tsymbursky, who was not principally anti-Western, opposed rapprochement with the West, particularly in countering terrorism in Central Asia and Afghanistan. He favored cooperation with China, India, and Iran to influence the territories adjacent to Russia but not with Western countries.[37]

The second significant weakness of Eurasianism was also associated with its focus on geopolitics and the related insufficient attention to the development of the values of Russian civilization. Trubetskoi and his supporters still set the task of formulating a new ideology. They showed an active interest in discussing the possibility of combining Eurasianist, Orthodox, and other traditional Russian values.[38] Others like Savitsky, Gumilev, Dugin, and Tsymbursky seemed less interested in the country's spiritual foundations. Characteristic in this respect is the criticism from the Slavophiles, some of whom blamed the Eurasianists for forgetting Orthodox spirituality.[39] The latter prompted some representatives of Eurasianism to migrate to the camp of Slavophilism.[40]

In post-Soviet conditions, the Eurasian tradition of fortress and expansion has continued in the work of supporters of Danilevsky and Savitsky, on the one hand, and those who, like Dugin, are inspired by the Western geopolitical theories of Mackinder and European far-right thinkers. Dugin's supporters worked to justify territorial expansion, while Danilevsky's followers continued to develop the ideas of geopolitical self-sufficiency and internal development of Russia (Mezhuev 2012; *In Memoriam* 2015). Both schools proceeded from the importance of confronting the West for the Eurasian survival of the country.

Eurasianism is not doomed to serve the purposes of Russia's confrontation with or estrangement from the western part of the world (or other civilizations). Russia remains at a cross-road. The new generation of Russian IR scholars is beginning to rethink the ethnocentrism and civilizational exceptionalism of Danilevsky, Gumilev, and other Eurasian thinkers. There have been those in Russia positioning it as holding a central position in the "greater Eurasia" and, therefore, able to benefit from the larger environment's economic, political, and cultural influences. Such "pragmatic Eurasianism" (Vinokurov 2013) may take root in the region. Although Russian officials often present Eurasian projects to strengthen the country's geopolitical power and security, they continue to be interested in global openness for economic and technological development.

Therefore, Eurasianist theory can contribute to a better understanding of the political dimension of global processes. The truth of Eurasianism lies in considering the region as culturally diverse yet integrated and interconnected. The geopolitical concepts of "independence" and the "spatial development" (*mestorazvitiye*) – the attention to borders, and a strong state – can find their application in current conditions.[41] The global realities of the world do not disqualify geopolitics but place countries and regions in new conditions for spatial development. In the ideas of Russian geographers-travelers of the nineteenth century, Eurasianist philosophers of the twentieth century, and their contemporary supporters, one can identify a deep understanding of the geopolitical and cultural roots of the continent's problems and solutions. They have reasons to insist on stabilizing the continent as a single political space. Faced with the threat of internal anarchy and external interference, many Eurasianists accepted – albeit with a heavy heart – the USSR as a form of such stabilization. Today, when the revival of the Soviet Union is impossible, Eurasianists again view Russia as an essential contributor to stabilizing this complex heartland and its diversity of peoples.

Notes

1 Arnold Toynbee's notion of "external proletariat" captures the violent potential of these borderland territories. In Russian geopolitics, Tsymburski (2007) theorized the areas as located in between "civilizations" introducing in their description the notion of Limitrof.

2 The Ottoman Empire developed similar relations with its Jewish and Christian minorities. See Lieven (2006, 149).

3 For a sample of studies of Russia in Eurasia, both critical and supportive of the heartland thesis, see Trenin 2001; Tsygankov 2003; Bassin and Aksenov 2006; Bassin 2009; Suslov 2020.

4 For the initial argument about continuity between the old and new Russia see Berdyayev (1937).

5 Danilevski's influence on Eurasianists is well recognized. On the impact of Leontyev, see Pashchenko 2000, 198–220.

6 This was noticed by Vadim Tsymbursky (2000).

7 Towards the end of his life, Leontyev became disappointed in the Russian ability to survive as an authentic culture. In a letter to the philosopher, Vasily Rozanov, Leontiev even wrote that "the Chinese are destined to conquer Russia when our *mixing* (with Europeans, etc.) reaches its highest point. And *such* Russia doesn't deserve another road." (Khatuntsev 2011).

8 Solovyev's reaction to Leontyev's work was also generally critical (Solovyev 1990, 418).

9 Solovyov, for example, was known for his negative attitude towards both the Muslim East and Asia and the "yellow danger" emanating from it (see Chapter 4 for more details).

10 In this regard, the definition of Eurasianism as "Slavophilism of the era of Futurism" by Fyodor Stepun is telling (about Futurist influences on Eurasianism, see Glebov 2017).

11 On this and other influences on Eurasianism, see also Riasanovsky 1967; Bassin 2011.

12 In the early twentieth century, some linguists viewed the Turanian family of languages as including most languages of the Eurasian region, while excluding those of Indo-European, Semitic, and Chinese.

13 Savitsky attached particular importance to the military-technical capabilities of the Eurasian culture to resist the hostile Romano-Germanic culture. Arguing with Trubetskoi in his desire to isolate himself from everything European, including "technology and empirical knowledge", Savitsky opposed the "preaching of cultural weakness" and actively borrowed technical achievements under the condition of ideological self-sufficiency (Savitsky 1998, 215–216).

14 On historical thinking of Eurasianists, see Пащенко 2000; Laruelle 2008.

15 Such an understanding, however, did not prevent supporters of the White Idea like Ivan Ilyin from accusing Eurasianism of switching to "the soil of Russian communism, socialism and populism", as well as "acceptance, cessation of the struggle, strong-willed admiration, adaptation, practical fact-worship" before the USSR (Isayev 1992, 424).

16 For more on conflicts within Eurasianism, see Shlapentokh 1997.

17 In his work *The Power of the Weak*, he wrote about the dangers of "cosmopolitan wanderings and temptations of the Russian godless, sinful intellectual spirit" responsible for the "Bolshevik International." He called for the reconciliation of the people and the intelligentsia under the "all-permissive dome of the Orthodox Church" (Suvchinsky 2002, c. 366).

18 For details on Suvchinsky's views on revolution, see Glebov 2006.

19 Gumilev 1990. The book's original edition appeared in 1979 and was unknown to non-specialists. However, among ethnographers and geographers, the book was widely discussed. Since Gorbachev's perestroika, it has become one of the most popular, along with other works of the thinker (Gumilev 1989; 1992; 1993a, b). See Bassin 2009, 2016 for a detailed analysis of Gumilev's theories and influence in modern Russia.

20 Gumilev refers here to Savitsky 1927.

21 On Gumilev's theory of inter-ethnic relations, see Gumilev 1990, 87–100. The community that arises at the junction of two super-ethnic groups, Gumilev called a "chimera."

22 The application of theory of ethnogenesis to Russia was developed in more detail in Gumilev 1992a.

23 For an analysis of Russian geopolitical theories, see Kolosov and Mironenko 2002; Gadzhiyev 2007; Tsymbursky 2007; Solovyev 2010; Silayev and Sushentsov 2017; Okunev 2019; Tsygankov 2022a.

24 For a similar triple classification of perspectives on Eurasia as the third continent, the anti-Western Eurasia, and the greater Eurasia, see Suslov 2020, 207.

25 This section draws on Tsygankov 2017.

26 For Danilevsky's influence on Ustryalov's ideology, see Agursky 1987.

27 For Western studies of Russian nationalism, see Dunlop 1983, 1985; Agurski 1987; Brudny 1998; Tuminez 2000.

28 In particular, Kirill endorsed *Russkaya doktrina* (2007).

29 Tsymbursky also took issue with Danilevsky's hopes for tactical cooperation with Germany as the nation capable of destroying Russia's favored cultural influence in Eurasia. Parts of Tsymbursky's have been published posthumously (*In Memoriam* 2015).

30 Besides Panarin, other Eurasianist thinkers listed in the survey as important are Nicholai Gumelev (10%), Nicholai Trubetskoi (8%), and Nicholai Savitsky (5%) (Tsygankov 2017).

31 Such broad definitions of Eurasia are often practiced by those who, like Dugin, believe in the possibility of ruling the continent from a single center. Among Western adherents of such definitions, the works of Zbigniew Brzezinski (1998) are especially well-known.

32 Among other Western intellectuals seeking to "wipe Russia out of history," Dugin mentioned Brzezinski, who once applied the colorful metaphor of a "black hole" in the middle of Eurasia to Russia (Ibid, 8). Another frequent target of Dugin was Francis Fukuyama (Ibid, 127, 179).

33 For details, see Tsygankov 2022a, chap. 4.

34 Even among the Westernizers, Andrei Sakharov defended the notion of Eurasia and wrote his project, "Constitution of the Union of the Soviet republics of Europe and Asia" (Sakharov 1990, 266–276). For details, see Tsygankov 2002.

35 The wording of the question was as follows: "Do you support the preservation of the union as a renewed federation of sovereign republics in which the rights of a person of any nationality are fully guaranteed?" The Yelstin-led Democratic Russia has actively campaigned against the referendum (Kotz and Weir 1997, 147).

36 For a discussion of the turn, see Blakkisrud and Rowe 2018.

37 After the terrorist attacks on the United States in September 2001, Tsymbursky (2001) criticized the Russian leadership, which, in his opinion, agreed to participate in a "foreign war" and "surrendered" Central Asia and Georgia to the Americans.

38 On the role of religion in classical Eurasianism, see Bazavluk 2020.

39 Such reproaches were made, for example, by Berdyaev.

40 For example, I mean the ideological evolution of Alexander Panarin, who in the 2000s took the position of an Orthodox Christian thinker. See chap. 3). Recognition of this problem is more common for contemporary Eurasianists, who develop their ideas in dialogue with Slavophiles and pay considerable attention to the value-spiritual dimension of Russian identity (*In Memoriam* 2015).

41 An example of the reformulation of traditional geopolitical principles to the conditions of globalization is Gadzhiev's (2007) work. He redefined the concept of geographic space by stressing "economic, cultural-civilizational, informational, etc." ways to stabilize the region and argued for creating a system of collective security with the participation of all the region's central states.

Further Reading

Konstantin Leontyev and Classical Eurasianism

Bassin, M. 2016. *The Gumilev Mystique*. Ithaca, NY: Cornell University Press.

Bassin, M., S. Glebov, and M. Laruelle, eds. 2015. *Between Europe and Asia*. DeKalb: Northern Illinois University Press.

Glebov, S. 2017. *From Empire to Eurasia*. DeKalb: Northern Illinois University Press.

Gumilev, L. N. 1992. *Ot Rusi k Rossiyi*. Moscow.

Hauner, M. 1990. *What Is Asia to Us?* London: Routledge.

Laruelle, M. 2008. *Russian Eurasianism: An Ideology of Empire*. Washington, DC: The Johns Hopkins University Press.

Leontyev, K. 1991. Vizantizm i slavyanstvo. In: *Rossiya glazami russkogo*, edited by A. F. Zamaleev. St. Petersburg: Nauka.

Pashchenko, V. Ya. 2000. *Ideologiya yevraziistva*. Moscow: Izdatel'tsvo MGU.

Riasanovsky, N. 1967. The Emergence of Eurasianism. *California Slavic Studies* 4.

Schimmelpenninck Van Der Oye, D. *Russian Orientalism*. New Haven, 2008,
Tolz, V. 2011. *Russia's Own Orient*. Oxford and New York, Oxford University Press.

Eurasianist Currents after the USSR

Bassin, M. 1991. Russia between Europe and Asia. *Slavic Review* 50, 1.
———. 2009. The Emergence of Ethno-Geopolitics in Post-Soviet Russia. *Eurasian Geography and Economics* 50, 2
Bassin, M, C. Ely, and M. K. Stockdale, eds. 2011. *Space, Place and Power in Modern Russia*. DeKalb: Northern Illinois University Press.
Dugin, A., ed. 2002. *Osnovy Yevraziystva*. Moscow: Aktogeya.
———. 2015. *Geopolitika*. Moscow: Akademichesky proyekt.
Katzenstein, P. J. and N. Weygrant. 2017. Mapping Eurasia in an Open World. *Perspectives on Politics* 15, 2.
Suslov, M. 2020. *Geopolitical Imagination: Ideology and Utopia in Post-Soviet Russia*. New York: Ibidem, Columbia University Press.
Tsygankov, A. P. 2003. Mastering Space in Eurasia. *Communist and Post-Communist Studies* 36, 1.
———. 2017. In the Shadow of Nikolai Danilevskii. *Europe-Asia Studies*.
Tsymbursky, V. 2007. *Ostrov Rossiya*. Moscow: Rosspen.
———. 2016. *Morfologiya rossiyskoi geopolitiki i dinamika mezhdunarodnykh system XVIII-XX vekov*. Moscow: Knizhnyi mir.

The "Greater Eurasia"

Diesen, G. 2017. *Russia's Geoeconomic Strategy for a Greater Eurasia*. London: Routledge.
Gadzhiyev, K. S. 2007. *Geopoliticheskiye gorizonty Rossiyi*. Moscow: Mezhdunarodnyie otnosheniya.
Karaganov, S, ed. 2017. *K velikomu okeanu 5: ot povorota na Vostok k Bol'shoi Yevraziyi*. Moscow: Valdai Club, September.
Kotlyakov, V. M. and V. A. Shuper, eds. 2019. *Russia in the forming Greater Eurasia*. Moscow: "Kodeks" Publishing House.
Lane, D. and V. Samokhvalov, eds. 2015. *The Eurasian Project and Europe*. London: Palgrave.
Lewis, D. G. 2018. Geopolitical Imaginaries in Russian Foreign Policy: The Evolution of "Greater Eurasia." *Europe-Asia Studies* 70, 10.
Lukin, A. and V. Yakunin. 2018. Eurasian integration and the development of Asiatic Russia. *Journal of Eurasia Studies* 9.
Lukin, A. and G. Diesen, eds. 2020. *Russia in a Changing World*. New York: Palgrave.
Malyavin, V. 2022. *Evraziya i vsemirnost': novyi vzglyad na prorodu Evraziyi*. Moscow: Shans.
Rogov, S. 1998. *Yevrasiyskaia strategiya dlya Rossiyi*. Moscow: Institute SshA i Kanadi.
Vinokurov, Ye. 2013. Pragamticheskoye yevraziystvo. *Rossiya v global'noi politike* 2.

References

Agurski, Mikhail. 1987. *The Third Rome: National Bolshevism in the USSR*. Boulder, CO: Westview.
Bassin, Mark. 2009. The Emergence of Ethno-Geopolitics in Post-Soviet Russia. *Eurasian Geography and Economics* 50, 2.

————. 2011. Environmentalist Discourses in Classical Eurasianism. In: *Space, Place and Power in Modern Russia*, edited by M. Bassin, C. Ely, M. K. Stockdale. DeKalb: Northern Illinois University Press.

————. 2009. The Emergence of Ethno-Geopolitics in Post-Soviet Russia. *Eurasian Geography and Economics* 50, 2.

————. 2016. *The Gumilev Mystique*. Ithaca, NY: Cornell University Press.

Bassin, Mark and Konstantin E. Aksenov. 2006. Mackinder and the Heartland Theory in Post-Soviet Geopolitical Discourse. *Geopolitics* 11, 1.

Bazavluk, Sergei V. 2020. Eurasianists on the Role of Orthodoxy and the Church in the National-State Development of Russia. *RUDN Journal of Russian History* 19, 1.

Berdyayev, Nikolai. 1937. *Istoki i smysl russkogo kommunizma*. Paris: IMCA Press.

Blakkisrud, H. and E. Wilson Rowe, eds. 2018. *Russia's Turn to the East: Domestic Policymaking and Regional Cooperation*. Springer.

Brudny, Y. M. 1998. *Reinventing Russia. Russian Nationalism and the Soviet State, 1953–1991*. Cambridge, MA: Harvard University Press.

Brzezinski, Z. 1998. *The Grand Chessboard*. Basic Books.

Crews, Robert D. 2006. *For Prophet and Tsar*. Cambridge, MA: Harvard University Press.

Danilevsky, Nikolai. 1990. *Rossiya i Yevropa*. Moscow: Kniga.

Dugin, Aleksandr. 2000. *Osnovy geopolitiki*, 2nd ed. Moscow: Arktogeya.

————. 2015. *Geopolitika*. Moscow: Akademichesky proyekt.

————. 2022a. Rossiya protiv anti-Rossyiyi: interesy i tsennosti. *Katehon*, March 28.

————. 2022b. Dlya Nezygaria. July 18. https://t.me/russica2.

Duncan Peter J. S. 2000. *Russian Messianism: Third Rome, Revolution, Communism and After*. London: Routledge.

Dunlop, John B. 1983. *Faces of Contemporary Russian Nationalism*. Princeton: Princeton University Press, 1983.

————. 1985. *The New Russian Nationalism*. Boulder, CO: Westview.

Gadzhiyev, Kamaludin. 2007. *Geopoliticheskiye gorizonty Rossiyi: kontury novogo mirovogo poryadka*. Moscow: Ekonomika.

Gefter, Mikhail. 1991. *Iz tekh i etikh let*. Moscow: Progress.

Glebov, Sergei. 2006. Le frémiss ement du temps: Petr Suvchinsky, l'eurasisme et l'esthétique de la modernité. par. In: *Pierre Souvtchinsky, cashiers d'étude*, edited by E. Humbertclaude. Paris.

Gumilev, Lev N. 1989. *Drevnyaya Rus' i Velikaya Step'*. Moscow: Khranitel'.

————. 1990. *Etnogenez i biosfera zemli*. Moscow: Mishel.

————. 1992a. *Ot Rusi k Rossiyi*. Moscow: Progress.

————. 1992b. *V poiskah vymyshlennogo tsarstva*. Moscow: Azbuka.

————. 1993a. *Drenviye tyurki*. Moscow: Klyshnikov.

————. 1993b. *Hunnu: stepnaya trilogiya*. Moscow: AST.

————. 2002. Skazhu vam po sekretu. In: *Osnovy yevraziystva*, edited by A. Dugin. Moscow: Arktogeya.

Gumilev, Lev, V. Yermolayev. 2002. Gore ot illyuziy. In: *Osnovy yevraziystva*, edited by A. Dugin. Moscow: Arktogeya.

Hauner, Milan. 1990. *What Is Asia to Us?* London: Routledge.

Hosking, Geoffrey. 1997. *Russia: People and Empire, 1552–1917*. Cambridge, MA: Harvard University Press.

In Memoriam. 2015. In Memoriam. V. L. Tsymbursky. *Tetradi po konservatizmu* 1, ISEPI.

Isayev, Igor' A., ed. 1992. *Puti Yevraziyi*. Moscow: Yurist.

Khatuntsev, Stanislav. 2011. Kitayskaya ugroza u Konstantina Leontyeva i Vladimira Solovyeva. *Russkiy zhurnal*, February 28 www.russ.ru/pole/Kitajskaya-ugroza-u-Konstantina-Leont-eva-i-Vladimira-Solov-eva-1.

Kolosov, Vladimir A. and Nikolai S. Mironenko. 2002. *Geopolitika i politicheskaya geografiya*. Moscow: Aspekt Press.

Kortunov, Sergei. 2009. *Stanovleniye Natsional'noi Identichnosti*. Moscow: ROSSPEN.

Kortunov, Andrei. 2019. Vossoyedineniye hartlenda. In: *Russia in the forming Greater Eurasia*, edited by V. M. Kotlyakov and V. A. Shuper. Moscow: "Kodeks" Publishing House.

Kotz, David and Fred Weir. 1997. *Revolution from Above: The Demise of the Soviet System*. London: Routledge.

Lamansky, Vladimir. 1916. *Tri mira Aziysko-Yevropeiskogo materika*. 2nd ed. Petrograd: Novoye vremya.

Laruelle, Marlene. 2004. *Ideologiya russkogo yevraziystva*. Moscow: Natalis.

———. 2008. *Russian Eurasianism*. Washington, DC: The Johns Hopkins University Press.

LeDonne, John. 2020. *Forging a Unitary State: Russia's Management of the Eurasian Space, 1650–1850*. University of Toronto Press.

Leontyev, Konstantin. 1991. Vizantizm i slavyanstvo. In: *Rossiya glazami russkogo*, edited by A. F. Zamaleev. St. Petersburg: Nauka.

Lieven, Dominique. 2006. *Empire: The Russian Empire and Its Rivals*. New Haven, CT: Yale University Press.

Lukin, Aleksandr. 2020. The Russia–China Entente and its Future. *International Politics*.

Mackinder, Halford. 1943. The round world and the winning of the peace. *Foreign Affairs* 21, 4.

Malyavin, Vladimir. 2022. *Evraziya i vsemirnost': novyi vzglyad na prorodu Evraziyi*. Moscow: Shans.

Martin, Steven. 2001. *The Affirmative Action Empire*. Harvard University Press.

McDaniel, Timothy. 1996. *The Agony of the Russian Idea*. Princeton: Princeton University Press.

MccGwire, Michail. 1991. *Perestroika and Soviet National Security*. Washington, DC: The Brookings Institution.

Mechnikov, Lev. 2019 [1889]. *Tsivilizatsiya i velikiye istoricheskiye reki*. Moscow: Yurait.

Mezhuyev, Boris. 2012. *Politicheskaya Kritika Vadima Tsimburskogo*. Moscow: Yevropa.

Narochnitskaya, Natalya A. 2004. *Rossiya i russkiye v mirivoi istoriyi*. Moscow: Mezhdunarodnyye otnosheniya.

Nartov, Nikolai A. 1999. *Geopolitika*. Moskva: Yuniti.

Novikova, Lyudmila and Irina Sizemskaya. 1997. *Russkaya filosofiya istoriyi*. Moscow: Rosspen.

Okunev, Igor. 2019. *Politicheskaya geografiya*. Moscow: Aspekt press.

Otunbayeva, Roza. 1991. V preddveriyi novogo miroporyadka. *Mezhdunarodnaya zhizn'* 3: 183–191.

Pantin, Vladimir I. 2022. Ideologicheskiye osnovy yevraziyskoi ekonomicheskoi integratsiyi. *RUDN International Relations* 22, 1.

Pashchenko, Vitaliy Ya. 2000. *Ideologiya yevraziystva*. Moscow: Moskovskiy universitet.

Potapov, Aleksandr. 2000. Spetssluzhby i Yevraziya. www.agentura.ru/library/eurazia/i

Riasanovsky Nikolas. V. 1967. The Emergence of Eurasianism. *California Slavic Studies* 4

Russkaya doktrina 2007, edited by A. Averyanov. Москва: Yauza.

Sakharov, Andrei D. 1990. *Trevoga i nadezhda*. Moskva: Progress.

Savitski, Pyotr. N. 1927. *Geograficheskiye osobennosti Rossiyi*. Prague: Yevraziyskoye knigoizdatel'sto.

————. 1998. Yevropa i Yevraziya. In: Orlova, I. B. *Yevraziyskaya tsivilizatsiya.* Moscow: Norma.

Semyonov-Tan'-Shansky, Vladimir. 1915. O mogushchesvennom territorial'nom vladenii primenitel'no k Rossiyi. *Izvestiya Imperatorskogo russkogo geograficheskogo obshchestva* LI,

Shakhnazarov, Georgi. 2001. *S vozhdyami i bez nikh.* Moskva: Vagrius.

Shlapentokh Dmitry. V. 1997. Eurasianism: Past and Present. *Communist and Post-Communist Studies* 30, 2.

Silayev, Nikolai and Andrei Sushentsov. 2017. Soyuzniki Rossiyi i geopolitichesky frontir v Yevraziyi, *Valdai International Discussion Club,* Paper No. 66, April.

Solozobov, Yu. 2022. Geopoliticheskiye smysly Tegeranskogo sammita. *Russkaya istina,* August 4.

Solovyev, Eduard G. 2010. *Rossiya v mire.* Moscow: IMEMO.

Solovyev, Vladimir. 1990. Danilevsky. In: *Sochineniya,* 2nd ed. Vol. 2. Moscow: Nauka.

Suslov, Mikhail. 2020. *Geopolitical Imagination: Ideology and Utopia in Post-Soviet Russia.* New York: Ibidem, Columbia University Press,

Suvchinski, Pyotr. 1929. Pax Eurasiana. *Евразия* 10.

————. 2002. Sila slabykh. In: *Osnovy yevraziystva,* edited by A. Dugin. Moscow: Arktogeya.

Taylor, Peter J. 1996. *The Way the Modern World Works.* Chichester and New York.

Tolz, Vera. 2001. *Russia.* London: Arnold.

Trenin, Dmitry. 2001. *The End of Eurasia.* Moscow: Carnegie Endowment for International Peace.

————. 2020. China–Russia Relationship Model for Major Powers. *Global Times,* July 15.

Trubetskoi, Nikolai. S. 1993. O turanskom elemente v russkoi kul'ture. In: *Rossiya mezhdu Yevropoi i Aziyei,* edited by L. Novikova and I. Sizemskaya. Moscow: Nauka.

————. 1998. Yevropa i chelovechestvo. In: Orlova, I. B. *Yevraziyskaya tsivilizatsiya.* Moscow: Norma.

————. 2002a. Naslediye Chingishana: Vzglyad na russkuyu istoriyu ne s Zapada, a s Vostoka. In: *Osnovy Yevraziystva,* edited by Aleksandr Dugin. Moscow: Aktogeya.

————. 2002b. Ob ideye-pravitel'nitse ideokraticheskogo gosudarstva. In: *Osnovy Evraziystva,* edited by Aleksandr Dugin. Moscow: Arktogeya.

————. 2002c. My i drugiye. In: *Osnovy Evraziystva,* edited by Aleksandr Dugin. Moscow: Arktogeya.

Tsygankov, Andrei P. 2002. The Return to Eurasia. In: *Economic Nationalism in a Globalizing World,* edited by Eric Helleiner and Andreas Pickel. Ithaca, NY: Cornell University Press.

————. 2003. Mastering Space in Eurasia. *Communist and Post-Communist Studies* 36, 1.

————. 2004. *Whose World Order?* University of Notre Dame Press.

————. 2008. Self and Other in International Relations Theory. *International Studies Review* 10, 4.

————. 2012. The Heartland No More. *Journal of Eurasian Studies* 1, 1,

————. 2017. In the Shadow of Nikolai Danilevskii. *Europe-Asia Studies* 69, 4.

————. 2022a. *Russia Realism.* London: Routledge.

————. 2022b. Russia, Eurasia, and the Meaning of Crimea. *Europe-Asia Studies* 74, 9.

Tsymbursky, Vadim. 2000. Skol'ko tsivilizatsiy? S Lamanskim, Shpenglerom i Toinbi nad globusom XXI veka. *Pro et Contra* 5.

————. 2001. Eto tvoi posledniy geokul'turny vybor, Rossiya. *Polis,* November www.politstudies.ru/universum/esse/7zmb.htm#14.

————. 2007. *Ostrov Rossiya*. Moscow: Rosspen.

Tuminez, Astrid. 2000. *Russian Nationalism since 1856: Ideology and the Making of Foreign Policy*. Boulder, CO: Rowman & Littlefield.

Valdai Club, July 1, 2019. Russia's Turn to the East: Expectations and the Reality. Moscow: Valdai Club.

Vinokurov, Yevgeny. 2013. Pragamticheskoye yevraziystvo. *Rossiya v global'noi politike* 2.

Woodburn, Stephen M. 2013. Preface to Danilevskii, N. Ia. *Russia and Europe*. Slavica, Indiana University Press.

Yakunin, Vladimir. 2013. Politicheskaia tektonika sovremennogo mira. *Polis*, no. 4.

Yevraziystvo. 2002. *Yevraziystvo*. Opyt sistemticheskogo izlozheniya. In: *Osnovy yevraziystva*, edited by A. Dugin. Moscow: Arktogeya.

Zyuganov, Gennady. 1999. *Geografiya pobedy*. Moskva: Unknown publisher.

————. 2002. *Globalizatsiya i sud'ba chelovechestva*. Moscow: Molodaya gvardiya.

6

THE "RUSSIAN IDEA" FOR RUSSIA AND THE WORLD

If we cannot learn to listen to others as they whisper their prayers, we may well confront them later on when they howl their war cries.

James Billington (1997)

The final chapter summarizes my review of the RI. At the center of Russian thinking is the attention given to the nation's identity resulting from relations with and contribution to the global world. The RI is inextricably connected to Russia's search for optimal relations with the West and the rest of the world and a better national and global future along the lines of preserving the spiritual, social, and geopolitical values formulated by the three schools of thought. The chapter identifies varieties of exceptionalism (fortress and expansion) and dialogue among the Slavophiles, the Communists, and the Eurasianists.

Apart from exceptionalism, Russian thinkers have promoted ideas of dialogue in spiritual–ideational, sociopolitical, and regional dimensions. The Russian concept of dialogue assumes the importance of not abandoning one's values but developing them in conversations and relations with others. Russian thought identifies the meaning of Russia's contribution to the world as the ideal of a free, integral personality developing in an interconnected and mutually responsible world. In such an ideal world without ideological and other extremes, spiritual freedom, economic development, and individual social and geopolitical values will not be affirmed through the exploitation of other peoples with their distinct histories and traditions. In this world, the global will grow from below without Western or other civilizations' dominance or attempts to present cultural values as universal. The latter especially concerns the West's ideals of secularization, capitalism, and liberal democracy. While in constant dialogue with European and Western thought, Russian thinkers continuously stress an alternative to the Western understanding of personality, tradition, and modernity.

DOI: 10.4324/9781003377573-6

In addition to summing up the reflections of Slavophiles, Communists, and Eurasianists, the chapter offers a brief assessment of Russian thought regarding the war in Ukraine. Russian exceptionalists, or advocates of strengthening the imperial state in the face of Western pressure, have supported the war, viewing it as the struggle for the very survival of Russia as a civilization. The position of supporters of dialogue and the establishment of a globally pluralist world turned out to be entirely different. Not desiring Russia's military defeat in a confrontation with Ukraine and its Western supporters, this group of Russian thinkers argued for creating conditions for a compromise and ending the war without achieving the goals set by the Kremlin for the complete "demilitarization" and "denazification" of Ukraine. The thinkers of the latter group have also proposed paths for building relations with the outside world based on dialogue, not national exceptionalism.

In attempting to move beyond the stereotypical interpretation of the RI as an apology for an aggressive anti-Western empire, I critically examine such arguments expressed by thinkers of liberal orientation. These interpretations have historical origins but have become especially prevalent in the context of the war in Ukraine, resulting in loud calls from different parts of the European and Western world to "cancel" the Russian culture of "aggression" and "decolonize" Russia and its internal political structure.

The final part of the chapter analyzes the promises of the concepts of dialogue and an integral personality in a globally interconnected world. Conditions for implementing these ideas include ending the war in Ukraine and establishing a just peace in the interest and security of all involved parties. The outside world should facilitate a resolution of the conflict by considering the complexity of its roots. Such an approach will likely reduce the appeal of nationalism and militarism on both sides of the conflict. Russia may then rediscover its mission of promoting global pluralism by opposing attempts to rule the world from one center and proposing ideas of international cooperation. The absence of such pluralism and cooperation is fraught with the growth of nationalism in the world.

Faces of the Russian Idea

The Fortress

A considerable part of those advancing the RI is supportive of viewing Russia as a fortress against foreign, especially Western, pressures. The ideals of the fortress grow influential in the context of weakening Russian–European relations. Such weakening prompts Russian thinkers to call for the country to build on its spiritual roots dating back to Byzantium, a unique system of social and political relations, and a particular geographic position. Another reason for the growing influence of the fortress ideals is the country's relative weakness and inability to actively promote Russian ideals abroad.

Of the Slavophiles whose views I have considered, the supporters of the fortress ideal were those who viewed Russian Orthodox Christianity and the peasant commune as the only valid values superior to those of all other peoples and who insisted on the preservation of these values in isolation from Europe. For example, Konstantin Aksakov was especially fearful of the rise of liberal and revolutionary concepts on the European continent. He argued for the need to shield Russia from these ideas. Aksakov traced the revolutionary development of the West and its influence on Russia to the reforms of Peter the Great. Aksakov's limited expansionism was evident in his support for the Crimean War, which he viewed as the liberation of the Orthodox Christians within the Ottoman Empire. However, at the same time, Aksakov wanted no relations with Europe to strengthen the Russian foundations inside Russia.

Following the Crimean War, Pan-Slavists supported strengthening Russia in separation from the European peoples. One Pan-Slavist thinker, Nikolai Danilevsky, shared Aksakov's anxieties while especially wary of the rise of Germany. Seeing the dangers of growing militarism in Europe, Danilevsky advocated a tactical improvement of relations with Germany. At the same time, he argued the importance of establishing a powerful militarist state and supported Peter's military-administrative reforms. While supporting such reforms, Danilevsky condemned what he viewed as Peter's pro-Western cultural attitudes insisting that Russia is a particular "cultural-historic type," different from European or "Romano-Germanic."

During the same period, the idea of a fortress developed among Russian Communists, who desired Russia's isolation from Europe. Like Slavophiles, Russian social thinkers feared the revolution on Russian soil. However, they associated the future of the country with the peasant commune. Following Alexander Herzen, Russian populists promoted the ideas of peasant socialism. For example, Nikolai Mikhailovsky created the theory of a holistic personality (*tselostnaya lichnost'*), whose development he considered impossible on the industrial basis of Western civilization. Politically, Mikhailovsky advocated the establishment of a powerful state to liberate the individual from above. Russian Anarchists also supported the commune of peasants, workers, and artisans as the foundation of emancipated and holistic human existence.

Following the Bolshevik Revolution, isolationist ideas were advanced by those fearful of Russia's spiritual, ideological, political, and cultural enslavement by European nations. Among Slavophiles, such fears were expressed by Ivan Ilyin and his supporters, who strongly opposed the Bolshevik system. Ilyin considered the establishment of the Soviet Union and the very idea of socialism as manifestations of Russia's spiritual capitulation to the powerful Western nations. He believed that these powers introduced socialist ideas to weaken Russia. Ilyin associated the country's spiritual revival with the Orthodox faith, strong state, and the rule of law. After the Second World War, Alexander Solzhenitsyn advocated similar ideas.

During Russia's post-revolutionary weakness and civil war, Russian Communists also began to consider the possibility of West-independent development. The Bolsheviks, who came to power, soon abandoned the theory of world revolution in favor of Joseph Stalin's idea of socialism in one country surviving under the hostile environment of world capitalism. Following the Second World War, the concepts of independent development and "building socialism" progressed within the Soviet Union in polemics with supporters of greater openness to Western countries.

Finally, during the post-Revolutionary weakness, isolationism progressed within the Eurasianist movement. Like Ilyin, many Eurasianists expressed an extremely negative attitude toward the Bolshevik regime in Russia while remaining fearful of European influence on the country. Following Danilevsky, they viewed Russia as a particular cultural and historical type, the emergence of which they associated with the country's unique geography and Turkic-Mongolian influences. Nikolai Trubetskoi, Pyotr Savitsky, and others viewed Russia's geographic, sociocultural, ethnic, economic, and political self-sufficiency as the foundation of the Eurasian continent. After the Second World War, Lev Gumilev, a student of Savitsky, continued to develop these same ideas. Gumilev created his theory of cyclical human development based on local cultures' internal laws, geography, and interaction with the natural and cosmic environment. In his way, he substantiated the idea of mutual cultural and geopolitical hostility between Russia and Europe.

The idea of a fortress received a new birth after the collapse of the Soviet state and failed attempts by Russia to integrate into the community of Western countries. Among the Slavophiles, the attitude of returning to the ideals of the Orthodox Third Rome and opposing Western "spirituality" has strengthened. Alexander Panarin and his supporters expressed these sentiments in their writings. Such views also developed among Communists who, like Stalin, advocated economic and political self-sufficiency within the former Soviet region. Gennady Zyuganov, the leader of the Communist Party of the Russian Federation, supported these ideas, as did others. At the same time, Communists endorsed the notion of geopolitical self-sufficiency by building on the views of the Eurasianists.

The Expansion

Relative to advocates of the fortress model, expansionists are less common among theorists of the RI, yet visible and potentially influential. Those advancing expansionist ideas believe the West is hostile and weak due to Russia's material and ideological capabilities.

Among Slavophiles, expansionism rises whenever there is a need to protect Orthodox Christians or those ethnically close to Russians. During the Crimean War, many Slavophiles advocated the liberation of the "Slavic brothers" from Turkish rule and, ultimately, the "liberation" of Byzantium and Constantinople as the spiritual foundation of Russia. The sentiments for liberating the Slavs in the Balkans grew strong during the last third of the nineteenth century, resulting from Russian victories over the Turks and the perception that Europe was too weak and fragmented to resist Russia's imperial advancement. Some of the late Slavophiles, such as Mikhail Pogodin, Rostislav Fadeyev, and others, advocated the capture of Constantinople and the unification of the Slavs into a single state. Others, including Ivan Aksakov, opposed such actions while supporting the pan-Slavist confederation.

Among Communists, those supportive of Russian expansion included Anarchists led by Mikhail Bakunin. Bakunin insisted on the need to destroy the state as an institution while sympathizing with the Slavic idea. He advocated the crushing of the Russian, Austrian, and German empires in the interests of a more universal, especially Slavic, unification. The revolutionary ideas of Vladimir Lenin and Leon Trotsky, who wanted to seize power in Russia and develop the world's revolutionary process on its basis, spread among the Social Democrats. Both theorists of world communism substantiated the world's readiness for a global breakdown in their works *Imperialism* and *Permanent Revolution*.

After the revolution, Lenin and Trotsky abandoned their ideas, but Nikita Khrushchev and Leonid Brezhnev revived the notion of expanding socialism following the death of Josef Stalin. Soviet leaders championed socialism as a world system opposed to global capitalism. In the 1950s and 1960s, the Soviet Union developed successfully and rapidly, giving confidence to the theorists of socialist expansion. Like early theorists of communism, they believed it would not survive internally without international development.

Expansionists also existed among the Eurasianists. Within classical Eurasianism, they included the Marxist-sympathetic group of Nikolai Suvchinsky. This group did not see the Soviet state as the enemy, instead opposing the West and the United States. In the postwar period, this line of thinking continued in the development of Soviet military planners. The latter sought to combine geopolitics and Marxism to win in a global struggle against America and European countries. These Soviet thinkers viewed the consolidation of the Euro-Asian continent as the foundation of a victory by the USSR over Western "imperialism."

Following the USSR's collapse and Russia's weakness, the ideas of expansion were not influential but did not disappear altogether. Until the development of the Russian-Ukrainian crisis, few Slavophiles defended expansionist ideas. However, within Eurasianism, the neo-Eurasianist school of thought has advocated global revolutionary expansion. According to its leader, Alexander Dugin, Russia has no choice but confront the United States bolstered by an alliance with other land-based powers. As the Russian state began to recover during the 2000s, Dugin's ideas became more influential, albeit not decisive, in shaping the country's foreign policy.

During the second half of the 2000s, left-wing thinkers began to develop theories of revolutionary expansion and transformation of global capitalism in response to the weakening of West-centered globalization. In a certain sense, these theories continued the logic of Trotsky and Lenin, arguing the importance of challenging the dominant capitalist position of the United States by the "peripheral" Russia. As an engine of resistance to Western imperialism, Russia had to rely on other countries of "peripheral" capitalism and global social movements inside and outside the West.

The Bridge

Finally, the development of Russian thought is inseparable from attempts to present Russia as capable of overcoming extremes and connecting different cultures worldwide. Generally speaking, Russians are inclined to learn and borrow from others, melting the acquired knowledge into their own toward some critical national goals. Such borrowing and openness to dialogue with others are possible if there is confidence in the value of the lessons offered by another culture and the Self's ability to absorb them. For other cultures, including the Western ones, not to be perceived as threatening Russia, it is necessary to have strong relations with them and the psychological stability of the country's internal foundations.

In relations between Russia and the West, such conditions existed when their political, spiritual, and cultural systems were not too far apart. The perception of such closeness, though by no means coincident with Western culture, is essential for theorists of the Russia-bridge identity. For example, the early Slavophiles felt a close connection to Europe and even admired some of its characteristics while wishing to strengthen Russian Orthodox and communal principles. Aleksey Khomyakov called Europe "the land of holy miracles," desiring a more complete unity with it, but on the spiritual and moral foundations of his beloved Orthodox Christianity. He thought that only such Christianity contains universal truths that allow and presuppose openness to the West. Maturing as a thinker in the first third of the nineteenth century – during the reign of Alexander I – Khomyakov, like many others, did not perceive liberalism, secularism, industrialism, and revolution as the main direction of future European development. He considered it possible and necessary for Russia and Europe to learn from each other and develop based on "pure," non-hierarchical Christianity.

As Europe moved institutionally apart from Russia, the theories of Russia–European dialogue and unity weakened. In the post-reform and pre-revolutionary times, such ideas nevertheless existed. Vladimir Solovyov was among those who sincerely believed in the strength of Russian–European relations. Russia was still an integral part of the European continent, and Solovyov, together with Russian liberal Westernizers, defended the country's European identity. However, unlike the Westernizers, he advocated a rapprochement between the two Christian principles of the Second and Third Romeos. The followers of Khomyakov and Solovyov defended his ideas of the Christian foundation of Russia–European relations. They did so before and after the revolutionary events of 1917. Because of the Bolshevik Revolution in the country, they already had to defend these ideas while in exile.

After the Second World War, ideas of dialogue with the West emerged in the Soviet Union following the death of Stalin. At the time, opportunities arose for some convergence of the positions between the USSR and the social democratic governments of European countries. During the 1960s and 1970s, the new generation of young people was often critical of Stalin's ideas and prepared for dialogue with the West. In the West, progressive intellectuals expressed views of "convergence" or mutual learning of the systems of socialism and capitalism. Within the Communist Party, some defended the concepts of "peaceful coexistence" of the two systems. They also partly shared social democratic ideas, although they had to be careful in expressing such views. This environment formed the future socialist reformer, Mikhail Gorbachev. Gorbachev called on the USSR and the West to learn from each other and compete for the best. While a supporter of dialogue with capitalism, he remained confident in the core values of socialism. Gorbachev titled his book *Perestroika for our Country and the Whole World,* assuming future integration of all the best in the world based on ideas of social equality.

The ideas of a socio-political dialogue of systems did not disappear after the collapse of the Soviet Union, although in many respects, they lost their attractiveness. They were defended by Gorbachev and his followers, who believed in learning from neoliberal globalization while protecting Russia's national interests. These ideas had little future, given the unpreparedness for a dialogue on the part of global American capitalism and the weakness of Russia itself.

The dialogue ideas turned out to be more suitable for discussing Russia's social, cultural, and political relations with non-Western countries. Eurasianists and Communists turned out to be more open to dialogue and interaction with non-Western countries than were the Europe-centered Slavophiles.[1] Under the influence of Eurasianism, political and economic organizations were established in the space of "greater Eurasia" to advance a continental dialogue and cooperation. Rather than opposing the West, as in the theories of fortress and expansion, the emphasis is made on the search for common interests and the co-development of the Eurasian space. The authors of such ideas expect European countries to gradually integrate into this space.

Table 6.1 summarizes the main divisions within Russian thought.

The "Russian Idea" and the War in Ukraine

On February 24, 2022, Putin launched a "special military operation" in Ukraine. The war in Ukraine has revived fears of Russian nationalism outside the country while generating radically different reactions to the war at home. Supporters and critics of the Kremlin's decision have clashed over various dimensions of the Russia-Western conflict and the Russia–Ukraine war. In particular, they have debated growing military ties between Ukraine and NATO, Western foreign and security policy, and Kyiv's negative attitude toward Russians and the Russian culture in Ukraine.

TABLE 6.1 The "Russian Idea" (RI): Positions and Conditions of Influence

	FORTRESS	*EXPANSION*	*BRIDGE*
WHAT? (Position)	Isolationism	Revolutionary change	External dialogue & internal reform
HOW? (Mode of existence)	National autarchy	Unilateral promotion	Bi (multi) lateral dialogue
WHY? (Condition of influence)	Low confidence & Western pressures	High confidence & Western pressures	High confidence & Western recognition

Revived Western Fears of Russia

A standard critique in the West of the RI stresses its cultural exceptionalism and anti-Western orientation (Pipes 2005). Scholars often assess Slavophiles and Communists as enemies of democracy and liberalism (Devlin 1999; Engelstein 2009), whereas Eurasianism is associated with nostalgia for empire and struggle with the West (Laruelle 2008; Katzenstein and Weygrant 2017). Western scholars tend to be skeptical of attempts by other cultures to formulate their civilizational ideas, viewing them as a challenge to the "universal" ideology of liberal democracy and market capitalism (Fukuyama 1989). Even Gorbachev's ideas of dialogue and Perestroika initially were received by many American and European experts as a ploy to undermine the West and prolong the existence of the "inhumane" Soviet system (Cohen 1986; English 2022).

Pro-Western liberals in Russia are equally suspicious of theories of nationally distinctive interests, values, and development paths. They assess such theories as driven by dangerous nationalist myths (Yanov 1987, 1995) and justifying Russia's backwardness relative to the "advanced" Western world. To leading Russian liberal, Pavel Milyukov, ideological hatred for European peoples motivated Danilevsky's *Russia and Europe* (Novikova and Sizemskaya 1997, 174). To contemporary Russian liberals, imperial nostalgia guides theories of national interests and values, contributing to the aggravation of Russia's relations with the West (Arbatova 2019; Shevtsova 2020; Kunadze 2021; Pavroz 2021).

The main problem with such criticism is its inability to see in the RI anything but a desire to confront the West, regardless of whether this concerns theories of exceptionalism or dialogue. The overall complexity and distinctiveness of Russian thinking are reduced to aggressive expansion and nationalism. Politically, such reductionism and ignored dialogue limit the space for engagement while encouraging policies of confrontation and containment. After all, if the RI is about nationalism and external aggression, then a serious discussion is not possible.

Accusations of Russia of aggression and fascism have been common in the context of the war in Ukraine (Dickinson 2022; Snyder 2022a; *The Economist* 2022). Their authors believe that the ideas of Alexander Dugin and other radical nationalists inspired Russia's invasion of Ukraine.[2] Renewed fears of Russia include her annexation of the entire Ukrainian territory and aggression against other European nations (Volker 2022; Burbank 2022).

The political influence of Dugin and his supporters remains questionable, however (Laruelle 2022b). Putin's (2021) claims of Russia–Ukrainian "national unity" (*odin narod*) are not rooted in Dugin's geopolitical thinking. Such claims also should not be confused with Putin's determination to strengthen the security and prestige of Russia. Before the crisis of 2014, he never directly questioned the legitimacy of the Ukrainian state. Even after the annexation of Crimea, Putin did not follow the recommendations of Russian nationalists to annex Donbas. His decision to invade Ukraine in 2022 primarily reflected the need to prevent Ukrainian membership in NATO (Hill 2022; Suny 2022) and to protect people residing in separatist regions of Donbas. The subsequent decision to annex Donbas, Kherson, and Zaporizhye also likely reflected the determination to weaken Ukraine as a potential threat to Russia's security.

The aggressive war launched by Putin led many to assert Russia's imperialism concerning Ukraine and its drive for freedom and independence. As stated by historian Timothy Snyder (2022b), Russia is conducting a colonial war and is prepared to destroy the Ukrainian nation through organized killing, rape, and deportation. Some other writers also see the war in Ukraine as a natural result of the development of the Russian imperial idea. They propose to dismantle Russia's "imperial" political system by internally "decolonizing" it (Etkind 2022). The latter could be accomplished by creating "truth and reconciliation committees focusing on both Soviet Russian and contemporary atrocities," granting greater autonomy to the country's regions, and even partitioning Russia for "moral and strategic" reasons (Kassymbekova and Marat 2022; Soldo 2022). The ideas of Russia's imperialism and forced subjugation of Ukraine and other parts of Eastern Europe (Etkind 2011) highlight only one side of Russia's domestic and foreign relations – coercion, ignoring other historically significant bonds: common past, similar cultural and religious values, perception of the outside threats, and others.

Therefore, Western observers tend to assess Russia's actions and thinking as driven by its culture and history, resembling how Russian exceptionalist theories make sense of the West. Some authors go as far as to blame the entire Russian culture and society for the aggression in Ukraine. Critics of Russia often want to see not only the humiliation and defeat of Russia in the war, rejecting any possibility of compromise and dialogue, but also insist on "canceling" the entire Russian culture as imperialist and aggressive. For example, some writers proposed to condemn great Russian writers like Fyodor Dostoevsky for their "explosion of pure, distilled evil and long-suppressed hatred and envy" (Buruma 2022 citing Zabuzhko 2022).

Related to the identified essentialist argument is the strategy of separating Russia and Ukraine in terms of their values. Scholars sometimes present the cultural values of Ukrainians as European and opposed to Russian-imperial and Eurasian ones (Torbakov 2014). However, Russia's ambition to be a part of

Eurasia may reflect the country's geopolitical position rather than fundamentally different values. Even more dangerous are presentations of Russia by Ukrainian nationalists, including those tracing their roots to Nazi ideology (Ishchenko 2017; Katchanovski 2020).

While the cultural and historical boundaries between Russians and Ukrainians are real, they should not be exaggerated. The two nations have shared religious, ethnic, and cultural similarities and were even a part of the same state for several centuries. In addition, neither Russia nor Ukraine is politically homogeneous. Within Russia, there are supporters and critics of the war. Within Ukraine, there are anti-Russian constituencies and those who gravitate toward Russia and view the policies of Kyiv as nationalist and threatening their interests (Sakwa 2015; Petro 2023). For the latter, it is not Russia that is imperial and trending toward "decolonization" but Ukraine and the West.

Exceptionalism and Dialogue inside Russia

Among those who supported Putin's decision to use force against Kyiv, it is important to differentiate between those who did so for military-political and civilizational reasons. The former are supporters of realist thinking in Russia's intellectual and political class, and their views deserve special consideration (Tsygankov 2022a, 2023). Here, I consider only those who supported and opposed the war for civilizational reasons. This section analyzes their assessment of the war and recommendations.

Those supportive of the war justify it by the need to confront the global expansionism of Western civilization. According to the exceptionalists such as Alexander Dugin, Yegor Kholmogorov, Alexander Prokhanov, Zakhar Prilepin, and others, Western values are aggressive and fundamentally anti-Russian. For the West, Ukraine merely serves as a platform for undermining Russian civilization associated with the Russian Orthodox Church, Russian language, culture, and historical memory (Engstrom 2022; Laruelle 2022a). Therefore, Putin's decision was inevitable and must only lead to victory. No compromise is possible and will only lead to even more brutal wars in the future. As the radio host of *Komsomolskaya Pravda* Sergei Mardan (2022) wrote this on social media:

> The Russian fighting army is the national idea around which Russia has always united. ... There is no more need to explain what patriotism is and what it resembles. It looks like a Russian infantryman storming yet another fascist Konigsberg. Russian patriotism is painted in the colors of the army field uniform, the national flag, and the guard's ribbon. As always. Nothing changed.

According to Dugin (2022a), the confrontation between Russia and the West over Ukraine is a struggle between tradition, on the one hand, and the Western ideas of progress, modernity, and postmodernity, on the other. He views Western ideas as racist and leading to a new enslavement of humankind, continuing the path of the West's imperialism. Russia, however, is capable of being the leader in building the world on non-Western foundations. The RI is, therefore, well-suited for this global struggle and should be defined as an idea of an anti-Western civilization (Dugin 2021). Critical of any compromise, Dugin proposed the "philosophy of Victory" to lead Russia to the final triumph and the "dismem-berment" of the West (Dugin 2022b). Such a victory requires internal mobil-ization, including cleansing all negative sentiments in the intelligentsia or other social strata. Dugin had already promoted similar views following the 2014 crisis but received no support from the Kremlin and even lost his job at Moscow State University (Medium 2014). This time he is confident that Putin has made the final choice in this struggle and now shares the "philosophy of Victory."

Another theorist of the RI as exceptionalist and anti-Western is a neo-Slavophile thinker Yegor Kholmogorov. He views Russia's preserved control over Ukraine as a condition for maintaining a Slavic, Orthodox Christian, and imperial identity. According to him, Russia must defeat global liberalism in Europe by uniting all territories and peoples that share Slavic Orthodox Christian values (Kholmogorov 2019). Like Dugin and others, Kholmogorov believes Ukraine is Russia and cannot exist separately. In a series of TV programs on RT, he insisted on Russia's imperial right to change Kyiv's "occupation" regime and return Ukraine to Russia (Engstrom 2022).

The position of Russian thinkers advocating compromise as a way to end the war in Ukraine is shared by supporters of the dialogue of cultures among philosophers and journalists. In their view, the causes of the war in Ukraine are the insensitive actions of the West and the growth of nationalism in the post-Soviet region that destroyed the Soviet state. In the words of the last presi-dent of the USSR, Mikhail Gorbachev (2022), "the conflict is fundamentally rooted in the disruption of Perestroika and the irresponsible decisions made in Belovezhskaya Pushcha by the leaders of Russia, Ukraine, and Belarus." In add-ition to nationalism, Gorbachev (2022) blamed the West for ignoring Russia's security concerns and prolonging the war in Ukraine instead of encouraging a peaceful resolution.

Philosophers Sergei Nikol'sky and Boris Mezhuyev pointed to the dehumanized nature of Dugin's "philosophy of Victory." Mezhuyev (2022) compared this philosophy with the ideas expressed in Fyodor Dostoevsky's novel *Possessed*. The novel's heroes were prepared to commit suicide in the name of Russia's civilizational victory. Nikol'sky (2022) compared Dugin's self-perceived role with the philosopher Martin Heidegger under the Nazi regime. Nikol'sky further compared Dugin's calls for an internal "cleansing" of traitors among the intelligentsia with the American McCarthyism of the 1950s. These authors countered ideas of a radical confrontation with the West with the idea of a responsible personality and political action guided by responsibility before future generations.

The publicist Gleb Pavlovsky (2022), who formed his views under the influence of Mikhail Gefter,[3] argued the importance of positive ideals and their realization through dialogue and compromise with the outside world. In assessing the decision on the war with Ukraine, Pavlovsky criticized the decision as an improvisation guided by the motives of historical revenge on the West. In his view, a way out of the crisis must be different. It must reject the idea of a final victory and be based on a compromise between Russia, Ukraine, and the West. Like Gorbachev, Pavlovsky (2022) found that not only Russia is to be blamed for the crisis but also the Western governments that have bet on a military victory and unleashed an "economic war."

The Slavophile thinker Alexander Tsipko (2022a) also stressed the importance of dialogue to avoid escalating relations between Russia and the West. Tsipko (2022c) further identified strong imperial and anti-Western sentiments inside Russia and the danger of their encouragement by the Kremlin. According to him, the government is responsible for strengthening the legal consciousness, and not imperial sentiments:

> Due to the relative weakness of cultural consciousness, Russians find no other way to justify the meaning of the state except deify the Tsar-father. ... To them, the religious idea of the Tsar-father personifies the Russian state, the church, and the entire Russian life ... until the Russians develop legal consciousness and the concept of human individuality, they are doomed to live under Tsar-fathers.

Tsipko (2022b) clarified that Russian thinking must not develop in isolation from the outside world, including contemporary European societies with their prioritization of a free personality rooted in Christianity.

Critical of the "special military operation," the above-considered supporters of the dialogue did not support the idea of Russia's military defeat. The politicians of Ukraine and Western countries and some pro-Western Russian intellectuals (Radchenko 2022; Gozman 2023) articulated the latter position. The supporters' views of dialogue are rooted in understanding the complexity of responsibility for the conflict. Such opinions are also sensitive to the fear that Russian anti-Western sentiments will not disappear if Russia suffers a defeat at war. On the contrary, such feelings may grow by pushing the country to a new war.

The "Russian Idea" and Global Dialogue after the War

As of this writing, it is impossible to predict when and on which terms the Russia-Ukraine war will end. The war has served to undermine stability in the wider world and empower the discourse of exceptionalists rather than advocates of the global dialogue. The longer the conflict lasts, the more likely it is to politically increase the influence of isolationist and expansionist policies inside Russia. If the war becomes a new normal, the worst fears of critics of Russia may come true. This concluding section considers the conditions for global dialogue and possible avenues for its future development, including using ideas articulated by Russian thinkers.

Conditions and Demand for Dialogue

The Russia-Ukraine war does not resemble the Second World War (Lieven 2022). Unlike the war with Nazi Germany, the contemporary conflict is not about the survival of human civilization confronted by an evil enemy. Although Russia is primarily responsible for launching the war, Russian officials have articulated several legitimate humanitarian and security concerns (Matlock 2022; Watkins 2022) that must be considered along with those of Ukraine and Western nations. It is important to listen rather than dismiss the ideas of others because they reflect strong values and aspirations. American scholar James Billington (1997) once argued for listening and understanding "the interior spiritual dialogue" inside Russia by outsiders. He warned, "if we cannot learn to listen to others when they whisper their prayers, then we may have to confront them later when they issue their battle cries."

Therefore, the global community has a vital role in ending the devastating conflict by proposing a comprehensive solution. Such a solution must address the complex roots of the war, including the lack of an inclusive security system and ethnically polarizing politics in Europe. Rather than encouraging victory or defeat in the war, the outside world should create conditions for negotiations and compromise. Such compromise will serve as the best hope for defeating voices of national exceptionalism and reviving ideas of global dialogue inside and outside Russia.

The development of such dialogue is challenging today. The contemporary world is transitioning from the West-dominant to a different system of international relations. International transitions are usually accompanied by tension and instability, potentially leading to the growth of nationalism and wars. In Russia, the ideas of national and civilizational exclusiveness are also on the rise (Tsygankov and Tsygankov 2021). In this book, I have explored some of these ideas. According to their authors, a dialogue with the outside world, especially its Western part, is a dangerous delusion that can only weaken one's cultural foundations.

Nevertheless, the development of global dialogue and interdependence remains essential for preventing even greater instability and the danger of conflicts, including among major powers with the possible use of nuclear weapons. Despite the risks of the contemporary situation, the potential for ideational and cultural interaction in the world is significant. In a certain sense, the declining influence of Western dominance presents the world with new opportunities for intercultural dialogue. Such a dialogue is practiced today between Russia and the non-Western countries that did not support the anti-Russian sanctions of the West (Lynch 2022). In the future, such a dialogue may become possible with

Western countries. When military-political stabilization is achieved, the ideas of Russian theorists of dialogue between peoples and civilizations may revive their significance. Russia's geopolitical and geocultural location in the world continues to position it for such development.[4]

In Russian thought, there has always been a strong appreciation of the world's diversity, unity, and interconnectedness. For example, the tradition of the Russian "planetary thinking" (*kosmizm*) has proposed various approaches to the notion of universal unity. Having been initially offered within the Slavophile philosophy by Nikolai Khomyakov, Vladimir Solovyov, Nikolai Fedorov, Pavel Florensky, Nikolai Berdyaev, and others, the idea of universal unity became part of the thinking of Russian geographers, biologists, sociologists, and natural scientists, including Konstantin Tsiolkovsky, Vladimir Vernadsky, Alexander Chizhevsky, and others.

Awareness of the world's complex interdependence led to the development of Russian thinking about intercultural, civilizational dialogue. Those who stressed such dialogue saw it as a "world of worlds" (Gefter 1994) or a "civilization of civilizations" (Karaganov 2022). They argued that being located at the crossroads of world civilizations and having benefited from their diversity, Russia is in a position to contribute to their reconciliation and global development. Because of its geographic location between Europe and Asia, its religious tolerance, and its political and economic "semi-periphery" status between the West and the non-Western periphery, Russia remains a cross-regional land of the world's significance. Russian thinkers also assume that facilitating global dialogue requires that the country remain strong and confident, capable, if necessary, of demonstrating force.

Three Bridges to the Future

Russian thinkers have alerted the world to three sets of global issues that remain essential and must be addressed today: cultural identity, socioeconomic justice, and regional diversity. These issues have historically prompted Russian theorists to ask about their nation's contribution to resolving them. While engaging with these issues, the Slavophiles, Communists, and Eurasianists have developed ideas that promote global dialogue.

• Dialogue of Cultures

The first Russian insight concerns the dialogue between cultures and civilizations. Aware of civilizations' cultural (values) and political (sovereignty) boundaries, Russian thinkers nevertheless believe in the possibility of improving cross-cultural understanding and reducing conflicts in international relations. Cross-cultural dialogue implies the importance of being impartial in mutual understanding while remaining confident in one's values and priorities.

That confidence can result from historically developed perceptions of national strength and distinctiveness, as highlighted by post-colonial thinkers and classical realists who challenge the idea of Western cultural domination (Karkour 2022). Along with others and even before them, Russian Slavophiles challenged Europe/West's cultural dominance arguing for a pluralistic and inclusive idea of Europeanness.

Russians have historically interacted with other people at the crossroads of great cultures and civilizations. Russians learned from the Scandinavians and Greeks during the period of the principalities, from nomadic peoples under the Mongols and the emergence of Muscovy, from the Turks and Tatars, Poles, French, and other Europeans and Westerners. Today, Russians are actively borrowing from the Chinese and other non-Western nations. Moscow has significantly contributed to ending ethnic conflicts in Central Asia, the Caucasus, and the Middle East. Russia also initiated the idea of an in-depth partnership with China, including within the format of a greater Eurasia. Finally, Russia has actively (co)established new multilateral organizations, including BRICS (Brazil, Russia, India, China, and South Africa), SCO (Shanghai Cooperation Organization), EAEU (Eurasian Economic Union), and others.

Such interaction with the non-Western world became possible due to the described capacity for intercultural understanding and the perception of sufficient confidence and security inside Russia. Dialogues are possible only if a nation has developed core values programmed for openness to other cultures. One historical evidence of such openness is Russia's avoidance of the path of ethnic nationalism chosen by several European countries in the first half of the twentieth century. The solution to important development tasks requires the nation's confidence to mobilize relevant national historical experience and learn from the experience of other peoples.

The absence of such confidence in relations with the West made it impossible to develop a dialogue with it. The contemporary confrontation between Russia and the West has two sources. The first is Russia's exaggerated fears of losing its political and civilizational independence. The second source is the West's unpreparedness for dialogue. Western societies are profoundly polarized and lack internal and external dialogue capacity. Scholars highlight the trend toward cultural monism in Europe and its hierarchical subordination to the United States (Sakwa 2017).

The context of the Russia-West confrontation and the war in Ukraine minimizes opportunities for dialogue. The sides cannot revive it without reviving mutual equality and national confidence. The latter will likely happen following the strengthening of Russia's position in the non-Western world. Mutual cultural respect, rather than "European values," would be a foundation for such dialogue (Kortunov 2019, 352). Even though some observers (Weichert 2022) assert that Russia has transformed its identity into that of Asia, it is more likely that Russia has preserved its traditional interest in having a dialogue with both Eastern and

Western nations. If so, the RI of civilizational mediation between the West and the non-West, the United States and China, may take on a new meaning.

- Social Justice and Development

Another possible bridge to the future is associated with the Russian belief in a particular political system as a prerequisite for social justice and sustainable development. Social inequality has deepened significantly in the contemporary world compared to past decades (Chancel and Piketty 2021), creating new conditions for global instability. Many in Russia and outside criticize the Western system of capitalism and individualism. They view such a system as responsible for exploiting the non-Western parts of the world. Despite their differences, many Slavophiles, Populists, and Social Democrats shared their criticism while advancing the Russian ideal of a "holistic personality" in harmony with oneself and the outside world.

These ideals do not correspond to the realities of growing social inequality, uneven development, and corruption. Russia's personalistic political system and confrontation with the West tend to perpetuate, rather than resolve, these issues. In attempting to find solutions, Russian thinkers revisit the ideas of a strong state capable of reducing inequality, stimulating development, and guaranteeing freedom (Tsygankov 2014, 2015). Demand for such a state exists in Russia and abroad, making the idea appealing to national and international audiences (Fishman and Martyanov 2022; Uchayev 2022).

In Russian thought, especially among Slavophiles and Communists, a strong state is a condition for releasing social energy and initiative rather than stifling them. In this area, Russians may also learn from other peoples, both Easterners, with their collectivist culture, and Western Europeans, with their prioritization of a socially oriented state. In a European state, social programs serve stability and economic development purposes. Such a socially strong state also requires a foreign policy to protect sovereignty and stimulate national development. The purpose of such a policy is integration into the most dynamically developing parts of the world economy on favorable terms for the country.

- Regionalism and Geographic Openness

In the contemporary world, regionalization is a powerful trend long studied by political geographers and scholars of global geopolitics (Gadzhiyev 2007; Okunev 2019; Koopman 2021). While economically interdependent, the world is becoming more local and centered on Eurasia, Euro-Atlantic, Asia-Pacific, Latin America, and other regions.

Under these conditions, the Eurasian dialogue and geo-economic development ideas indicate new regional thinking and particular importance for Russia. Russian experts frequently discuss the construction of a "greater Eurasia," the establishment of which serves the interests of both national and regional development. The creation of such a region presupposes an awareness of Russia's civilizational identity and its openness to other civilizations. The idea of such Eurasia results from the Russian understanding of inter-civilizational dialogue with its emphasis on national identity and "universal responsiveness" (*otzyvchivost'*) (Fyodor Dostoevsky). Slavophiles also commonly relied on notions of Russia as the "great Euro-East" and "the unifier of Europe and Asia."

These ideas can contribute to openness and stability in the Eurasian region in conjunction with inter-civilizational dialogue and a just state. In Russian history, the traditions of such open regionalism arose as early as the ninth century based on trade interaction between Russians, the Greeks, and northern Europeans. In this tripartite system, the Russians acted as intermediaries and protected the commercial river routes. The interests of the Russians required maintaining a civilizational dialogue and trade openness while preventing the dominance of other regional powers (Tsygankov 2022b). The early Eurasian system broke due to the rising activities of Mongols, the crusaders, and the nomads in the region. However, trade routes reopened after the strengthening of the Muscovy principality.

Today, against the backdrop of the rise of China and India in Eurasia, new conditions may appear for building a system of geographical openness. In the new Eurasian system, the interests of the Russians, as before, require the development of an inter-civilizational dialogue, maintaining transport and economic transparency, and preventing regional hegemony by other major powers. Such global dialogue also requires that Russia and other powers have the internal confidence to pursue international cooperation.

Russian civilizational thinkers have, therefore, developed valuable insights into resolving the dilemma of how one can be national and valid to your culture while advancing a path for global cooperation, security, and prosperity. Many Russian thinkers believe in resolving this dilemma without adopting one of the extreme positions. Global and national dialogues about cultural identity, social justice, and regional diversity occur worldwide. However, nationally exceptionalist discourses continue to be powerful, and the shadow of war looms. It remains to be seen if ideas of the global dialogue prevail over those of war and nationalism.

Notes

1 Danilevsky and Lamansky may be considered exceptions from this rule.
2 For a recent analysis of accusations of Russian state and non-state actors of fascism, see Laruelle 2022c.
3 For analysis of Gefter's views, see Pavlovsky 2015, chapter 5.
4 For complexity of forming national and global identity of Russia and Russian cultural influence, see Ageeva and Akopov 2022.

Further Reading

The RI and the War in Ukraine

Dugin, A. 2021. Russkaya ideya – eto ne nashi tvoreniye. *Portal-kultura*, October 7.

Engstrom, M. 2022. We don't support the 'special operation', we're carrying it out. *Russia.Posts*, May 3.

Karaganov, S. 2022. Why Russia Believes It Cannot Lose the War in Ukraine. *The New York Times*, July 19.

Tsipko, A. 2022. Neuyemnyye fantaziyi russkoi idei. *Nezavisimaya gazeta*, May 11.

Tsygankov, A. P. 2023. Russian Realism and the War in Ukraine. *Journal of Military and Strategic Studies*.

Putin, Ukraine, and the RI

Burbank, J. 2022. The Grand Theory Driving Putin to War. *New York Times*, March 22.

Putin, V. 2021. "On the Historical Unity of Russians and Ukrainians." Moscow, Kremlin, July 12.

Laruelle, M. 2022. The intellectual origins of Putin's invasion," *UnHerd*, March 16.

Fears of Russia

Buruma, I. 2022. Stop Blaming the Russian Soul. *Project-Syndicate*, Jun 7.

Laruelle, M. 2022. So, Is Russia Fascist Now? Labels and Policy Implications, *The Washington Quarterly* 45, 2.

Sakwa, R. 2023. *The Russia Scare: Fake News and Genuine Threat*. Routledge.

Snyder, T. 2022. We Should Say It. Russia Is Fascist. *New York Times*, May 19.

Yanov, A. 1987. *The Russian Challenge and the Year 2000*. New York: Blackwell.

Contemporary Visions of Russia's Future

Etkind, A. 2022. The Future Defederation of Russia. *Moscow Times*, June 8.

Fishman, L. G. and V. G. Martyanov. 2022. Esli ne urok, to proyekt. *Rossiya v global'noi politike* 20, 4.

Trenin, D. 2022. «Переиздание» Российской Федерации. *Россия в глобальной политике* 20, 2.

Tsygankov, A. 2023. The World After: The War in Ukraine and Russian Visions of the Future. *Russian Politics* 2

References

Ageeva, Vera and Sergei Akopov, 2022. "Global Russians": Case study of transnational actors in world politics. *Europe-Asia Studies.*

Arbatova, Nadezhda. 2019. "Three Faces of Russia's Neo-Eurasianism," *Survival* 61 (6).

Berdyaev, Nicolai A. 1990. Русская идея. In: *О России и русской философской культуре.* Отв. ред. Е. М. Чехарин. Москва.

Billington, James. 1997. "Religion and Russia's Future." The Templeton Lecture on Religion and World Affairs, *FPRI Wire*, October www.fpri.org/articles/1997/10/religion-and-russias-future.

Burbank, Jane. 2022. The Grand Theory Driving Putin to War. *New York Times*, March 22.

Buruma, Ian. 2022. Stop Blaming the Russian Soul. *Project-Syndicate*, Jun 7.

Chancel, Lucas and Thomas Piketty. 2021. *Global Income Inequality, 1820–2020: The Persistence and Mutation of Extreme Inequality*. ffhalshs-03321887 https://halshs.archives-ouvertes.fr/halshs-03321887/document.

Cohen, Stephen F. 1986. *Sovieticus: American Perceptions and Soviet Realities*. New York: W. W. Norton.

Devlin, Judith. 1999. *Slavophiles and Commissars: Enemies of Democracy in Modern Russia*. New York: Palgrave Macmillan.

Dickinson, Peter. 2022. Putin admits Ukraine invasion is an imperial war to "return" Russian land. *The Atlantic Council*, June 10.

Dugin, Aleksandr. 2021. Russkaya ideya – eto ne nashi tvoreniye. *Portal-kultura*, October 7.

———. 2022a. Rossiya protiv anti-Rossyiyi: interesy i tsennosti. *Katehon*, March 28.

———. 2022b. Dlya Nezygaria. July 18. https://t.me/russica2

Engelstein, Laura. 2009. *Slavophile Empire: Imperial Russia's Illiberal Path*. Ithaca, NY: Cornell University Press.

English, Robert D. 2022. "Disparaging Gorbachev, Distorting Perestroika: Lessons of the Cold War's End," *The National Interest*, October 29.

Engstrom, Masha. 2022. We don't support the 'special operation', we're carrying it out. *Russia.Posts*, May 3.

Etkind, Alexander. 2011. *Internal Colonization: Russia's Imperial Experience*. Cambridge: Polity.

———. 2022. The Future Defederation of Russia. All empires eventually fall apart. *Moscow Times*, June 8.

Fishman, L. G. and V. G. Martyanov. 2022. Esli ne urok, to proyekt. *Rossiya v global'noi politike* 20, 4.

Fukuyama, Francis. 1989. The End of History? *The National Interest*.

Gadzhiyev, Kamaludin. 2007. *Geopoliticheskiye gorizonty Rossiyi: kontury novogo mirovogo poryadka*. Moscow: Ekonomika.

Gefter, Mikhail. 1994. *Мир миров - российский зачин*. Moscow: old.rus

Gorbachev, Mikhail. 2022. Gorbachev nazval prichiny voiny na Dobasse. *Politeka*, March 17.

Gozman, Leonid. 2023. Europe's freedom depends on Ukraine winning a decisive victory over Russia. *Moscow Times*, January 23.

Hill, Alexander. 2022. Curious Kids: Why did Putin invade Ukraine now? Is it for the U.S.S.R. again? *Conversation*, March 17.

Ishchenko, Volodymyr. 2017. Far Right Participation in Ukrainian Maidan Protest. In: *Ukraine in Crisis*, edited by Nicolai Petro. London: Routledge.

Karaganov, Sergei. 2022. Why Russia Believes It Cannot Lose the War in Ukraine. *The New York Times*, July 19.

Kassymbekova, Botakoz and Erica Marat. 2022. Time to Question Russia's Imperial Innocence. *Ponars*, April 27.

Katchanovski, Ivan. 2020. The far right, the Euromaidan, and the Maidan massacre. *Journal of Labor and Society*.

Katzenstein, Peter and Nicole Weygrant. 2017, Mapping Eurasia in an Open World. *Perspectives on Politics* 15, 2.

Karkour, Haro L. 2022. *E. H. Carr: Imperialism, War and Lessons for Post-Colonial IR*. London: Palgrave.

Kholmogorov, Yegor. 2019. Pochemu Rossiya —Yevropa, a Yevrosoyuz … ne ochen'. August 28 https://tsargrad.tv/articles/pochemu-rossija-evropa-a-evrosojuz-ne-ochen _213564.

Koopman, Sara et al. 2021. Critical Geopolitics/critical geopolitics 25 years. *Political Geography*, https://doi.org/10.1016/j.polgeo.2021.102421.

Kortunov, Andrei. 2019. Heartland reunion: geopolitical chimera or historical chance? In: *Russia in the Forming Greater Eurasia*, edited by V. M. Kotlyakov and V. A. Shuper. Moscow: "Kodeks" Publishing House.

Kunadze, Georgi. 2021. "Put' izgoya: kuda vedet vneshnyaya politika Rossiyi," *Novaya gazeta*, July 3.

Laruelle, Marlene. 2008. *Russian Eurasianism: An Ideology of Empire*. Washington, DC: The Johns Hopkins University Press.

———. 2022a. The Russian Radical Right and the War in Ukraine. *Ponars*, July 12.

———. 2022b. The intellectual origins of Putin's invasion," *UnHerd*, March 16.

———. 2022c. So, Is Russia Fascist Now? Labels and Policy Implications, *The Washington Quarterly* 45, 2.

Lieven, Anatol. 2022. Ukraine's War Is Like World War I, Not World War II," *Foreign Policy*, October 27.

Lynch, Colum. 2022. The West Is with Ukraine. The Rest, Not So Much. *Foreign Policy*, March 30.

Mardan, Sergei. 2022. *Telegram*, July 8 https://t.me/mardanaka.

Matlock, Jr., Jack F. 2022. Today's Crisis Over Ukraine. *ACURA ViewPoint*, February 14.

Medium 2014. "Putin's 'Mad Philosopher' Is Out of a Job," *Medium*, June 29.

Mezhuyev, Boris. 2022. Opyaneniye dukkha, ili osada Instituta Filosofiyi. *PublicO*, July 12.

Nikol'sky, Sergei. 2022. Chto neset s soboi 'filosofiya Pobedy'. *Nezavisimaya gazeta*, June 1.

Novikova, Lyudmila and Irina Sizemskaya. 1997. *Russkaya filosofiya istoriyi*. Moscow: Rosspen.

Okunev, Igor. 2019. *Politicheskaya geografiya*. Moscow: Aspekt Press.

Pavlovsky, Gleb. 2015. *Tretyego tysyacheletiya ne budet*. Moscow.

———. 2022. Predrassudok mira v dni voiny. *Eurasia Insight*, June 26.

Pavroz, Alexander. 2021. "Geopolitical Contradictions of Contemporary Russia," *Comparative Strategy* 40 (4).

Petro, Nicolai. 2023. *The Tragedy of Ukraine: What Classical Greek Tragedy Can Teach Us About Conflict Resolution*. Berlin and Boston: De Gruyter.

Pipes, Richard. 2005. *Russian Conservatism and Its Critics*. New Haven: Yale University Press.

Putin, Vladimir. 2021. On the Historical Unity of Russians and Ukrainians. Moscow, Kremlin, July 12.

Radchenko, Sergey. 2022. Why Russia needs to be humiliated in Ukraine. *The Spectator*, May 15.

Sakwa, Richard. 2015. *Frontline Ukraine*. London: I. B. Tauris.

———. 2017. Europe and the political: From axiological monism to pluralistic dialogism. *East European Politics* 33, 3.

Shevtsova, Lilia. 2020. "Putin ostalsya v polnoi izolyatsiyi," *Gladred*, December 22.

Snyder, Timothy. 2022a. We Should Say It. Russia Is Fascist. *New York Times*, May 19.

———. 2022b. The War in Ukraine Is a Colonial War. *The New Yorker*, April 28.

Soldo, Nicollo. 2022. Delusion. The US Government's Commission on Security and Cooperation in Europe (CSCE) holds a briefing on the "moral and strategic" necessity of partitioning Russia. https://niccolo.substack.com June 22

Suny, Ronald G. 2022. Ukraine war follows decades of warnings that NATO expansion into Eastern Europe could provoke Russia. *The Conversation*, February 28.

The Economist. 2022. 'A dark state.' Vladimir Putin is in thrall to a distinctive brand of Russian fascism, July 30.

Torbakov, Igor'. 2014. " 'This is the Strife of Slavs among Themselves': Understanding Russian–Ukrainian Relations as the Conflict of Contested Identities." In *The Maidan Uprising, Separatism and Foreign Intervention*, edited by Klaus Bachmann and Igor Lyubachenko. Frankfurt am Main: Peter Lang.

Tsipko, Aleksandr. 2022a. Svet apokalipsisa opyat' v rukakh russkogo naroda. *Nezavisimaya gazeta*, February 9.

———. 2022b. Neuyemnyye fantaziyi russkoi idei. *Nezavisimaya gazeta*, May 11.

———. 2022c. Vo vlasti mutnoi intuytsiyi. *Nezavisimaya gazeta*, June 6.

Tsygankov, Andrei P. 2014. *The Strong State in Russia*. Oxford University Press.

———. 2015. Сильное государство: теория и практика в 21 веке. Moscow: Валдайский клуб.

———. 2022a. *Russian Realism*. London: Routledge.

———. 2022b. Russia, Eurasia, and the Meaning of Crimea. *Europe-Asia Studies*.

———. 2023. Russian Realism and the War in Ukraine. *Journal of Military and Strategic Studies*.

Tsygankov, Andrei and Pavel Tsygankov. 2021. Constructing National Values. *Foreign Policy Analysis*.

Uchayev, Yevgeny. I. 2022. Sokhranit' chelovechestvo v epokhu Antropotsena. *Rossiya v global'noi politike* 20, 1.

Volker, Kurt. 2022. The (Russian) Empire Strikes Back. *The Center for European Policy Analysis*, January 10.

Watkins, Susan. 2022. An Avoidable War? *New Left Review* 133 / 134, January-April.

Weichert, Brandon J. 2022. Russia becomes an Asian nation. Sanctions may be empowering Russia to create the pathways for financial and economic independence from the West. *Asia Times*, April 25.

Yanov, Alexander. 1987. *The Russian Challenge and the Year 2000*. New York: Blackwell.

———. 1995. *Weimar Russia and what we can do about it*. New York: Slovo.

Zabuzhko, Oksana. 2022. No guilty people in the world? *Times Literary Supplement*, April 22

INDEX

Note: Page numbers in **bold** refer to tables.

Printed and bound by CPI Group (UK) Ltd, Croydon, CR0 4YY

05/12/2024

01801029-0018